Contents

iv

HIGH SPEED TRAINS
FAST TRACKS TO THE FUTURE

edited by

John Whitelegg,
Staffan Hultén
&
Torbjörn Flink

*L*eading *E*dge™
press and publishing

In association with Stockholm School of Economics

HIGH SPEED TRAINS: Fast Tracks to the Future
Published by Leading Edge Press & Publishing Ltd
The Old Chapel
Burtersett
Hawes
North Yorkshire
DL8 3PB
☎ (0969) 667566

© Leading Edge & the individual contributors, 1993

ISBN 0-948135-45-X

A CIP Catalogue record for this book is available from the British Library.

Text editing and index: Midge Whitelegg
Final editing and design: Stan Abbott
Cover design: Ruth Abbott
Cartoons: Bill Lehan
Type: Leading Edge Press & Publishing Ltd
Colour reprographics: Impression, Leeds
Printed and bound in Great Britain by Ebenezer Baylis and Son Ltd, Worcester.

About the Editors

Dr John Whitelegg is Head of Geography at Lancaster University and a world authority on public transport.
Staffan Hultén is Assistant Professor at Stockholm School of Economics, where Torbjörn Flink is a researcher.

Foreword

LEADING EDGE is pleased to have been able to assist the Stockholm School of Economics in bringing the collection of papers in this book to as wide an audience as possible.

There is much to interest many different groups of people. Rail enthusiasts will find here arguably the most comprehenisve collection to date of writings on the subject of high speed trains, with a historical perspective on developments in all those countries which have, as it were, gone down the high speed track.

Those to whose interest in railways can be added a concern for the general concept of publicly-owned transport infrastructure may well bristle at the thoughts of Mendoza on the role of the train in the burgeoning Spanish economy, or at Hawke's perhaps cursory dismissal of the argument that railways rarely compete for funds with roads on a "level playing field". But they will surely find inspiration in Whitelegg and Holzapfel's thought-provoking championship of the cause of local and regional rail services.

Equally, as much as the above may choose to skip some of the more theoretical chapters, it is precisely these which make this collection a work of considerable importance to academics in a variety of disciplines — economists, historians, economic historians and others.

And those whose interests touch the romance of rail travel, or the great buildings which railways have created, will surely delight in the enthusiasm of Richards and MacKenzie and their vision of the railway palaces of the future.

May I thank all those who have assisted in the production of this book and offer particular thanks to those who have contributed photographs, especially David Briginshaw, at the *International Railway Journal*.

Stan Abbott, Leading Edge Press & Publishing, December 1992

Picture credits

Notes

* International Railway Journal

While every endeavour has been made by the publisher's correctly to attribute the origins of pictures supplied, this may not have been possible in every case.

Preface

THIS BOOK analyses and evaluates the development of high speed trains in Europe, Japan and the USA. At present there are only a limited number of research reports on the economic and social impact of high speed trains. In general these have focused on national high speed train ventures. In contrast, this book is intended to compare diverse national high speed train systems and projects, and discuss thematically the overall impact of high speed trains.

Railways were an important object of study for social scientists when railways dominated the inland transport of goods and passengers. In geography, the focus centred on the contribution of railways to the total supply of transport. In economics, evolutionary theorists, like Schumpeter and Rostow, saw in railways one of the decisive factors behind the second industrial revolution. Hotelling used railways and bridges as two classical examples of the case for marginal cost pricing in industries with large fixed costs and extremely small marginal costs. In economic history, railways were used as one of the key examples of the advantages of the measurement-oriented new economic history, compared with the more descriptive traditional practice.

We envisage that the spread of high speed trains and high speed train technology will again prompt social scientists and policy-makers to place railways on the research agenda. High speed trains will certainly not have the same impact on society as the railways had in the 19th century, but they have nevertheless already proved the competitiveness of rail against both air and road.

They have also contributed to the growth of demand for travel, with consequences for both spatial structures and the environment. The evaluation of these impacts is an important research issue for social scientists.

The majority of the contributions to this book were originally presented at the Conference on High Speed Trains, Entrepreneurship and Society, organised by Torbjörn Flink and Staffan Hultén, at the Stockholm School of Economics in June 1990.

We wish to express our gratitude for financial support from NUTEK (Swedish National Board for Industrial and Technical Development), TFB (Swedish Transport Research Board), SJ (Swedish State Railways) and EJR (East Japan Railways) for organising the conference and undertaking the work on this book.

We are very grateful to the Economic Research Institute at the Stockholm School of Economics for its assistance throughout, from organising the conference to doing the editorial work on the book. We would especially like to thank policy adviser Marika Jenstav at Swedish State Railways, formerly at the Swedish Transport Research Board, for her invaluable support, as well as all those organisations which supplied photographs.

The Editors, Stockholm and Lancaster, October 1992

RADICAL DEPARTURES: *To date, the world's high speed rail systems have, almost without exception, used a conventional system of two parallel steel rails, although other solutions have been tried...*

Above: *The Brennan Monorail*

Below: *Tracked hovercraft research test vehicle*

8

Part One

1.

Introduction

By the Editors

THE EUROPEAN railway system is currently developing rapidly, and on a wide front — most of Western Europe's major cities will in due course be linked by a new high speed train network. The driving force behind this development is the saving in time which can be achieved by passenger trains on journeys up to 1,000kms, in comparison with other means of transport.

Some of these high speed services are already in operation, while others are in the construction or planning stages. Planned investments in high speed railways over the next 25 years are expected to amount to $100 billion. This massive wave of investment in a new railway infrastructure and rolling stock represents a challenge to social scientists. How will these investments affect the environment, research and development, suppliers to the operating companies, other competitors in the transport industry and, last but not least, consumer attitudes and travel behaviour?

In 1964 Japan launched the first passenger train with an average speed of more than 160kmh, on the newly built line between Tokyo and Osaka. Since then, Shinkansen trains have been a symbol of modern Japan, and have developed into a national railway network reaching from Morioka in the north to Fukuoka in the south. The total length of the system is 1,836kms. The system has carried more than three billion passengers without any serious accident.

In January 1989 the Community of European Railways presented a plan for a European high speed inter-city network. This envisaged the inter-connection of a large number of European cities by a high speed network by 1995. The whole network would be completed in 2015-2020.[1] Plans like that of 1989 are not new. Back in the early 1970s, the UIC (International Union of Railways) proposed just such a high speed inter-city network for Europe.[2]

The high speed train era in Europe began in the late 1960s with the initiation of a number of projects. One common feature of these was that they incorporated new technology. Three types of research projects were started.

● **projects that tried to increase railway speed on existing track with new rolling stock**

● **projects that used new lines and new rolling stock and**

---

[1] Community of European Railways, 1989

[2] Knall, G, 1974

● projects that used new rail technologies, for example, the French Aérotrain and the German maglev Transrapid.

Other projects with unconventional track systems were later launched in Great Britain, the USA and Japan. So far, no alternative high speed rail technology has been commercially introduced.

In the history of railways, increased speed has always been a prime aim of railway companies. This book, however, will not record this development in detail, although occasional references will be found.

We define a high speed train as one with a much higher average and maximum speed than other trains. Today the most common definition of a high speed train is one that has a maximum speed of more than 200kph and an average speed of more than 150kph. Europe's first modern high speed train (HST) was introduced in 1975 in Great Britain. Since 1983, France has enjoyed the world's fastest train service — the TGV from Paris to Lyon, while Italy started its Milan-Rome high speed service in 1988. The French network was expanded in 1990-91, with the opening of the TGV-Atlantique lines. In Britain, the electrification of the East Coast Main Line, north from London and the introduction of the new Electra locomotive permits speeds up to 225kph. Plans are now well developed for the introduction of a new type of train capable of 250kph in Britain.

In Germany, the new ICE train was introduced on the "neubau" track sections in 1991, and in Spain AVE — a modified TGV Atlantique train — entered service on the high speed line from Madrid to Seville on the day of the inauguration of the World Expo, on April 20, 1992.

In Italy, a new generation of high speed trains was developed, called ETR 500. In a more modest form, the same kind of development can be seen in Sweden, where a new highspeed train, capable of 210kph, was introduced in September 1990. The most important improvements in the near future are the opening of the Channel Tunnel network in 1993, the building of a French national high speed network and the construction of the PBKA network linking Paris, Brussels, Köln and Amsterdam into a high speed network in 1998.

The impact of railway investments on society

Social scientists have regarded the rapid development and growth of railway networks in the 19th century as synonymous with the breakthrough of industrialism. The railways affected society in many ways. The most obvious improvements were lower-cost carriage of goods and people, dramatic reduction in travelling times and the extension of travelling to all social classes.

Railways enlarged the market for goods because they gave cheaper and faster carriage, and the construction of new railway lines generated enormous investments. But the railway also influenced society indirectly, by placing new demands on engineers, politicians, capitalists, the labour force and other groups.

Apart from developing locomotives and rolling stock, the engineers were faced with totally new technical problems in the construction of bridges, viaducts and tunnels. The construction of the great metropolitan railway stations gave architects and engineers the opportunity to use new building materials and to experiment with new designs. The railways presented the capitalists with a challenge, since the rapid extension of this new transport system required the reorganisation of the capital market.

Contractors and operating companies had to organise the labour force to meet the demands of a production process which required high standards of punctuality and precision. Local time was abandoned in favour of national time zones. The impact of the railways was observed from an early stage by social scientists and railways were regarded as the primary motive force behind industrialisation in continental Europe and the USA.

Heckscher's doctoral dissertation[3], for example, described the effects of late 19th century railway construction in Sweden, while Schumpeter[4] repeatedly cited the railway as illustrating the difference between static and dynamic economics.

More recently, authors such as Fishlow and Fogel have questioned whether the effects of the development of railway systems really were as significant as some of the more extreme positions taken by Schumpeter and Rostow would imply. Fishlow and Fogel criticised Rostow's claim that railways were historically the most powerful single initiator of the American take-off[5] and Fishlow complained that Schumpeter lacked restraint when "he wrote that it is possible to treat the economic history of the United States in the last half of the 19th century solely 'in terms of railroad construction and its effects'."[6]

Fishlow and Fogel claimed that the evidence for the idea of the indispensability of railways for the industrial take-off was weak and failed to establish a causal relationship between the railway and the economic and social changes that characterised the American economy in the 19th century.[7]

Both Fishlow and Fogel acknowledged that the railway was the most important innovation in the 19th century but they opposed the view that the railway was necessary for the American takeoff. In Fogel's words, "no single innovation was vital for economic growth during the 19th century. Certainly if any innovation had title to such distinction it was the railroad".[8] And Fishlow presented nearly the same interpretation: "Such an affirmation of the importance of the railway does not imply that it was singularly crucial to the increased pace of economic activity before the Civil War. Without the innovation, growth would surely have been slower, but the country would not have withered: five per cent or even ten per cent of 1859 income is a small sum in this context. Few innovations can be expected to become indispensable within

---

[3] Heckscher, E, 1907

[4] Schumpeter, J, 1934 and 1939

[5] Fogel, R W, 1964, p13 and Fishlow, A, 1965, p13

[6] A Fishlow, 1965, p13

[7] R W Fogel, in P Temin (ed), 1973, p184f "The idea of a crucial nexus between the railway and the forward surge of the American economy following 1840 appears to be supported by an avalanche of factual evidence. There is, first of all, the impact of the railway on the growth of cities… Further, the decisive victory of the railways over canals and rivers in the contest for the nation's freight is beyond dispute… Finally, there is the high correlation between new railway construction and both population growth and commercial activity."

[8] R W Fogel, 1964, p234

brief years of their introduction. Certainly the steam engine, or electric power, did no such thing."[9] The debate therefore focused on just how important the railways were. No-one questioned the fact that they did have some importance. And the constructive conclusion to draw from the works of Fishlow and Fogel is that the axiom of indispensability of railways for the industrial take-off can not be taken as proven and demands careful investigation.

Earlier empirical work has not detailed the various effects that the railways had on society. From a methodological point of view, Fogel and Fishlow showed that it was possible to measure a large number of effects that the railways had on the 19th century American economy. According to Fishlow, who gave a more thorough account of the railways' influence than Fogel, transport innovations have three major economic effects:

● the lower cost of carrying goods and people

● the increased size of the market that follows from cheaper and faster transportation, and

● the resource demands generated by railway construction and operation.

What was missing to a large extent in Fishlow's and Fogel's work was the inclusion of dynamic influences like innovations[10] or induced development sequences.[11] Fishlow explicitly excluded other paths of influence, such as the "lateral effects".[12] Such effects are often difficult to measure and on a macro level they are captured in a "residual", loosely referred to as "technical progress", which can be seen as a "coefficient of ignorance".[13]

The evolution of high speeds in the railway system[14]

The introduction of railways produced an impressive improvement in inland passenger transportation. In England it took 20 hours in 1830 to go from London to Manchester before the first railways were opened. Twenty-five years later, after the building of a railway network, the journey took five hours 30 minutes.

The setting of railway speed records and the construction of new railway lines have often coincided. One of the first high speed railway records was achieved when the line from Liverpool to Manchester opened in 1830. The record was set because a Member of Parliament had been injured by a train and needed to go to a hospital.

So George Stephenson — one of the designers of the train — drove it as fast as

---

[9] Fishlow, A, 1965, p305f

[10] Tonnolo, G, 1983, p227f

[11] Fishlow, A, p305 "Although we can identify induced development sequences, whether arising from derived demands or forward linkages, it is a herculean task to assign values to them because the alternative path of growth is largely unknown."

[12] According to Rostow these are the induced set of changes which tend to reinforce the industrialisation process on a wider front. See Fishlow, A, 1965, p. 13ff

[13] See O'Brien, P, 1977, p17f

[14] This section is based on the following publications: Freeman Allen, G, 1985, Hollingsworth, B and Cook, A, 1987, Hobsbawm, E, 1969, Hughes, M, 1988 and Marshall, J, 1985.

The various British railway companies sought to push up speeds between the wars. The streamlined Duchess of Hamilton was the London Midland and Scottish Railway's answer to the Pacific Class of the LNER. It is pictured here near Crewe in about 1938

possible — 58kph. It was to no avail, as W Huskisson MP later died in hospital. The most recent high speed record was achieved in 1990 on a section of the newly built TGV-Atlantique line. After a large number of test runs, a modified TGV-Atlantique train was able to reach 515kph.

Higher railway speeds have been made possible through experiment, new technologies, incremental innovations and competition between existing railway lines and other technologies. In the 19th century, gradual improvements to the steam technology raised the maximum speed of trains to 145kph. The records for steam traction were generally held by British railway operators, with the exception of a record of 144kph set on the Paris-Dijon line in 1889.

The railway speed record, held by steam technology for more than 90 years, was beaten by an experimental German electric locomotive built by Siemens & Halske in 1902. The electric locomotive reached 162kph but a disturbing side-effect was that it severely damaged the track. New experiments followed with electric railcars built by Siemens & Halske and AEG. The later railcar reached 210kph in October 1903 on an experimental railway south of Berlin.

The next speed record was also set by an experimental vehicle, in 1931. It was a petrol railcar driven by a propeller and designed by Kruckenberg. This railcar reached 230kph. A large number of trains and railcars reached high speeds in the 1930s and many of them were used on commercial services. Two of best known are the Fliegender Hamburger, in Germany, and Gresley's A4 in Great Britain.

The Fliegender Hamburger was a diesel railcar that held the world speed record for trains in commercial service in 1933. This diesel and similar diesel railcars formed an impressive network of high speed railway services in Germany before the World War II. The A4, designed by Sir Nigel Gresley, was developed as a consequence of the German success with railcars. The London North Eastern Railway (LNER) was so impressed by the Fliegender Hamburger that it asked the German builders to estimate the possible timings for similar units between London and Newcastle or Leeds.

The reply was disappointing because the LNER routes had much more difficult running conditions than the Fliegender Hamburger lines in Germany. So the LNER set out to explore what speeds its existing Gresley locomotives could reach. Within two years, the LNER had produced a high speed steam locomotive, the Gresley A4, that in commercial service could outperform the German diesel railcars. In 1938 one A4 locomotive set the all-time record for steam traction with 201kph.

Year	Speed (kph)	Country	Type of train
1903	203	Germany	Electric railcar
1903	210	Germany	Electric railcar
1931	231	Germany	Petrol railcar driven by a propeller
1953	240	France	Electric locomotive with passenger cars
1955	331	France	Electric locomotive with passenger cars
1981	381	France	Electric train set
1988	407	Germany	Electric train set
1989	482	France	Electric train set
1990	515	France	Electric train set

Table 1.1 Railway high speed records 1903-1990

After the war, the French state railways and the French railway industry took the lead in the development of higher railway speeds. In 1953 and 1955 two new world records were set by electric locomotives of the Series CC 7100 type. On a later occasion, the track was severely damaged by the train running at high speed. The 1955 record was not beaten until 1981 when a TGV train reached 381kph on a test run on a section of the newly built, but not yet opened, Paris-Lyon line. Seven years later the German ICE train beat this record on a test run on a section of the German "neubau" track, and in 1989 and 1990 the French took a firm grip on the high speed record with two impressive runs.

The present railway record of 515kph means that the speed capability of traditional rail technology is equal or better than the competing rail technologies — magnetic levitation or Bertin's Aérotrain.

High speed trains determinants, activities and effects

The current investment in high speed trains and high speed lines constitutes the third wave of investment in railway infrastructure. The first investment wave brought about the building of the network, as investigated by Fishlow and Fogel. The second investment wave was the electrification of the railway network.

The situation today for the railways is quite different from these earlier investment waves. First of all, the competitive position of railways has gradually deteriorated after the era 1840-1920 when railways dominated inland transport markets. Secondly, most developed countries have a large railway network. Thirdly, it has become increasingly difficult to construct new infrastructure because of the effect on the environment. Finally, major railway investment plans must not only compete for capital with other projects, they also compete with other state controlled services for political support.

These four circumstances, and the fact that high speed trains will have a much smaller impact on the development of society, explain why we have chosen a wider approach than Fishlow in our studies of high speed trains. Figure 1.1 shows the relationships that will be discussed in this book.

The basic logic of Figure 1.1 is that the initiation, development and introduction of high speed trains have been affected by a set of determinants, external or internal to the railway system. The determinants have directly influenced the character and content of the activities. Subsequently, different types of effects emerge that feed back to the determinants. This picture of the process is obviously amplified because the real world processes are not as clear-cut as our figure indicates.

A few schematic examples may explain the relationships presented in Figure 1.1.

1) The decision in Japan to build the first Shinkansen line between Tokyo and Osaka produced investment in high speed trains and new infrastructure. The construction of the trains and the building of the infrastructure gave the railway material suppliers a market for their products. Later on, the success of the Tokyo-Osaka line, through a feed-back to the determinants, promoted the building of an additional number of Shinkansen lines.

2) The delay and the subsequent failure of the British APT project, discussed in Chapter 14 by Potter, redirected the British high speed railway system towards an incremental strategy and delayed other projects with tilting trains.

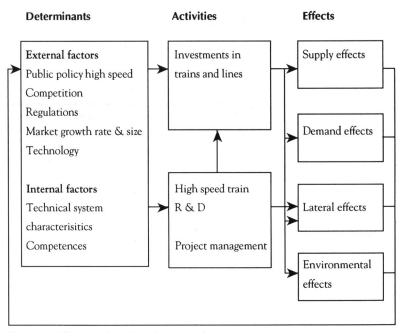

Figure 1.1 The general analytical framework

3) Investments in high speed railway lines have an impact on the environment through the changes they create in the demand for passenger transport. They have a beneficial impact on the environment through the substitution of air and road transport. But they can be presumed to have a negative environmental effect through their contribution to long-term expansion of total transport demand.

Organisation of the book

The book is divided into four sections. The first comprises this chgapter and a discussion on the historical perspective of railway research. Section 2 consists of studies discussing the development of high speed train services in France, Germany, Great Britain, Italy, Japan, Spain, Sweden and United States.

Section 3 deals with thematic issues related to the growth of high speed train services, such as environmental questions, modern railway stations, standardisation of railway equipment, management of high speed train projects, public policy issues and design of high speed trains.

The last section consists of two chapters which discuss high speed trains as a research agenda for social scientists, evaluate the social and economic effects of high speed trains and discuss their future development.

Bibliography

Community of European Railways, Proposals for a European High-Speed Network, January 1989

Fishlow, A, American Railroads and the Transformation of the Ante-Bellum Economy, Cambridge, Mass, 1965

Fogel, R W, Railroads and American Economic Growth: Essays in Econometric History, Baltimore, 1964

Fogel, R W, A Quantitative Approach to the Study of Railroads in American Growth: A Report of some Preliminary Findings, in New Economic History, in P Temin (ed), Penguin Books, 1973

Freeman Allen, G, The Illustrated History of Railways in Britain, London, 1985

Heckscher, E, Till belysning av järnvägarnas betydelse för Sveriges ekonomiska utveckling, Stockholm, 1907

Hobsbawm, E, 1969, Industry and Empire, Penguin Books, 1969

Hollingsworth, B and Cook, A, The Great Book of Trains, London, 1987

Hughes, M, Rail 300, Newton Abbot, Devon, 1988

Knall, G, Snabbtågen halverar dagens restider, in Teknisk tidskrift 1974:4, 1974

Marshall, J, Rail, The Records, Enfield Middlesex, 1985

O'Brien, P, The New Economic History of Railways, London, 1977

Schumpeter, J, The Theory of Economic Development, Cambridge, Mass., 1934

Schumpeter, J, Business Cycles Volume I, New York, 1939

Tonnolo, G, Railways and Economic Growth in Mediterranean Countries: Some Methodological Remarks, in O'Brien, P (ed), Railways and the Economic Development of Western Europe, 1830-1914, Oxford, 1983.

2.

Research on railways in an historical perspective

By Erik Dahmén
Professor Emeritus of Economics and Economic and Social History at Stockholm School
of Economics

THE INFLUENCE of railways upon long-term economic growth has proved a stimulating field of research for economic historians. Besides its historical interest, this research is important because it has raised a number of more general theoretical and methodological problems.

Views on the influence of railways have changed and differed considerably through time. This can be illustrated by reference to two basic questions.

The first refers to the causality issue — why were railways built? Did they appear on the economic scene mainly for "external" reasons, in the sense that a "technological push" was decisive? Or were they predominantly the result of a pressing need for improved transport facilities to keep a growing economy going at full speed?

The second question is "counterfactual". Did railways generate economic growth which would otherwise have been much slower and very different? Or, in their absence, would substitutes have appeared providing transport services sufficiently efficient to leave growth unimpaired?

The fact that the answers to these basic questions have been so different is only partly due to differences in the economic and institutional conditions in different countries at different times. It is also, which is less evident and more interesting, a product of the differences between various analytical approaches and conceptual frameworks used by researchers. Let us amplify these answers and then discuss some general methodological problems met with in studies of the importance of railways.

The first research on railways was almost purely descriptive — as was most economic history research towards the end of the 19th century. The dominant, so-called Historical School noticed that railways had been built; when and how this happened; and how many other things occurred around the new facilities. The visible facts, as such, were supposed to reveal everything with a minimum of guidance from mainly implicit theory. Description might foster and generate theory but this was considered to be of secondary interest.

This descriptive research was soon subjected to criticism. The so called neoclassical economists introduced an all-round **price theory** and thus also a **resource allocation** theory, dealing with the formation of prices and preconditions for market equilibrium and optimal use of factors of production at a given point of time. Dynamic entrepreneurship was accorded no role in the core of this mainstream theory and technological progress was seen as an exogenous (external) factor.

This, of course, did not mean that the theoreticians were unaware of the importance of entrepreneurs and technology. Certainly, many of them underestimated these factors but the general reason for excluding them was, firstly, the aim of concentrating on the fundamentally important resource allocation function of price mechanisms, and secondly, to make clear the reactions of the price system to exogenous changes, that is new technologies.

Such changes led to a reallocation of resources and a new market equilibrium, but the fact that this also enhanced productivity and growth was not analysed more closely.

Due to the static nature of this theory the questions posed were fairly easy to answer — the costs of moving goods and people across space and time were reduced. This in its turn widened the markets for products, as well as for factors of production, and helped to attain a productivity promoting division of labour and economies of scale. The need to hold large stocks was also reduced, which made it possible to transfer substantial funds to growth-stimulating real investments, instead of having them locked up in stocks. Furthermore, many geographical and social barriers to competition were broken down. Last, but not least, there were technological spin-offs in which price mechanism played a role.

Because price theory talked this clear language it could, combined with casual observations of the main obvious factors, bring better insights into causal chains than a more detailed description. This being so, there was no need to bother about complicated statistical tests which would have been particularly difficult to undertake as the search for, and collection of, reliable statistics, if at all available, would have required much additional, and possibly frustrating, work.

Thus, in the early 20th century, researchers pretended to have given answers to the basic questions with pure description as well as with price theory — the railways were mostly seen as having been built ahead of industry and trade. Economic growth would have been much slower, in some cases even absent, without railways.

Those who were content with pure description did not even raise the question whether approximately equivalent substitutes would have appeared or not. According to the neoclassical economists the conclusion followed from a quite simple counterfactual proposition. They saw no need to work with detailed alternatives in order to conceptualise how things might have turned out without railways.

Some critics of the neoclassical theory did appear before World War One but did not command much attention until much later. The most constructive criticism was launched first and foremost by the young J Schumpeter. Its core was the focus on economic development as a result of interactions between entrepreneurial activity and technology. A capacity to generate economic development by innovations and "creative destruction" (not only by enhanced productivity) — rather than the optimal allocation of given resources — was seen as the essence of capitalist systems. Accordingly, static price theory, however indispensable, could only give a very limited understanding of economic development.It could not be replaced but had to be supplemented by an "evolutionary" theory that by definition implied "institutional" economics with focus on the preconditions for well functioning capitalist systems.

The Schumpeterian approach did little to change the picture of the importance of railways. Railways were looked upon as one of the most obviously important innovations in the 19th century. They not only facilitated the industrial break-through, but played a very active role as a generator. There was little need, according to the Historical School and the neoclassicists, for sophisticated counterfactual propositions and complicated statistical tests. To quote Schumpeter: "Just look around you!"

It was not until World War Two that the consensus on the economic impact of railways was challenged. Those who now entered the scene, representing the so called "New economic history", started from a neoclassical basis but nevertheless arrived at very different conclusions about the importance of railways. The essence of this new school of thought can be summarised as follows.

The research was based on the use of production function analyses in order to measure the contribution to growth by different inputs of factors of production. On that basis, a first attempt was made to exploit the potential of a combination of economic theory and econometrics[1] in studies of economic growth. So far, only business cycle theories had been tested with econometrics. The application of theory to the railway issue was made in order to assist historians to specify mechanisms through which investments in railways operated on the growth rate.

Attempts were then made to quantify these mechanisms, using advanced statistical methods. A main thesis was that it is useless to discuss the consequences of railways unless one knows whether the railway services represented more than would have been contributed by alternatives. One of the conclusions of the new economic historians was that cheap inland transportation was a necessary precondition for the industrial breakthrough. But its satisfaction did not necessarily entail the specific form of transportation represented by railways. Substitutes did exist with a high development potential.

This assertion was supported by calculations that pretended to show that GNP (gross national product) at a certain point of time would not have been much lower in the absence of railways. It was unlikely that their "social savings", measured as the additional costs incurred by sending the same freight between the same points by other means, was substantial.

The new economic history launched its criticism and new ideas with, so it seems, some overstatements in order to challenge the "received wisdom" in a way that could not possibly leave more traditionally oriented colleagues in the economic history profession indifferent. And, indeed, the new approach did not pass unchallenged. A lively discussion followed, dealing not only with the interpretation of historical events as such, but also with research methodology.

All could agree that the new economic history raised well specified and logically consistent questions. It was also conceded that causal chains had been too loosely specified in the old approach and that the contribution to economic growth by 19th century railways might have been exaggerated. It was not without justification that the burden of proof was laid on those who had launched the "axiom of indispensability".

On the other hand, the interpretation offered by the new economic history of

---
[1] The application of mathematics and statistics to economics.

what actually happened, that is the strong downward assessment of the role of railways, was not left unquestioned. Critics turned the burden of proof back and took issue particularly with the research methodology.

Some criticism was directed at the empirical basis for the new research on railways. The reliability of statistical information varied a great deal and was in some cases less than satisfying. However, the new economic history could not, in fairness, be accused of having been generally careless on this point. The quality of statistics was not the most important issue.

Some of the methodological issues referred to the use-production functions. Could such an analytical tool, at best, do more than raise interesting problems? And could it result in anything but fallacious post hoc probability conclusions about causal chains, thus leaving the search for real answers to other analytical methods?

It was not denied that the new economic history had been fairly successful in employing production functions on a low aggregative level, referring to fairly homogeneous groups of firms and well defined branches of industry. But attempts at aggregated "macro" levels were of little use and could be misleading when new production functions, new products and raw materials — as well as other aspects of continuous structural changes — represented much, or even most, of the growth-promoting dynamics. Is it really meaningful to calculate how much one or the other factor of production and the, mostly large, residual, loosely and quite misleadingly labelled "technical progress", have contributed to the growth rate? Actually this residual (technical progress) can be seen as a "coefficient of ignorance" concerning the most important dynamic factors.

A number of other critical questions were more specific. Are the results of attempts to measure the "social savings" of railways at a certain point of time convincing? Is it sensible to assume that, in the absence of railways, an increasing transport demand derived from developments unrelated to railways would have led to substantial improvements to other means of transportation, and to the invention and practical use of substitutes... and thus to the same transportation cost structure? Some critics have considered these questions to be rather rhetorical.

The controversies concerning these and related questions have now receded. As far as the railway issue is concerned the results have been judged inconclusive and two burdens of proof remain. This has contributed to a tendency towards bridging the gap between, on the one hand, traditional, mostly micro-based, historical research and, on the other hand, that part of the macro economic theory conducted by economists with a greater interest in economic history than the majority of theoreticians. There are, however, some points on which there now seems to be much less disagreement than before.

Economic development is seen as too complex and diversified a process to permit statements on prime movers. An increasing number of economists are less confident about pure economics than before and more interested in a broader social science approach. This has led to an increasing interest in methodological issues. Today, sophisticated counterfactual propositions are mostly looked upon as an intellectual exercise that may be an eye-opener and possible a barrier to hasty conclusions. But it is an indisputable fact that railways actually meant much more than other carriers of freight and people.

A counterfactual proposition need not go further than stating that a different course of events would have occurred without railways. Not even a sophisticated counterfactual scenario can be constructed with anything but gross margins of error. It is also agreed that there is no satisfactory technique, nor any need, to give precise measure to the importance of railways. And accordingly there is no basis for quantifying their share of the economic growth rate. What is held to be more important, and an interesting subject for research, is why railways were conceived and constructed, and how they interacted with other factors in contributing to the actual growth rate.

This last statement may seem to boil down to a preference for something in between the descriptions favoured by the Historical School and the neoclassical theoretical approach. This, however, is not so. What it means is — and this is of fundamental importance to observe — first, that much more theory than was implicitly entailed in the research of the Historical School is necessary in causal analyses. Secondly, that there is actually a need for more theory than in the static neoclassical approach, or more exactly, a need of supplements in the form of *evolutionary* theory.

Certainly, this is still seen by many economists as something too distant from strict, operational and testable theory. But those who do not hold this view are more numerous than in the 1970s. And it is exactly this that is narrowing the gap, in a more successful way than that ambitiously tried by the new economic history, between professional economic historians on the one hand, and economists who want to work with theory and empirical material in causal analyses but not with advanced theoretical and mathematical modelling, on the other.

Let us conclude by looking, subjectively, at examples of analytical tools that have proved useful in research on what can be suitably characterised as *transformation processes*.

The focus on transformation processes instead of on their result as measured at aggregated macro levels — that is, on growth — implies analyses at the micro level, because it is only here that it is possible to study the core of the process, represented by entrepreneurial activities and their interplay with technological and institutional factors.

However, as the ultimate aim is to obtain insights into the mechanisms behind macro developments, the analyses have to be conceptually anchored on what is called the meso level, that is the relations and interactions between micro entities through time. Analytical tools on the meso level should be used as "divining-rods", with a view to identifying activities and causal chains which appear repeatedly and have some common characteristics, but are mostly, so to speak, differently dressed in different areas and different times.

Price theory and many other parts of mainstream economics as presented in ordinary textbooks are, of course, examples of such tools. But there are other tools which, contrary to the neoclassical ones, are fitted to grasp transformation processes, that is those in which railways have been, still are, and can be expected to be, central.

Thus, for example, a situation may be dominated by a demand pull and/or by other opportunities to increase production and to make headway into new technologies and new fields of profitable activities. If so, there is a prevailing *"positive transformation pressure"* or rather suction.

There may also be a *"negative transformation pressure"*, that is a situation that is dominated by declining demand and which may call for countermeasures. When such a pressure depends on too high a general cost level, attempts to reduce costs across the board will, of course, be close at hand, as well as, perhaps, various measures to attain a more cost-effective branch structure.

On the other hand, if the pressure is mainly due to circumstances other than too high costs, that is non-competitive or obsolete products, or vanishing markets (which often are possible to diagnose only with the benefit of hindsight) such defensive measures may prove misplaced. Economic history, and of course business history, offers many examples of such experiences.

In addition to successful defensive countermeasures we can consider those with an "offensive" character. These are particularly interesting as illustrations of a special kind of economic dynamics, and comprise cases where innovations are induced by a destructive threat and thus would not otherwise have been forthcoming. This means that primary innovations may be creative in a double sense — both in their own right, and as stimulators of innovative countermeasures. One example which illustrates the point is the appearance of fast-sailing clippers as a response to the arrival of steam ships.

This basic analytical approach is useful in research on railways.

During the great railway era most railways were almost everywhere constructed mainly in response to a combination of technological and economic opportunities, that is in situations characterised by positive transformation pressures.

In recent decades, railways have instead been subject to negative pressures. Large parts of the networks have lost competitive power, very much as a consequence of the expansion of domestic airlines and, of course, due to rapidly increasing road traffic. The response to this pressure raises many questions which are interesting also in view of the present schemes for high speed trains.

To what extent are high speed trains to be seen as a defence, yielding new technologies and new ways and means of offering railway services? Do they in this case represent the same kind of economic dynamics — offensive countermeasures — that has been common in the history of industry, shipping and trade? If so, to what extent has this reaction been preceded by cost-reducing and, possibly, restructuring measures such as discontinuing of non profitable parts of the "old" railway network and closing of many stations, or by other kinds of passive defence, instead of immediate, more innovative measures? Would it in this case be correct to talk about "observation lags" or rather, which would be of particular interest from a social science point of view, about "decision lags" due to institutional rigidities or vested interests?

Perhaps these questions are beside the point? Has, after all, the negative transformation pressure right from the beginning played a minor role compared with "technological push"? Have spin-offs from other technological areas opened up new, unexpected opportunities? Maybe the development of networks of high speed trains offers the only alternative to shutting down large parts of old networks. Or perhaps it is necessary because of the serious environmental effects of continuously expanding road and air traffic?

However, the following question remains: to what extent can high speed trains be expected to offer examples of a creative destruction, with some domestic airlines and road traffic becoming the "victims"? If this is the case, are these "victims" likely to react in a rather passive way, or actively by various countermeasures, some of which may contain innovative elements with repercussions for high speed trains?

With this basic approach some additional analytical tools fall well into place. They refer to *complementarities* in technological, economic and other factors interacting through time. The economic success of certain stages in a transformation process often requires completion of particular complementary stages. As long as this condition is not fulfilled there is a *"structural tension"*. This could mean a depressive pressure, or at least a lack of profitability, in the "premature" stages, but also a development potential, as such tensions may give rise to initiatives and activities so as to bring the missing stages into place.

Such initiatives may be taken by existing, or new, actors without concerted activities, that is simply as a reaction to market "price signals", or within the framework of network-relations outside what is traditionally called a "market".

In order to catch important aspects of such "structural tensions" and their implications for transformation processes I introduced, about 50 years ago, a special concept, namely *"development block"*. This concept refers to a *"sequence of complementarities"* which, through a series of released structural tensions, result in a more, possibly completely, balanced situation. New technologies and new or expanding enterprises, as well as infrastructure, represent examples of such complementary links.

Then, in a second analytical step, a distinction has to be made between two kinds of development blocks, namely those of an *ex post* character and those which are an *ex ante* phenomenon.

An *ex post development block* is characterised by linkages in which, first of all, "signals" within the price system are the indicators. Such linkages have, of course, been recorded by economic historians and geographers, though without conceptualising the process in analytical categories beyond the realms of the static price theory. And without ambitions to integrate the results with a macro theory of economic development.

A *development block ex ante* is even more interesting as an example of economic dynamics, not least because it illustrates possibilities of such an integration. In such a development block, entrepreneurs visualise *in advance*, without any clear market signals, potentials embodied in already existing or perceived structural tensions. This gives incentives to activities of various kinds, for example concerted initiatives, to solve the problems that have to be solved in order to release the potentials, thus reducing the risks of making bad investments.

Such a release is not a matter of advertising, sales promotion or marketing activities but of entrepreneurship in order to find opportunities to invest, or make others invest, in related branches or sectors of the economy which represent the missing links. The core of the dynamics is, so to speak, in procuring one's own

24

customers by separate entrepreneurial activities, mostly in the hope of starting a self-generating process.

What about the implications for the railway issue of these further analytical steps? Apparently, many railways have been built as links within development blocks which have been mostly of the *ex post* character, sometimes ahead of other links, and in other cases as a response to market "signals". As the completion of such blocks has often been quite time-consuming, tight capital markets and shortened time horizons in downward phases of business cycles have not rarely led to financial difficulties.

However, the history of railways also offers examples of *ex ante* development blocks. Some of those who were active in railway companies, or in their financing, were also engaged in other entrepreneurial activities within industry and trade that were expected to interact with the railways.

To what extent, if any, are high speed trains to be seen as integrated parts of development blocks? If so, can they be expected to set in motion such blocks mainly *ex post*? Can their profitability from a business or socioeconomic point of view be supposed to be dependent on their completion? Is the completion likely to be a more or less automatic, though of course time-consuming, market process? Or will concerted activities to that end be necessary in order to minimise the risks of economic difficulties? In other words: is there a need for *ex ante* elements in the development blocks of high speed trains?

So these are the main questions:

● To what extent do high speed train investments present much of the same type of dynamics we have seen in the earlier history of railways and in shipping, industry and trade?

● Is it correct to say that the current and planned activities can be seen as a second offensive phase of a response, in many cases preceded by various kinds of cost-reducing measures, to many years of negative transformation pressures?

Insofar as they do comprise such an offensive response, there is but a very short step to expect them to open up a process of self-generating advance along a track, the end of which may be perceived only by those who are equipped with an entrepreneurial vision.

Part Two — Country Studies

3.

Introduction
By *the Editors*

THIS PART of the book presents a number of studies of high speed trains in different countries. Some chapters give an historical overview of the development of railway transport, while others deal with more recent events in detail. History clearly matters if we want to understand what is happening in the railway sector today.

This is so because early choices of, for instance, technology tend to lock railway systems into specific patterns of evolution. It will also become evident that the striving for higher speed on railways, in competition with other modes of traffic, is a far from recent phenomenon. The first wave of high speed trains did, in fact, start in the late 1920s in both the USA and Europe.

Even though the examples exhibit a great diversity of characteristics and content, some common themes can be found. Public policy towards the transport sector in general, and railways in particular, is one such theme. The increasing competition from road and air traffic is another. In historical perspective, the railways have, since the Second World War, been facing the threat of substitution by new modes of transport, in the same way as railways rendered horse-drawn coaches and canals obsolete in the 19th century. We can thus see the following chapters as an exposé of the railways' struggle for survival, and how they have taken advantage of the possibility offered by the steadily growing demand for faster transport.

In the first chapter, Beltran describes the origin and early development of the TGV (Train à Grande Vitesse). The first turning point was the creation of a national railway administration, SNCF, in the 1930s. Through standardisation and investment in electrification, the service level improved. In the 1960s several public utilities in France met severe competition. This problem was dealt with in the Nora Report, following which major reorientations in the strategies of these companies were initiated.

The organisation of SNCF was changed to permit a better and more rapid adaptation to new market conditions. An interesting detail here is the closer cooperation between technicians and economists at the research and development department. As a result, it was concluded that SNCF should direct its efforts towards a long-distance, inter-city network.

The second part of the first chapter deals with the TGV story from 1976 onwards. Polino describes how the high speed train system in France evolved from one line, the Paris-Lyon connection, to a network. An important choice was whether or not to make the new system compatible with the existing network. This way the TGV trains could reach destinations beyond the high speed lines and use the existing stations, albeit at less than top speed.

The technical and economic success of the TGV-Sudest line spurred further development. This line is to be extended to Marseille and connected to the Italian network. A second line out to the Atlantic coast and further south has been partially completed and put into service. Presently, work on the TGV Nord and the TGV interconnection around Paris is under way. Despite numerous and thorough investigations, some of the effects of the TGV on employment, industrial activity, and its long-term environmental and energy conservation implications, remain unknown. Still, many see the French experience, together with that of the Japanese, as exemplifying the real potential of conventional railway technology.

In Spain the choice has fallen on the French type of high speed line. A completely new line has been built using rolling stock of TGV type, manufactured by GEC Alsthom subsidiaries, with assistance from Spanish partners. The enthusiasm over the Olympic Games in Barcelona and the World Expo in Seville in 1992 served as motivation and provided a stiff deadline and, indeed, the connection was completed in record time. However, Gómez-Mendoza is questioning the economic rationale for building high speed lines in Spain at all. He argues that the potential of road and air traffic systems has not yet been fully utilised, and that the railways in Spain seem to be most competitive on short-haul routes.

An interesting feature of the Spanish high speed train adventure is that the new system was made internationally, but not nationally, compatible. The plans are to connect the new lines to the emerging French TGV network, and possibly also westwards to Portugal, while the Iberian broad gauge network will slowly be converted to the international standard gauge.

The Italian history of high speed trains is quite long and intriguing. In the 1930s, the fascist regime invested heavily in the railway system and used it as a symbol of progressiveness. During this period a new generation of fast train, the ETR 200, was built, some examples of which are still in service.

After the war, the reconstruction of the railway demanded large efforts. A new, straighter connection between Rome and Milan was put in hand early on, and several types of high speed rolling stock were tested. The Pendolino project, initiated in 1969, had the purpose of providing a tilting train capable of 250kph, to be used on both new and existing tracks. At the very moment when the first prototype was put on the rails, the politicians cancelled plans for higher speeds.

According to Giuntini, one major obstacle throughout has been the mismanagement of the railway system, because of continuous friction between politicians and the administration. It was not until 1988 that a second generation of tilting trains could start commercial service. The experience so far is not all positive. Putting sophisticated new trains, running at a high frequency, into a system close to total collapse is likely to produce major difficulties. A successful high speed train service demands more than a fast train. Possibly, the planned 1,200kms of semi-privately financed new lines will prove more successful.

Why did the USA, despite its large and highly developed railway system at the beginning of this century, lose its position as a leading railway nation? To begin with, Klein argues, the regulations imposed on railways about 1920 represented a major obstacle to their competitiveness and further development. Several operators did, however, manage to launch the so-called Streamliners in the 1930s. The higher speed of these trains was made possible by the use of efficient diesel engines and lightweight alloy construction technologies borrowed from the aviation industry.

The war drastically changed conditions for the railways. The strategically important aircraft technology was improved through intensive research and development activities while the railway system deteriorated through heavy use without reinvestment. Attempts to create high speed train services in the 1960s and 70s all failed, as did those with public (Federal) support. The initiative has therefore been left to private actors and state authorities. No doubt, the story of high speed trains in the USA is puzzling. The institutional aspect of railway development in the USA is discussed in the closely related contribution by Dobbin.

The British experience of high speed trains in the post-war period can be characterised as the victory of gradualism over radicalism. The technologically sophisticated APT (Advanced Passenger Train) project failed, while the less advanced InterCity 125 could safely be put into service in the mid-1970s (see also Chapter 14). The latter proved successful on the fairly straight, unelectrified East Coast Main Line, and later on other routes.

Nash presents an overview of the effects of high speed on rail in Britain. He concludes that the gradual measures taken so far have paid off well, both commercially and socially. The effects of increased speeds on traffic volume seems to be in the order of one to one, that is an elasticity of -1. That is to say, that if speed is increased by ten per cent, then traffic will, similarly, increase by ten per cent. However, the elasticity seems to be a stepwise function of reduction in travel time. We have evidence from the introduction of the TGV which points to much higher elasticities, somewhere between -2 and -3. But then, the investments have been much larger.

In the Swedish case, the authors' main question is why it took so long to develop a high speed train. When answering this question, attention is given to a broad range of factors, including intra- and inter-organisational action, economic and technical problems and political action. This gives us a picture of the far-reaching and complex interactions involved in this type of project. Solving all the different types of problems that occurred called for levels of coordination and cooperation beyond what could be accommodated within the normal routines.

The aim of having a tilting train, like the British APT and the Italian Pendolino, meant that additional technical problems were encountered. It is concluded that no single factor could account for the delay, and that lost potential revenues were to some extent traded for a higher technical quality when the X2000 train was completed.

According to Aberle, the German Neubaustrecken came about because of three factors:

● the expected bottlenecks in the system due to increasing freight transport

● the successes of high speed trains in Japan, and

● the possibility of re-establishing a competitive passenger service.

The decision to run both freight and passenger trains on the new lines posed some problems. Construction costs became very high and, as it turned out, freight traffic actually decreased by 20 per cent before services could start. Mixing slow freight trains and fast passenger trains on the same line sharply reduced capacity.

Furthermore, the German ICE trains are not compatible with the systems in the surrounding countries, which limits their usefulness. Nevertheless, Germany plans to invest heavily in its railway system during the coming years, in both new and upgraded lines.

The last contribution in this part tells the story of the post-Tokaido Shinkansen development. Japan exhibits two counteracting features with respect to high speed train services. On the one hand, a concentrated population with high purchasing power, on the other, a topography which, in combination with large urban areas, sharply raises construction costs. Matsuda describes in some detail the sometimes extraordinary solutions needed to overcome these problems. In fact, the greater part of the lines run through tunnels or on viaducts. The benefits of high speed trains have so far been considered to offset the adverse effects of high construction costs and environmental disturbances.

Unlike the French TGV, the Shinkansen trains are not compatible with the old lines. It therefore took quite a long time to create a coherent network. Meanwhile, several new generations of Shinkansen trains appeared. The latest 400 series is particularly interesting since these trains, through their smaller loading gauge and the addition of an extra rail on the narrow gauge line, are compatible with parts of the old network.

4a.
SNCF and the development of high speed trains
1950-1981

Economic rationale and technological choices
Alain Beltran, Institut d'Histoire du Temps Present (CNRS), Paris

SNCF IS proud of its high speed network. The "grande vitesse" history is quite a long one, dating back to the Fifties and Sixties. This paper puts forward some hypotheses and focuses on the political and economic framework in which the French TGV has been launched.

The development of trains travelling at high speeds — whether in Europe or on other continents — is clearly a general phenomenon. However, each country and enterprise involved has its own peculiar approach to the development and its own solutions to the problems. Understanding this diversity can teach important lessons to today's decision-makers.

But before embarking on such an analysis, we must delve into history. We shall consider here the technical and economic choices made by the Société Nationale des Chemins de Fer Français (the SNCF, or state-owned railway company) during the 1950s and up to 1981 with the introduction of the high speed train or TGV (Train à Grande Vitesse) linking Paris to the southeast of France.

A new context

THE RISE OF COMPETITORS

The SNCF had to face the realities of a competitive market sooner than other state-owned monopolies and in this respect the 1960s were a real turning point. Rail transport had to fight increasingly hard for its share of the market against roads (cars for people, lorries for freight) and aeroplanes. Thus a public company was obliged to make the "intellectual shift" in attitude from that of a monopoly to being one player in a highly competitive sector.

The time at which these events occurred was a difficult one for SNCF in any case. There had been a dramatic decrease in traffic, especially freight, thanks to competition from road haulage. The operation's overall deficit became dangerously large. To cut losses and enable modernisation, the company was obliged to close part of its network and progressively reduce the number of its employees. Moreover, during the 1960s, the government favoured investment in roads, especially motorways (France definitely had a lot of catching-up to do in this field). The only remaining profitable sector for the railways, or so it seemed, would be inter-city connections (the regional planners were keen to promote such developments).

What seemed to be taking shape was the creation of a network with its own particular hierarchy where the most interesting items for the SNCF would be first class passenger travel and the Trans-Europ Express trains (TEEs). Finally, the achievements of the classic trains were being challenged by new technologies. In the 1960s, competition also came from the Bertin's Aérotrain, a new, non-railway invention for travelling at high speeds, developed by an engineer. Were trains as they had been known, condemned?

Comparative passenger traffic

France, 1946/73 passenger-kilometres (millions)

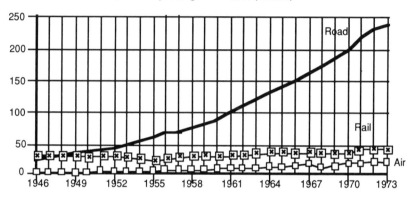

Figure 4.1

THE NORA REPORT AND THE TURNING POINT IN THE MARKETING OF PUBLIC COMPANIES

With France undergoing intense modernisation, where the keywords were profitability and concentration, the large sector comprising the state-owned industries could not afford to lag behind. Its role inside the French economy had to be more precisely defined. In the mid-1960s, the repercussions of the Nora Report were far-reaching. This dealt with the management of the large state-owned companies. Inspired by Electricité de France's example (the publicly-owned utilities company), it recommended overhauling the structures of the state-owned companies to improve their capacity to respond to the demands of competition. This free-market orientation provoked ample discussions, debates and proposals concerning new sales and marketing policies. The future of the railways was described as "disturbing". The network had to adapt itself to a competitive environment and concentrate its activities on profitable areas. At this point, the SNCF established a medium-term programme to improve its productivity and its profit structure.

Another public document dating from the same period and annexed to the Fifth Five-Year Plan (called "group 1985") insisted on the central importance of the transport system. An inefficient system could be a real hindrance to modernisation. Consequently, after the Fifth Five-Year Plan, transport policies were studied more

31

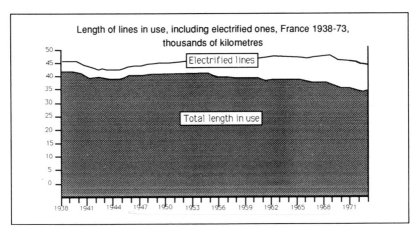

Figure 4.2

carefully and took the fierce competition into account. Previously, heavy goods and the TEEs (with supplementary fares) had been regarded as the profit-makers, but now, the competitive market tipped the balance in favour of quality of service on national long-distance connections, rather than internal productivity improvements. The new strategy would concentrate on the development and operation of long-distance networks.

RESTRUCTURING AND MODERNISING AT THE SNCF

Before the Second World War the maximum speed attained by French trains was 120kph (less than in many other countries). The existence of separate railway systems precluded network-wide innovation (before nationalisation of the different companies in 1937). Electrification had begun but was far from widespread: in 1938, of the 42,600kms of rail in service, only 3,340kms were electrified.

After SNCF was established in 1937, there was an increase in the maximum speeds attained: 130kph for steam, 140kph for electric. After the war, the traction units were standardised by importing a large number of American locomotives. The SNCF initiated a modernisation programme based on the use of industrial electricity (alternating current) on the major connections. Initially, France had opted for direct current at 1,500 volts (the military had a strong influence on this decision, wanting to ensure technical options distinct from those of the Germans).

However, Louis Armand, SNCF Director General, insisted on the choice of alternating current as the way to standardise the system, affirm the SNCF's role and promote the railway industry's access to the rest of the world. It would thus be possible to have fewer electrical substations and fewer expensive catenaries, since they would be connected to the general electricity network.

The first monophase 25,000-volt rail connection was the line from Charleville to Valenciennes. Even in 1955, the world train speed record (331kph) was still held using direct current. But as technological progress advanced, electric locomotives using alternating current attained equal results. After a while, locomotives able to use different types of current were introduced, which allowed standardisation of traffic and helped promote links with the other countries.

Various factors underlay the different nationalisation schemes implemented in France after the war. Sometimes the motivation was political (the vehicle-maker Renault for instance), but in other sectors engineers supported the idea of nationalisation because of the advantage to be gained from amalgamating production and research resources. This was the case with electricity, which was given enormous resources to devote to research.

The nationalisation of the railways in 1937 did not proceed in a similar fashion. It was not until the 1960s that SNCF developed a research department which played a vital role in the decision-making process concerned with the TGV. Just as the economists at Electricté de France became increasingly powerful (to the point of taking command of the company), so the economists in the research department played a crucial role in the SNCF.

It is said that the research department first made its appearance after a trip to Japan. It was simply tacked on to the existing organisation however, and did not constitute a remodelling of the research structure (thus representing a compromise). The research department personnel introduced new methods, particularly those which the Corps des Ponts et Chaussées (Corps of civil engineers) had used to promote its motorway policy. Thus, the research department developed a bias towards high speeds. At the same time, in 1967, a Development Department (which has since become the Marketing Department) appeared within the Sales Division. The somewhat lax organisation of the SNCF was tightened up. In 1976, the research department became a part of the Department of General Development and Research.

Economic rationale and technological choices

THE ECONOMIC ENTICEMENTS OF HIGH SPEED

We have seen that, for a long time, the SNCF was almost exclusively preoccupied with the overall improvement of the railway network. Consequently, research on high speeds became almost clandestine after the 1955 speed record. The emphasis was, rather, on regularity. It was the research department which, in 1966, first introduced the idea of thinking seriously about the economic advantages of high speed trains. Towards the end of the 1960s, a change in attitude emerged, recognising that it was important to save time as well as money.

The context was one of intense competition and the objective was to find solutions quickly to rescue the SNCF. It was therefore essential to limit new technological options. Having opted for the high speed train, the priority was no longer technological innovation, but innovation in sales and organisation.

The high speed development projects from 1965 to 1969 readily opted to use the existing infrastructures. A fluid synergy emerged between research and application. Very rapidly the accent was placed on compatibility between the existing rail network and the "new" high speed network, unlike the Aérotrain, which required special lines to be constructed.

A major advantage was that the train could use the existing infrastructure to enter cities. Gradually, with economic considerations taking precedence, well-tried technologies were chosen in preference to the complete innovation the Aérotrain represented. The fact that the attempts to set speed records for the TGV occur at the end of the process (just before the sales phase) and not at the beginning of the tests, as was the case in 1955, epitomises this approach.

THE CHOICE OF MATERIAL

Although the late Sixties restored high speeds to a place of honour, there were many who thought the railway could not evolve much further technologically. The limits were thought to have been reached. Only new technology could produce high speeds. From among the new technologies, the main contender was M Bertin's Aérotrain. The SNCF had been approached as early as 1957, but did not consider that the amount of traffic between Paris and Lyon warranted a trip of only one-and-a-half hours.

Bertin, however, had the support of the DATAR (Délégation à l'Aménagement du Territoire et à l'Action Régionale) which favoured rapid links between regional centres of population. In 1966, the Aérotrain reached 300kph and was highly regarded by both the government and the general public. A Lyon-Grenoble connection was promised (as well as other projects, like connections between the capital and the new towns). An experimental line near Orléans was built in the same year to test the Aérotrain in real life conditions.

However, these projects never became reality. Unsolved technical problems, difficulties in integrating the line into urban networks, the energy crisis, a too-broad array of technological options due to imprecise market study, and inertia on the part of the transportation industry were among factors which constantly delayed the launch of the Aérotrain. The idea was finally abandoned at the beginning of the 1970s.

The Aérotrain, however, was not without consequences for the SNCF. It focussed interest in working on high speeds and encouraged a more aggressive style in the nationalised company.

In the same period, the SNCF was interested in the experience of the Japanese with the Shinkansen (1964). Some sources speak of a "Tokaido complex"... After 1965, studies were done in France to adapt the gas turbine for use on railways. The first studies date from 1967/1968 and raised the question of the best kind of energy to use for traction, how to transmit it and which braking systems should be used. Essentially, these studies concluded that the gas turbine project was feasible.

In 1968/1969, the Paris-Lyon project was finished. In 1969 the first prototype TGV 001 trains (with gas turbines) had no tilt mechanism. But a subsequent decision to construct a new line between Paris and Lyon made tilting unnecessary. Furthermore, the straight alignment, following the undulations of the terrain made many constructions, such as tunnels and viaducts, unnecessary and thus turned out to be less expensive.

The high-speed project became official in 1970/1971 (after a report by Mr Coquand in 1970 and a favourable decision of the Cabinet). The period from 1972 to 1976 was characterised by detailed design and political decisions. The very positive results of 1972 (318kph with the gas turbine) had won over the railway employees, despite their initial scepticism. Electricity was chosen as early as 1974 (it followed the

The TGV Postal mail train on a stretch of new track

first oil crisis and almost President Pompidou's last decision).

NETWORK EFFECT AND NEW APPROACHES

Economic factors were the determining element through the entire process of choosing between the different technical options. The Paris-Lyon connection — close to saturation point — needed reinforcing. User studies highlighted the need for an integrated railway service and not just a Paris-Lyon connection. It was a question of planning for the whole of southeastern France.

The TGV was perceived as a means of servicing a whole region, as opposed to the Aérotrain which emphasised linear connections. The economists in the SNCF foresaw an entire high speed network (like the motorway system) where trains would be so numerous there would be no need for timetables. The pressure that came from elected representatives to locate a station and connections in their area — plus continued development on a European level — confirmed the demand for this network concept.

When the project was presented to the government, the economic plans were well advanced — much more so in fact than the technological side. These economic studies were a complete departure from the usual SNCF activities. Traffic forecasts, and not actual traffic volumes on given connections, and planning in terms of travel time were entirely new. The department economists now stressed the quality of the service and new methods of calculating prices. They had calculated future levels of profitability and the results were surprising. For example, they demonstrated how the TGV project would generate a sturdy profit by diverting Paris and southeast-bound traffic away from road and air, and on to rail.

Figure 4.3

Figure 4.4

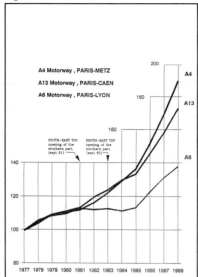

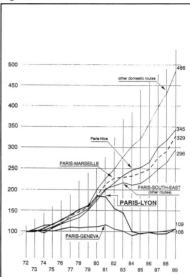

The figures illustrate the effect of the opening of the TGV service on other transport modes between Paris and Lyon. Left: motorway traffic, right, air traffic

The rate of return for the state, as opposed to the SNCF alone, was twice as high. It made possible the revitalisation of the railways. As had happened with Électricité de France, the research department's accounting methods and its problem-solving techniques spread throughout the entire enterprise. In fact, the research department played a major role in influencing SNCF's economic recovery, while paradoxically, the research on technology played a minor role. Once the experts' economic calculations had legitimated the project, it could be presented to the government.

The political side of the project was facilitated by close collaboration with the Ministry and an alliance with the builders of the system. The problem of the saturated Paris-Lyon connection was thus resolved: for the state, investment in the TGV was much more preferable in terms of productivity than doubling the track provision.

France thus chose a compromise solution: the TGV track to the southeast was dedicated (a new track of more than 250kms) but its compatibility with the rest of the network was ensured. Everything was done to harmonise the TGV with other trains: the same prices (but mandatory reservations and price supplements at times of heavy traffic); the same conductors; the same personnel. It was the same service... but with two hours sliced off! This continuity largely contributed to the TGV's success in 1981. The SNCF, sometimes against its own will, had successfully accomplished its evolution without causing any revolution.

Bibliography

Beltran, A; Picard, J F. 1992. *Histoire d'une décision : le chemin de fer à très grande vitesse en France, 1945-1990*, unpublished report, AHICF/Institut d'histoire du temps présent

Fourniau, J M, 1988. *La genèse des grandes vitesses à la*

SNCF, de l'innovation à la décision du TGV Sud Est, rapport INRETS n° 60

Hughes, M. 1988. *Rail 300, The World High Speed Train Race*, London.

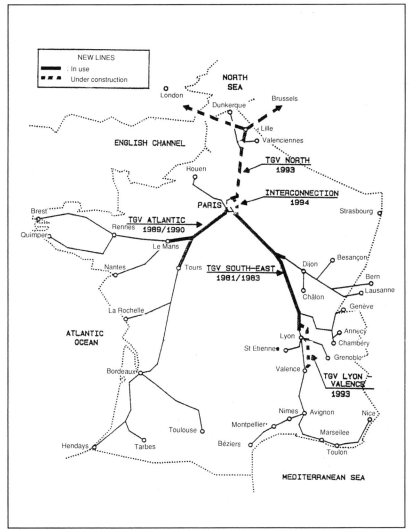

The TGV network, 1994

4b.
The TGV since 1976

A few hints for historical research

Marie-Noëlle Polino, French Railways Historical Society (AHICF), Paris

TWENTY YEARS ago, the question "What will things be like in the year 2000?" was a favourite subject for elementary school children in France. Landscapes that were too green and too calm, where the only movement came from a few air or space shuttles cruising high over tall apartment towers: such was the monotonous image that emerged from these predictions solicited from French youngsters. Never a train, except perhaps here and there a refined metro.

At the end of the Sixties, French youngsters imagined that trains would be left behind, along with cumbersome departures for August vacations or trips organised by their grandparents. In short, the train was outmoded. It had become an accessory of military service or student life quickly forgotten by the dynamic young managers of this period of economic growth. They left the train behind as soon as they could, in favour of the private car ownership and air travel that their society afforded them.

This past prediction does not describe our present reality, however. Even if it has not changed completely, the image of rail travel has been given a new lease of life in the Europe of the Nineties.

This new image and the events that have built it are a reality of which the primary characteristic for the contemporary historian, is its complexity. A variety of indicators all tend to show the same thing, whether they be studies commissioned by AHICF into the various positions of the people involved in development of the French (very) high speed railways; data obtained by transport research institutes[1]; or the images, myths and dreams inspired by high speed trains, and found in the media.

We shall therefore examine some of the concepts which, within the railway industry, government agencies and the public at large, have given shape to the reality of high speed trains in France.

1. **What circumstances have produced the demand for a TGV system? What arguments have continuously defended this system, and its modifications, over the past 15 years?**

2. **How was the high speed network designed, being initially conceived as an integration of the first high speed line with the existing network, and only later as the superimposition of a system of interconnected high speed lines on a**

---

[1] Bonnafous, A. A Synthesis of the Results of Other Case Studies: France. *High Speed Rail Workshop*, May 18-19, 1987, Groningen

conventional network?

3. In what terms, depending on the perspective taken, were the cost-effectiveness of the system and its effects on the transport market measured?

4. What is the role (central or otherwise) of speed, of its perception by the individual and the community, and of the trials at very high speeds, in the definition and in the perception of the "TGV effect"?

These few remarks will be all the more summary since the subject we are dealing with is so vast: 670kms of dedicated high speed lines are already in use in France, while very high speed trains also operate on a significant proportion of the conventional network. In addition, the long-term plan for development, published in June 1990, provides for the construction of 3,172kms of new line.

The momentum of the TGV system: from system to line; from system optimisation to network

According to studies cited by SNCF at international conferences and in accounts of the TGV over the past 15 years, the development of very high speeds followed a strictly logical sequence, a function of the internal logic of the railway system.

1974	Decision in favour of electric traction
1976	Work on the new Paris-Lyon line begins
1981	The first (south) section begins operation
	Plans for construction of a new Atlantic line are announced
1983	The second (north) section of the new Paris-Lyon line begins operation
1983-1985	Further development of services
	The first SNCF evaluations of the new line's results from a business and financial point of view are made; technical and economic evaluations are also undertaken
January 7 1985	Work on the new Paris-Le Mans line begins
October 9 1987	The French government decides to build a real TGV network, with the construction of the North line (TGV Nord), the Greater Paris area interconnection link for very high speed lines, and extension of the Paris-Southeast line to Valence
January 31 1989- April 1990	Studies for the "Draft for a national long-term development plan of very high speed rail connections" are commissioned by the French government
September 29 1989	Law declaring construction of the North line (TGV Nord, from Paris to Lille and Channel Tunnel) "to be in the public interest" (*Décret déclarant d'utilité*

publique et urgents les travaux) [2], allows the work to begin

October 26 1989	Law declaring construction of the line skirting Lyon (first step of the extension of the Paris-Southeast line to Valence) "to be in the public interest"
October 1989	Publication of a report on a possible eastern line (TGV Est) Paris-Strasbourg-Germany
December 1989-May 1990	A series of high-speed tests carried out on equipment to be used on the new Atlantic line (December 5 1989: 482.4kph; May 18 1990: 515.3kph)
May 31 1990	The Ministry of Research and Industry, SNCF and the builders sign a contract for research and development of "third generation" equipment
June 3 1990	Law declaring the Greater Paris area interconnection link for very high speed lines "to be in the public interest"
June 12 1990	Publication of the "National Long-Term Plan" (*schéma directeur national des liaisons ferroviaires à grande vitesse*)
September 30 1990	The Paris-Tours section of the Atlantic line begins operation. TGV reaches the Spanish border on con ventional network
December 1 1990	French and British teams meet in the Channel Tunnel
January 17 1991	Proposals of routes for the TGV Méditerranée (from Valence to the Italian border) presented to the Press
September 1991	Celebration of the tenth anniversary of the Southeast TGV line [3]

THE FIRST STEP: FROM 'SYSTEM' TO LINE[4]

The characteristics of the new Southeast TGV line are the result of various technical and economic choices. The choices made, partly under the pressure of circumstances and defined in relation to other very high speed trains either already in use or planned (Shinkansen and new air or magnetic suspension technologies, in particular), became the characteristic features in defining a *system* capable of replication at other sites and

---

[2] Current state of construction work in *Revue générale des chemins de fer*, 1992/1-2 (Jan.-Feb. 1992), Special issue, Le TGV Nord et la jonction

[3] For an overview of technical developments during these ten years, see *Revue générale des chemins de fer*, 1991/10, Oct. 1991, Special Issue, 10 ans de TGV

[4] Synthetic presentation, bibliography, figures in Roth, D. *The TGV System : a Technical, Financial and Socio-Economic Renaissance of the Rail-Mode*, "Mémoire" prepared under the supervision of M Georges Wagner, Columbia University Programs in Paris, June 15, 1990

producing the same effects.

Once their value had been demonstrated by the technical and commercial success of the new line, the general principles of the system were presented on several occasions during the period 1984-1985 by Michel Walrave, then assistant director general at SNCF in charge of development[5].

These can be summarised as follows:

● the compatibility of lines and equipment designed for very high speeds with the existing rail network

● specialisation of new lines — designated exclusively for passenger transport and consequently most capable of being adapted to a single type of equipment which is light and designed for very high speeds

The major technical choice made for the French system, electric traction, although not presented as having been a determining factor in this systemic approach, was nonetheless a major decision for the later development of the TGV system, as shown in the previous chapter.

After the first oil crisis, the need to reduce energy consumption became a major factor in the national administration's choice of a new line that would increase the efficiency of electric traction, continuing the electrification policy launched by Louis Armand.

The defence of electric traction by comparing the energy consumption of different modes of transport, and reference to competition from domestic airlines, became two basic features of studies undertaken when operations began in 1984 on the completed line, and of those used in preparing the long-term development plan. These common elements were presented in increasingly simplified ways, but this should not obscure the importance of this reasoning in initial decision-making processes.

The choice of electric traction was also important as it determined the technical limitations of other railway systems, as is shown by articles in the Press covering speed records attained by TGV equipment on a line designated for commercial use[6].

Moreover, the decision to use electric traction seems to have put pressure on the railway company (SNCF) to invest more in electrifying existing lines connected to the new TGV lines.

At the same time, the image of the TGV is changing: the "equivalent of the aeroplane" has become "the best train in the world". The official attitude of SNCF with regard to automobile competition is far more complex, however.

THE SECOND STEP: OPTIMISATION OF THE SYSTEM, AND THE TGV EFFECT

In his studies completed in 1984-1985, Michel Walrave combined technical and economic approaches to the construction and operation of a very high speed line: the financial balance of the first two years of full operation of the Paris-Lyon line permitted him to argue for the "optimisation of the TGV system" as defined below:

---

[5] Now General Secretary of the International Union of Railways

[6] See for example the article by Alain Faujas in *Le Monde* of May 20-21, 1990: "Le record du monde du TGV à 515,3 km/h : un avantage décisif pour le matériel français face au train à sustentation magnétique japonais"

"To put it simply, there can be said to exist two levels of system optimisation. The first of these consists of striving for optimum service characteristics in terms of quality and price, and more particularly of defining commercial speed, train frequency and comfort in terms of space and on-board services, primarily in relation to customer needs. In other words, this means working out, using appropriate economic models, the demand-based reaction to the different possible options.

"With this approach, one must obviously bear in mind that this demand also depends on general social and economic factors as well as on the service offered by rival modes and their predictable patterns of development.

"On a second level, the problem involves technical and economic factors and the optimum mix between resources used for operations, on the one hand, and investment in infrastructure and rolling stock, on the other, in order to obtain the desired results at least cost. In fact, there is mutual interaction between the overall optimisation process and technical and economic optimisation."[7]

At this time, preliminary studies for the path of the new Atlantic line clearly show the magnitude of the TGV effect: the French population and their elected officials have high expectations from what they perceive as a new mode of transportation.

Optimisation of the system throws into question the first objectives established for the commercial speed of the tracks. In fact, it appears necessary to find "a compromise between the value — whether commercial or social — of the time gained, and the corresponding cost increases"[7]. The "time gain" factor, which is the primary characteristic of the TGV system for the French public, as well as the main feature advertised for the opening of the Paris-South West line, varies with the distance to be travelled: while the passenger gains very little time in travelling a distance of 500kms (average radius of the surface area of France) at over 300kph, the objective recently established by the SNCF for the European highspeed network of "1,000kms in three hours" will require speeds peaking at 330 to 350kph on the new lines.

Can the systemic approach that predominates in the SNCF studies integrate changes in network scale and respond satisfactorily to the needs of clients and government? One answer seems to have been given by the accelerated development of the main components of the system, that is the technical characteristics of the rolling stock.

Third step: from system optimisation to network

Initially, the expression "network effect" was used with reference to the new Paris-Lyon line, and this justified its being called the Paris-Sud Est. The new line improved service to a region, or rather, improved railway connections between the second economic region of France and the first; the operating agency used the term network to express this improvement, even though the new line excluded transversal links and at times seemed to detract from inter-regional connections.

Nevertheless, since the best feature of the TGV system, as defined by its developers, is its speed, the idea of very high speed service on new lines, and of high speed service on existing lines, implies that the increase in the frequency of departures compensates for the paucity of stops, despite the demands of the cities it passes through.

The concept of a network appeared more often in studies commissioned by the French government from SNCF in January 1989, the results of which led in early 1990 to the publication of a "Long-term Plan" for new lines. Since these new lines had been planned on a European scale, they could be described as the beginning of a network of specialised lines superimposed on the existing network, with which it would connect without transfer of passengers, according to the principle of compatibility.

At the same time, marketing of the TGV system abroad confirmed the optimal conditions for its application: existence of a corridor, comprising a densely populated zone with concentrated economic activity, and high frequency of service.

At this point political decisions come into play, since the TGV is regarded as a tool in national and regional development, while the operating agency, functioning as a business, is primarily concerned with the commercial output of the first two lines built.

Two questions are raised at this point: is the very high speed train, as conceived in France, capable of creating a network without contradicting the fundamental choice of compatibility with the conventional system?

Are the requirements of public service and social cost-effectiveness for the new lines compatible with an essentially economic approach to system operations?

From technical choices to economic necessities, from economic results to political and social imperatives: the TGV effect and the network effect

Is the TGV capable of creating a network effect?

Passenger traffic on TGV trains in 1995, after the opening of the Northern TGV line and its connections, is expected to reach 35 billion passenger-kilometres. This is the equivalent of the whole of French long-distance passenger traffic in 1970, and of 50 per cent of long-distance passenger traffic in 1995. It will cover over 1,260kms of new line (currently: 670kms) and 6,000kms of compatible traditional line, referred to as the "network revived, thanks to use by the TGV".

This quantitative analysis does not take into account the quality of service to the towns and regions crossed, nor the routes "favoured" by speed, often presented as a value in itself.

Lines favoured by high speeds, and French tradition

Is the drafting of a long-term plan for very high speed lines a plan for a network, or an attempt to improve a group of lines connecting Paris and the Greater Paris area with the other major cities of France?

This question was raised at the time of the construction of the first French network between 1835-1850. It was raised again when the very high speed lines, with their stated purpose of improving connections on long-distance lines (as opposed to regional or Greater Paris area networks), reaffirmed a development tradition that has provoked criticism ever since the engineer Legrand adopted a radial network of lines centred on Paris in 1842.

---

[7] *Ibidem*

HIGH SPEED AND QUALITY OF SERVICE WITHIN AND BETWEEN THE REGIONS OF FRANCE

Planners have protested against the unequal treatment of the various French provinces in terms of service by the traditional system, while railway workers and passengers have protested against the preferred treatment of high speed trains in railway operations. This has been taken up by the Press and by community organisations[8].

SPEED FOR EVERYONE: A DEMOCRATIC VALUE?

In a 1984 report, the French Ministry of Transport made public its preference for a train that would be accessible to all and that would "democratise speed"[9].

The pricing system adopted for the Paris-Lyon line respected this priority: the supplement affects 30 per cent of passengers during peak hours while the price of the basic ticket remains the same.

In effect, as the new line is 20 per cent shorter than the old one, it was possible to raise the price per kilometre without any effect on the price paid by the passenger. This is not the case on the new Atlantic line.

The spread of passengers in terms of social and occupational categories remained unchanged from 1981 to 1983[10], after the opening of the new line, except for the higher professional categories travelling for business who preferred the train to the plane.

It can be said that it is the average traveller's access to high speed that constitutes a revolution within railway travel comparable, in air travel, to the advent of the jet plane and the subsequent lowering of fares.

TOWARDS A MULTI-MODAL NETWORK THANKS TO INTERCONNECTION?

The interconnection of very high speed lines, expected around, but outside, Paris (stations planned for Charles de Gaulle airport, Euro-Disneyland, the Massy Southwest autoroute entrance etc[11]), can be interpreted in various ways.

It is possible to see it as "the correction of an historical error", that is the existence of several separate Paris termini, a situation which has so far made it difficult for rail

---

[8] Varlet, J. Réseau ferré et relations interrégionales en France. *Revue d'histoire des chemins de fer*, n°2, Spring 1990, pp. 87-101

An example from the weekly press: David, Frank; Fainsilber, Denis, "La France du TGV à l'horizon 2000: géographie, où es-tu? [where are you gone, geography?]", *Le Nouvel Economiste*, n°746, 5/18/90, pp. 18-19

Concerns over service to major metropolitan areas: *Transports urbains*, n°74, janv.-mars 1992, Numéro spécial TGV: 1. la logique de la grande vitesse

[9] Frybourg, A; Moisi, F. La politique française dans le domaine de la grande vitesse ferroviaire, *in Les aspects socio-économiques des trains à grande vitesse, actes du Séminaire international du programme "technique, croissance, emploi"* tenu à Paris les 5-8 novembre 1984. Paris, La Documentation française, 2 tomes, 1985, pp 163 *ssqq*

[10] Vialle, G. Le TGV, un lancement commercial réussi [the TGV, a Successful Commercial Launch]. *Revue générale des chemins de fer*, 102e année, n°9 September 1983. Special issue, le TGV, bilan et perspectives, pp 496-504

[11] Iarovay, D. Interconnexion des TGV en Ile de France. *Revue générale des chemins de fer*, 109e annee, n°5. May 1990 pp 5-16

passengers to avoid going into the capital; and it can be seen as reinforcing the traditional pattern of lines radiating out of Paris.

Yet in all the interpretations, the interconnection is seen as constituting a network of very high speed lines that are superimposed on the existing network.

This view ignores the compatibility of the very high speed network with the existing one, as well as the multi-modal nature of a transportation network of which the railway is but one element[12].

In fact, the principle of the high speed train was initially borrowed from the autoroute (a railway platform has even been suggested for the median strip on the Autoroute du Nord) with which it was supposed to compete[13]. One can say that competition from highways has been as decisive, if not more so, in the development of projects for very high speed trains, as the competition from air transport. The autoroute supplied both models of operation and a commercial goal.

However, the expected transfer of traffic, while it did indeed occur, did not last. In addition, the private car was catered for with the construction of park and ride stations outside several urban centres served by very high speed lines, like for example Montchanin-Le Creusot on the Paris-Sud-Est line.

The interconnection of very high speed lines in the greater Paris region is also, and indeed especially, an interconnection between highway, railway and air links.

A choice was made, in the context of the competitive environment for railway travel, to redraw the map of passenger flow as a function of distance travelled: the car for short distances, the train for medium distances and the aeroplane for long distances.

The economic approach, planning and social cost-effectiveness

THE ANALYSIS OF THE OPERATING AGENCY

The evaluation of the cost-effectiveness of a new line, in the context of public service and controlled pricing, has been formulated by SNCF on the basis of the following criteria, used for the Paris-Sud-Est TGV line: profitability for the operator; saving for the client; effects on competition; cost-effectiveness for the state; cost-effectiveness for the public.

Studies show the breakdown of passenger traffic between air and rail travel and between highway and rail travel. On the other hand, the real effects of the very high speed trains on industrial activity, employment and regional isolation remain unknown, as indeed does the evaluation of energy conservation or environmental preservation that could result from the transfer of passenger traffic away from air or automotive transport in favour of the train.

The *systemic* approach to the TGV takes into account the financial effects of operations and traffic increase. It can elucidate neither the effects of increased

---

[12] Le concept de réseau dans l'univers ferroviaire. Actes de la journée scientifique du 11 octobre 1989. *Revue d'histoire des chemins de fer*, n°2. Spring 1990, in particular Orientations bibliographiques sur le concept de réseau dans l'univers ferroviaire, by Marie-Suzanne Vergeade, pp 227-236

[13] Geais, R. Contribution à l'histoire du TGV français. *Revue générale des chemins de fer*, 109e annee, n°3, March 1990, pp 9-15

transport speed on the operation or structures of the regional economy, nor the reasons for the transfer of passenger traffic from one type of transportation to another.

Qualitative evaluations of the TGV

EFFECT ON THE REGIONAL ECONOMY

Not enough time has elapsed to permit an evaluation of the long-term effects of the high speed links on the structure of French economic regions and on the hierarchy of French cities.

A 1985 study commissioned by DATAR (Délégation à l'aménagement du territoire et à l'action régionale/ regional development policy), INREST (Institut national de recherche sur les transports et leur sécurité), the Ministry of Transport, OEST (Observatoire économique et statistique des transports) and SNCF showed that in the short term the economic activity of the regions served by the Paris-Sud-Est TGV line was not structurally affected by reduced journey time for people travelling to the capital nor by the attraction of novelty. On the other hand, expectations for a "mechanical" TGV effect on regional prosperity, with the train presented as a "new mode of transport", were often disappointed[14].

In making decisions on the construction of new lines to the Atlantic and the North, the lessons learned by operating the Paris-Sud-Est TGV line have led SNCF to count not only on traffic drawn away from other modes of transport but also on new types of passenger traffic elicited by the specific advantages of the very high speed train.

Nevertheless, it seems that the quality of TGV transport — perceived as qualities of the train ("punctuality, spaciousness, comfort, communication, landscape"[15], as well as safety and low fares) — together with the speed itself, has a greater effect than frequency of service. Choices were made, and the competitive environment seems to have been considered in the initial choices, just as it is today with freight transport.

Conclusion: The logic of the system

SPEED AND TECHNICAL PROGRESS

Speed still remains the defining characteristic of the TGV system, in that it is responsible for the very high speed train being perceived as a new mode of transport by potential users and buyers.

Increases in commercial speeds cannot continue indefinitely on a given distance without corresponding increases in operating costs (in particular, energy costs, since the power to be applied grows as a cube of the speed) which cancel out any profits deriving from time savings.

On the other hand, when the average distance of rail connections is doubled by the international extension of a network of new lines capable of being used at high speeds, or at very high speeds, it is the performance of the rolling stock that is critical[16].

In addition, the safety of very high speed transport has to be continuously monitored in trials. This is what was at stake in the trials undertaken on the commissioning of the second new French line, in addition to the competitive performance of different technical systems under consideration by international markets such as Korea, Australia or Brazil.

Double-deck TGV

Faced with such a complex phenomenon as a new mode of transport, the historian may — and perhaps must — ask questions of general relevance. The usual connection made between speed and modernity should not blur the consequences of choosing speed as the standard of passenger transport — consequences that are also cultural. The effects of the TGV system in terms of national and regional development policy should also be stated and taken into account.

We are the lucky witnesses of a complete change in the operation of an old system. Now it is up to us to evaluate, appreciate, and perhaps enjoy, this innovation.

---

[14] Plassard, F. ed. *Les effets socio-économiques du TGV en Bourgogne et Rhône-Alpes*. Document de synthèse, Laboratoire d'économie des transports/interalp, June 1986. For an example of a sector study, see Buisson, M A, *Effets indirects du TGV et transformations du tertiaire supérieur en Rhône-Alpes*, LET, Décembre 1986.

Since the publication of a 'Long-term Plan' for new lines in 1990 and the protests and demonstrations against TGV in the South of France (the Valence-Nice line, called TGV Méditerranée), studies on the economic impact of the TGV are abounding : see the plentiful bibliographies in the publications of the Laboratoire d'économie des transports (Lyons), of the Groupe de recherche Réseaux du CNRS (Paris) etc

[15] Von Lubke, D. Le système ICE. *Le rail*, n°13, Sept 1989, Special issue La grande vitesse dans le monde, p 49

[16] Example of the presentation by the non-specialized press of the research project currently carried out in Nexon, Marc, Les paris du TGV de 3e génération (the challenges of the third generation TGV), *Le Nouvel Economiste*, n°2341, 28.11.91

5.
History and the AVE[1]

Antonio Gómez-Mendoza, Universidad Complutense, Madrid

IN 1986 the Spanish government embarked upon a vast railway programme. It was part of an ambitious public works scheme to improve the transportation system by 1992. In the first stage, the cabinet agreed to build a high speed railway line to service the southern city of Seville which was due to host that year's International Exhibition. This line came into operation in April 1992. On completion of the second stage, high speed trains will run from Madrid to Barcelona and from there to the French border to connect with the Paris-Marseille TGV. The project will integrate Spain in Europe's high speed network. The original initiative was later supplemented by the decision to adopt the standard international gauge for both lines, thereby opening the door to modifying the gauge through the whole Spanish network.

The 1986 scheme is regarded by government officials as a means of restoring the railway to its natural position in the transportation market. Since the interwar period, the Spanish railway undertaking has had to watch as competing modes gradually undermined its lead as the principal mode of transportation service.

As early as the 1920s, railway managers observed, with mixed feelings, the emerging competition of motorcars and lorries. The trend was temporarily interrupted after the Civil War, when an acute fuel shortage necessitated the expansion of public transport. In 1947 the monopoly enjoyed by the state railway company, RENFE, was further consolidated when the government limited the granting of road operators' licences to those routes where there was no competing rail transport. Yet in spite of this official support, the railways' share in the aggregate demand for passenger services declined rapidly through the 1960s. Between 1950 and 1980, this share decreased from 60 per cent to 7.6 per cent, to the advantage of the private motor vehicle which has met 77 per cent of the additional demand for transportation services.

Thus, in 1980, road transport supplied 89 per cent of passenger traffic. Two main factors accounted for this declining share of the market: firstly, in the face of rapidly rising per capita incomes, the shift to private motor vehicles and aeroplanes must be explained by the low income elasticity of railway traffic — railway services have become an inferior good in present day Spain.

Secondly, increasing numbers of potential travellers were discouraged by the poor quality of the service which RENFE usually provided. In sum, travellers showed their preference for motorcars and aeroplanes rather than rail.

---

[1]AVE — Alta Velocidad Española, or Spanish High Speed

Map showing the old rail route between Madrid and Seville and the line taken by the AVE

We may wonder whether it is desirable to allocate £10 billion sterling to "restore the natural position" of the railway when its market share has declined so sharply. The scarcity of published data on major traffic flows precludes a cost-benefit analysis in this transport sector. Fortunately however, we may look to historical experience to cast some light on the economic impact of high speed trains and the problems they will have to face.

The high speed line between Madrid and Seville is expected to fulfil a double objective:

● **to set the railway on an equal footing with road and air transport;**

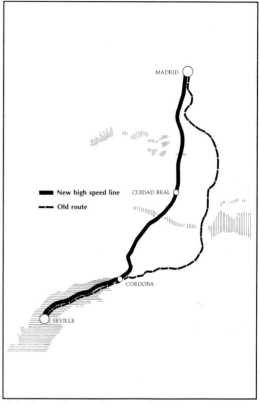

● **to promote economic growth in the southern regions once the present transport bottleneck is removed.**

To meet the first objective, trains will have to provide a new consumer good, just as the low speed trains did in the early railway period. It seems quite clear that the standard of comfort in particular will be a great improvement over standard train or coach services. Undoubtedly the major asset of the new train will lie in its high speed. But time savings in the conveyance of passengers and freight seem much less impressive if the increase in speed is viewed from a long-term perspective.

It should be borne in mind that some 84 hours were required to travel from Madrid to Seville before the advent of the railway. When a railway line was finally completed in the 19th century, the journey time was cut to 20 hours (Gómez-Mendoza, 1989, p166). Compared with this revolution in speed in the second half of the 19th century, the impact of the high speed train seems quite trivial. Indeed the AVE has "only" reduced by half the time needed to travel between Madrid and Seville.

There is little doubt that the substitution of the railway for the pack animal, the cart and the stagecoach meant a dramatic improvement in the living standards of 19th century Spaniards. The greater efficiency of the train, compared with traditional road carriers, in a country devoid of waterways, turned the railway into a major resource saver (Gómez-Mendoza, 1983, pp149-154). The real costs of moving goods by rail were cut by a factor of 40 in 1878, and by a factor of 60 in 1912. With no competition from other means of transport, the railway soon became an important component in the economic modernisation of Spain — unlike the experience of England, France or Germany (O'Brien, 1983). Thus, social savings accounted for 11 per cent of Spain's national income in 1878, and for 21 per cent in 1912. Though no similar calculation has been made for passenger traffic, I would estimate the savings might have been quite substantial on account of the important fare and time reductions effected by the railway.

The advantages over road carriers in price, speed and safety gave the railways a near monopoly in moving people and freight across the regions of 19th century Spain. Professional carters were driven out of business, not only on long distance routes but on the shorter hauls too, whenever access to a railway station was convenient. This situation has only recently been reversed.

Today, motor vehicles have succeeded in reducing the market share of the railway to a minimum. In view of experiences in England or the United States in the 19th century, where there was a close substitute for the railways (Fogel, 1964; Hawke, 1970), I maintain that the social saving of the AVE is necessarily quite low. Moreover, the AVE runs through an area of low population density, and the inhabitants have some of the lowest per capita incomes in Spain. In my opinion, these two factors will further prevent the AVE from producing a beneficial impact on the region.

As far as the second objective is concerned, several issues must be carefully assessed. Firstly, the government has set as a major target the removal of the existing transport bottleneck between central and southern regions. To this end, the AVE will necessarily have to absorb a substantial quota of the traffic which is presently channelled through the Despeñaperros Canyon. At present the section is running at 122 per cent of capacity and this must be reduced to 75 per cent. To this end, passenger as well as freight trains will have to be diverted onto the new line. This might sound familiar to students of the history of the Spanish transport system. By the mid-19th century, an inefficient and expensive transportation system threatened to precipitate the collapse of the internal economy (Ringrose, 1970). Indeed, increased competition between humans and animals for grain and fodder revealed a shortage of transportation services. Moreover, the precipitous topography and the extreme continental climate limited the scope of transport innovations, particularly the building of canals.

Although railway engineers faced serious difficulties, a 10,000-mile railway network was nevertheless completed by 1914. Railway operation released enough resources to ensure that economic development was not checked towards the end of the century. None of the arguments of technical constraint stand today, thanks to the innovatory technology that has been developed in road and air transport in the 20th century, and the scope for innovation being wider today than for the last 150 years.

It can therefore be argued that the answers to secular problems need no longer follow the patterns of the past. Yet the 1986 transportation scheme has once again laid emphasis on the railways and their potential as the unique means of promoting growth. It is appropriate to look at some of the background to the development of the AVE. Again, historical experience provides a useful framework for assessing decisions in this matter too. In the second half of the 19th century, the policy-makers opted for building the railways over a short period of time. Equipment, both for the track and for the rolling stock, was imported from abroad in huge quantities (Gómez-Mendoza, 1983, pp157-61). The argument is that, given the small scale of the iron and steel industry of the 1850s and its lack of technological development, to have pursued the alternative protectionist policy would have seriously delayed the opening of the first railway lines (Gómez-Mendoza, 1983, pp161-163). Thus, public policy sentenced the domestic iron industry to a slow growth over most of the period.

To some scholars, this meant a lost opportunity to develop a modern iron and steel industry in Spain (Harrison, 1978, p52). Today the political urgency of having the AVE ready for the 1992 International Exhibition obliged the Ministry of Public Works to place orders with French and German manufacturers. Yet the situation today is obviously quite different from that of the 19th century. Domestic producers are currently competitive in external markets for the manufacture of technologically advanced rolling stock[2]. I maintain that the decision constitutes the loss of an opportunity to promote further growth in this area.

AVE's capacity for promoting economic growth in the southern regions should be analysed with regard to the positioning of the high speed lines. In this respect, present day initiatives seem to be duplicating past initiatives. Indeed the recently built line to Seville and the proposed line to Barcelona follow almost exactly the radial pattern of the 19th century network. It was argued in the literature, that this network was designed to benefit certain areas while others suffered from the lack of a modern transportation system (Harrison, 1983, pp53-54).

While new evidence has shown that railway operation played a crucial role in promoting integration of the domestic market, there is still some uncertainty about the future performance of the new fast trains. On the Barcelona-Madrid corridor, the proposed high speed train will meet an intensive demand for transportation services[3]. Yet the distance separating these two cities (400 miles) is not likely to see rail services competing successfully with the air alternative.

In contrast, the distance between Madrid and Seville falls within the range over which rail can successfully compete with air. However, modest traffic flows between Madrid and Seville suggest that the AVE has been built ahead of demand[4].

It must be remembered that the transport bottleneck in this corridor is not the result of excess demand, but of a poor level of transportation capacity. As explained above, technical constraints in Despenaperros in the 19th century prevented the laying of double track along that section of the line.

The 1986 scheme to provide high speed trains was supplemented by the decision to adopt the international gauge on the new high speed lines. It was later agreed to extend the standard (international) gauge to the entire railway network. This

---

[2] An important contract was won, for example, to supply several modern Talgo trains.

[3] It is estimated that air traffic stood at 1.7 million passengers in 1987, while 500,000 travelled by train.

[4] The estimated number of air passengers between Madrid and Seville in 1987 was 500,000.

decision will obviously involve major reconstruction, affecting all the permanent way and most of the rolling stock. Work will stretch over 20 years.

There is general agreement among economic historians that the decision to build Spanish railway lines to a broad gauge was not a strategic move (Tortella, 1981, pp108-109). Technical factors prevailed over other considerations when the decision was first made in 1844. It is true that many inclined planes would have been necessary if the narrower gauge used in other countries had been adopted at that time. When the first lines were laid in the early 1850s, the locomotives had to be fitted with large boilers to withstand the stress of the gradients, and this led to the requirement for a broader gauge. However, a few years later, new locomotive designs obviated the need for this broad gauge. But the Railway Act of 1877 insisted upon the advantages of the 1.67m gauge.

It might, therefore, be argued that the 1844 decision eventually proved a gross miscalculation which prevented the integration of Spanish railways with the European network. Additional transit costs were involved for goods traded across the French border at a time (1880s) when France was Spain's major trading partner, absorbing 42 per cent of exports and providing 29 per cent of imports.

Once the extent of the damage became clear, the largest railway companies considered the possibility of changing the gauge. Despite the losses to the economy from this serious obstacle to foreign trade, the actual cost involved in a change of gauge seemed far too large. Private companies were repeatedly deterred from such an undertaking.

In the early years of the 20th century, new attempts were made to change the gauge. In 1914 a Royal Committee was set up to consider the pros and cons of opening a new standard gauge line from Madrid to the French border. The Rothschild's Railway Company in Spain, MZA, estimated that the total cost of changing the gauge through the entire network would amount to one billion pesetas. It is interesting to recall the words of Mr Maristany, MZA's general manager at the time, when he expressed his views on this fantastic challenge:

"The sacrifice which is involved in an investment totalling 1bn pesetas to obtain very limited benefits... will have little compensation. However, if there is still a willingness to invest such a huge amount of money, I think that it would be far more profitable to allocate it to the improvement of the lines, to the building of a double track, feeders and trunk lines which will boost traffic in general..."

The argument remains valid in the context of present day issues. The declining share of the railways in the transportation market is reflected in the share of foreign trade currently carried by rail. Trade statistics show that a mere 1.6 per cent of imports and 1.5 per cent of exports are carried on the railways[5]. Do these percentages justify an estimated investment of £1.35bn (excluding the social and economic costs to railway users)? To modify the gauge would mean building an entirely new railway network from scratch, at a time when the economic viability of the railway is in question. In the words of Mr Caballero, the former Minister of Transportation and Tourism:

"The gauge issue is a spurious problem and not much of a problem really. First

---
[5] In value terms, the respective percentages are 4.7 and 8.0.

Above: The AVE in full flight and, below, interior view

of all, because it has been technically solved (in reference to the Talgo)... Secondly, because the economic cost would be dreadfully high, and finally because we will end up with no railway at all" (on account of the 20 years needed to complete the transformation of the gauge).

The argument was further reinforced by RENFE'S chairman himself:

"...If there were enough money to change the gauge and if someone were to ask me what I would do with that money, I can sincerely state that I would never undertake such a transformation because there are so many other things to do..."

As I have argued above, such an investment could never be justified by an estimate of social saving, given the present level of railway performance. As for the high speed lines, it is quite evident that to lay a track with a broad gauge would be to repeat the errors of the past.

In conclusion, the emergence of new production functions in the 20th century has completely transformed transportation services in Spain. The railway played an important role in the promotion of the economic modernisation of the country in the 19th century because efficient alternative modes of transport were absent.

In the present day, short-haul passenger traffic is RENFE's fastest growing market[6]. It would appear that RENFE's most promising market for the future lies in commuter services. For long-distance trips, travellers clearly prefer the aeroplane or the private car.

Ignoring this fact, RENFE is concentrating upon a policy which shares many features with the well-known 19th century philosophy of promoting welfare and wealth through expansion of the railway network. If past experience were to be used to predict future developments, we must argue that history does not support the decision to promote high speed trains. Furthermore, to select the Madrid-Seville line as the start of the new high speed network, and to adopt the standard gauge would appear to be a hasty repeat of past misjudgments.

References

Fogel, R W. 1964. Railroads and American Economic Growth, Essays in Econometric History. Baltimore

Gomez Mendoza, A. 1983. "Spain" in O'Brien (1983) pp148-169

Gomez Mendoza, A. 1989. Ferrocarril, Industria y Mercado en la Modernizacion de España. Madrid

Harrison, J. 1978. An Economic History of Modern Spain. Manchester

Hawke, G. 1970. Railways and Economic Growth in England and Wales, 1840-1870. Oxford

Lopez Pita, A et al. 1988. El Desarrollo de Nuevas Infraestructuras en el Ferrocarril. Madrid

Ministerio de Transportes, Turismo y Comunicaciones. 1984. Informe de la Comision para el Estudio de los Ferrocarriles Españoles. Madrid

Nadal, J. 1975. El Fracaso de la Revolucion Industrial en España 1814-1913. Barcelona

O'Brien, P K. 1983. Railways and the Economic Development of Western Europe 1830-1914. Oxford

Ringrose, D R. 1970. Transportation and Economic Stagnation in Spain 1750-1850. Durham

Tortella, G. 1981. La Economia Española 1830-1900, in Tuñon de Lara (ed) Historia de España, Vol VIII, pp11-167

---

[6] With a growth rate of 3.1 per cent per annum between 1970 and 1983, compared with 2.3 per cent for long-haul traffic and 2.6 per cent for freight. Short-haul passenger traffic absorbs nearly 40 per cent of the aggregate transport capacity.

6.

High speed trains in Italy

From Fascism to the ETR 500

Andrea Giuntini, Assistant Professor, Istituto di Storia Economia, Firenze

Origins

ONE OF the few good things with which fascism is usually credited is its railway policy. The most familiar and oft-quoted maxim — the one about the trains running on time — undoubtedly forms part of the common heritage of a large proportion of Italians.

Though it might not seem entirely serious, this observation is perfectly consistent with the way in which Italians, even today, perceive the 20-year period of Fascist rule. Moreover, the railway policies implemented by the Fascist government, especially during the 1930s, do have a number of interesting features. Even with high speed, at that time simply called speed, the progress made by Mussolini's regime was not inconsiderable.

During the decade preceding the war, the Fascist regime's railway policy had two central concerns: to increase the speed of rail transport throughout the whole network, and the introduction, in spring 1932, of light trains to cater for mass transport. The idea was to increase the level of passenger traffic to compensate for the diversion of goods traffic to the roads. On the other hand, less attention was paid to lengthening the network, which was extensive enough in any case. In fact, between 1930 and 1939 only 836kms were added.

The introduction of light trains for mass passenger transport, together with a sustained reduction in fares, was something quite new. Indeed the diesel-powered locomotive, the Littorina, was first introduced in the early months of 1933. It was produced by Fiat and Breda, the latter being one of the most important manufacturers of rolling stock at the time, which still figures among rail-stock companies today.

The general reduction in journey times over a large part of the Italian railway network was also a very significant factor. It was an indication that the regime was strongly influenced by the notion of speed. At a time of autarchy and increasing international isolation as a result of military activity in Africa, a policy which encouraged this kind of consumer behaviour served as a prop to shore up popular support for the Fascist creed.

It should not be forgotten, however, that aspirations of achieving high speeds date back still further. In 1927, after years of preparation, the line between Rome and Naples was opened, the first of the two express lines (Direttissime) built in the Fascist period[1].

On December 6 1937, a group of French technicians travelled between Rome and Naples at a speed of 201kph aboard an ETR 200 electric train. The sole intention of this demonstration run was to impress the French guests who had been invited for that purpose. National pride had been aroused because the train featured in the trial had emerged from the Breda factories just a year before.

Designed by the research department of the Rolling Stock and Traction Service of the State Railways, the ETR 200 had the first aerodynamic profile to appear on Italian railways: the front of the locomotive was pointed, the side windows were fixed and as far as possible lay on the same plane as the external walls to avoid air turbulence.

The addition of shock absorbers on the bogies and the great flexibility of the auxiliary suspension system, together with the distance between the bogies and transmission via hollow axles, accounted to some extent for the extraordinary success of this train. It was built with innovatory technology and had particular features for convenience and comfort, such as air conditioning and a restaurant. As the model upon which subsequent fast trains were built, both in Italy and abroad, it was probably with the introduction of the ETR 200 that Italy first entered the world of high speed[2].

The first Italian electric train had three carriages: two for the passengers and a third for auxiliary services like the luggage compartment, mail car, kitchen and storage. There were 54 seats in the first carriage and 46 in the second. Six models were built in 1936 and a further batch of 12 in 1938, when certain modifications were made to ensure greater comfort for the passengers.

In short, the Fascist government had no lack of success with speed. On July 20, this time on the line between Milan and Florence, the ETR 200 broke the world speed record for a commercial train, recording an average speed of 165kph, while on the stretch between Pontenure and Piacenza it touched 203kph. Sitting beside the driver were Mussolini himself and the Minister of Communications, Stefano Benni. The record-breaking electric train was built precisely to deliver supremacy in speed and therefore no expense was spared.

The world record attracted attention from all over the globe and a model of the ETR 200 was put on display at the World Trade Fair in New York.

The electric trains, along with other new trains and service reorganisation, effected a significant increase in speed on rail transport in general. The high degree of efficiency thus achieved was nevertheless won by crushing all claims put forward by one of the most militant groups of workers in Italian history. Yet — in an Italy severely constrained by the weakness of its economic infrastructure, by technological underdevelopment in numerous sectors and by inequality between North and South, which the factious regime had certainly done nothing to correct — the results obtained on the railways were, by contrast, by no means insignificant.

---

[1] The other one, which followed seven years later, was between Bologna and Florence: Giuntini, A. I giganti della montagna. Storia della ferrovia Direttissima Bologna-Firenze 1845-1934; Olschki, Florence, 1984

[2] D'Angelo, A. I treni del futuro. Saranno veloci, in Berengo Gardin, P. (ed) Ferrovie italiane; Editori Riuniti, Rome, 1988, p390

Reconstruction

The option of motorised transport and the Settebello

At the end of the war Italy faced many problems. Obviously, the conflict set back the progress of Italian railways by several years. Damage to the railway infrastructure was extremely heavy. In 1945 the railways' transport capacity had been reduced to 40 per cent of its former level, and only ten per cent of the electrified lines were capable of functioning. Only a very small proportion of carriages — 20 per cent — was serviceable, as was an almost equally limited proportion — 40 per cent — of locomotives.

Fortunately the overall state of the transport industry was less serious. The few existing electric trains, 18 in all, had suffered enormous damage and two had been completely destroyed. Once those which could be had been repaired, and with improvements to their suspension and air-conditioning, they were gradually able to re-enter service.

In the task of restoring the Italian transport system, the aim was to return to the standards of the pre-war years. Without a precise programme, the governments that succeeded one another during the delicate reconstruction period could think of no alternative but to look back and try to reproduce the conditions that existed before the fateful year of 1940.

They did this while oscillating between temptations of an interventionist and a free-market kind, setting aside structural reforms, which they decided to tackle later, and urgently trying to ensure adequate living conditions for the people. Not to include communication and transport in their structural reforms was undoubtedly a grave error of judgment on the part of both the government and the opposition. Eventually a kind of neoliberalism came to dominate the economic strategies of the period, even in the transport and communications sector.

In essence, two factors underlay the move in favour of motorised transport, a move made in the second half of the 1940s:

● The absence of a systematic plan, and

● The presence of a strong and aggressive motor industry (above all Fiat) and other industrial sectors equally interested in the development of private transport.

However, the psychological aspect of the encounter with private transport should not be underestimated: for many years the car was the supreme object of aspiration for Italians — it was the status symbol of the masses, the American dream *par excellence*, and, in the final analysis, the way out of the tunnel of misery that had dramatically enveloped the entire country.

A population that, until then, had few opportunities for movement, discovered the joy of mobility and a capacity to affirm its dearly-bought freedom by changing location under its own power, without restrictions or limits. The increase in available leisure time, the trend towards internal migration and the reopening of a market that had remained closed for several years, all required freedom of movement. The train could not meet such needs, but the car did so perfectly.

In 1949, when the transport of goods by road overtook that by rail, there was a distinct impression that a profound change was underway. During the 1950s, the trend towards motorisation, transport of goods by road and unrestricted shipping was unstoppable. In 1951, year one of a decade in which the fate of Italian rail transport was sealed, a new law was passed which laid the foundations for a policy distinctly biased towards road[3]. Four years later, the motorway plan was introduced, which was subsequently to become the very cornerstone of the national car industry. In the space of a few years, a set of laws had been passed which clearly favoured what was called the "Road Federation", that is the grouping bringing together the powerful industries of cement, oil, pneumatic tyres and cars.

The decade thus saw a heavy wave of investment in national transport infrastructure, though this time little was invested in the railways. Once the network had returned to normal — and in 1950 almost all lines returned to normal service — there began a period of reorganisation and invigoration, though always within a context of complete subordination to road transport. The inevitable demands of technological and scientific progress were expressed in sectors other than the railways. For integration into the international market, a move necessary for political and economic purposes, railways were superfluous. Now that railway development and reconstruction had undoubtedly come to an end, the battle could be declared lost.

The idea of a prestigious train capable of restoring the railways to their former glory was conceived in 1948. In a country with a lot to offer tourists and where the phenomenon of mass tourism was in its infancy, a train of this kind would serve to attract foreign tourists in particular. The new train was called the ETR 300. It marked the beginning of a period of growth and was the symbol of an Italy that was changing its skin, of poverty that was giving way to incipient wealth. In the final analysis it was the symbol of the economic miracle which began in the 1950s and through the course of the following decade would make its mark on history.

After five long years of planning, the first two models emerged from the Breda factories in 1953. In terms of railway technology, the new luxury electric train, entering daily service on the line between Milan and Rome, represented an extraordinary leap forward. It combined very modern technical features with distinct qualities of elegance and comfort.

In many respects its design was highly original: indeed the two ends, which had been given a roundish aerodynamic shape, and the elevated driver's cab had never been seen before. Equally unusual was the introduction of observation cars, one at the front and one at the rear, an idea borrowed from American trains. Of the seven carriages — hence the name Settebello — four were reserved for passengers, another housed the restaurant and bar, a sixth was used for the kitchen and store, and the last provided the luggage compartment and service areas[4]. From the large window the passengers could enjoy the view, thus recreating the typically 19th century pleasure of travelling by train.

[3] Bortolotti, L. Viabilita' e sistemi infrastrutturali, in De Seta, C. (ed) Storia d'Italia. Annali 8. Insediamenti e territorio; Einaudi, Torino, 1985, p358

[4] Minoletti, G. Estetica dell'allestimento interno, in Ingegneria ferroviaria, a. VIII(1953), n. 7-8 p535

In reality, in the case of the Settebello, it is premature to talk in terms of high speed. The principles adopted in its planning were not, in fact, designed to meet the requirements of speed, but rather were inspired by a need for comfort and prestige. Nevertheless the Settebello did contribute to a noticeable reduction in journey time along the main Italian rail route. It continued to link Milan and Rome for 30 years before its well-deserved retirement.

The ETR 250, called the Arlecchino and regarded as the smaller brother of the Settebello, had an equally glorious career, running between Rome and Naples. Composed of four carriages, the Arlecchino was the fruit of collaboration between Breda and the state railways, the former undertaking the construction, the latter the planning. Successfully tested in July 1960, the Arlecchino, like the Settebello, reached a speed of 160kph. The Arlecchino's profile was similar to that of the Settebello: two rounded ends and driver's cabin raised above the level of the tops of the carriages gave the train a daring, aerodynamic shape.

The way in which the interior layout and aesthetic considerations had been conceived was highly original. In particular, laminated, pre-pressed panels with pop-cubist designs decorated the restaurant car. The variety of colours used for the upholstery of the four carriages was the inspiration for the train's name: for the rampant Italy of the 1960s, the personality of the character, who was poor but shrewd and finally victorious, was particularly fitting.

The trail blazed by the Settebello was followed by other fast trains which significantly improved the prospects for Italian railways in the late 1950s and early 1960s. It is worth mentioning the introduction of the Trans-Europ Express trains in 1957 and of the ETR 220, which was evolved through certain modifications to the electric train, the 200. To the previous three carriages was added a fourth, bringing the train's capacity up from 100 to 154 passengers. The additional carriage also housed a bar, and the train's length increased from 62.86m to 87.55m.

But the fast trains were only a fragile top layer. Beneath it the railways were in difficulty; the development of motorisation had thrown them into a state of crisis. Government spending was diverted over several years to projects aimed at strengthening the road network rather than meeting the needs of rail traffic. The apple of the government's eye continued to be the motorways, planned in great abundance to cover, gradually, almost the whole peninsula. For the railways, on the other hand, there was talk of cut-backs and pruning.

The 1955 motorway scheme, named after the minister Romita, was only interrupted by the 1971 credit squeeze; otherwise it dominated transport funding, relegating the railways to a decidedly subordinate role. The destiny presaged at the end of the war was being fulfilled. Moreover, the persistent government failure to intervene led to hypertrophy of the roads and atrophy of the railways. The first national transport conference was not convened until 1978, and even then it was not at the instigation of the government or the Minister of Public Works, but at the request of the trades unions. Italian industrialisation was proceeding without the railways[5].

---

[5] Lando Bortolotti writes: "The Italy of motorways corresponds precisely to the grossness and lack of culture of a bourgeoisie incapable of playing a hegemonic role, and thus unable to reabsorb, in a new synthesis, the heritage of the past." Bortolotti, L. op cit, p364

To equate economic progress with roads was an idea imposed by a power bloc created around private transport, and it severely compromised the whole of Italian economic development. Motorways were built alongside railway tracks, decisively penalising the latter, unable as they were to sustain the unequal competition[6]. The dynamism which characterised the transport sector from approximately 1959 to 1964 barely touched the railways. The considerable social change was expressed in motorisation. With the extraordinary growth in the country's productive capacity, there were changes even in deeply-rooted traditions and lifestyles; but the train was not the means by which such changes were expressed, it was merely an onlooker.

Appeals for integration, which were particularly prevalent after the formation of the EEC, were of little account; as were the appeals to redress, as a matter urgency, the historical inequality between North and South — an imbalance which a more rational use of the railways might perhaps have helped to reduce.

The plans for the railways served no purpose, or at least very little. The first scheme was introduced in 1958 and came to and end in 1963. The intention behind this five-year plan was to strengthen and modernise the network, as well as an attempt to block the collapse of investment in the sector. The second plan for the railways, this time a ten-year plan, was launched in 1962. In neither plan was there any mention of high speed; thus confirming that the Settebello and similar trains were isolated experiments without any coherent follow-up.

The Rome-Florence Direttissima

In the second half of the 1960s, the railway crisis hit what was perhaps its nadir. In the persistent absence of a policy favouring public transport, by now firmly subordinate to private transport, the opinion began to spread, even at the highest levels of government, that rail transport had only a residual role to play and that modernisation of the lines to allow journeys at 150-180kph was entirely superfluous — in spite of the experience of other countries where a fruitful debate on high speed was beginning to take shape.

Despite a considerable increase in Trans-Europ Express services — leading to greater coordination of the Italian passenger rail system with certain foreign networks, particularly France and Germany — and despite the successful trials of the electric locomotive E 444-001, called the Tortoise, and which reached a speed of 200kph between Naples and Rome, the germ of the idea of high speed was planted only with great difficulty.

In these circumstances the project of the Rome-Florence Direttissima was conceived. It was the first step taken in the direction of high speed in Italy. The project was initiated in 1966. Work began shortly after and, despite numerous complications, the Direttissima project is finally almost finished. The first section between Settebagni, on the outskirts of Rome, and Città della Pieve was opened in 1976. The production of the Direttissima has been a real *via crucis*: its construction has been one of the most troubled of the post-war period, marked by rising expenditure, inflation which reduced the initial capital, and wastage and delays due to technical errors. Yet along

---

[6] Di Gianfrancesco, M. Politica dei trasporti e sviluppo economico regionale: aspetti storici del disequilibrio italiano, in Rivista di politica economica, a. LXII(1972)

the route there are works of great achievement, such as the San Donato tunnel which is 11km long, and especially the viaduct over the Paglia river which, at 5.4kms, is one of the longest in the world.

The new track is shorter than the previous one by 61kms, being 255kms compared with the previous 316kms. At many points along the line there are connections with the old track, thus allowing for more efficient regulation of traffic.

Throughout the 1970s, the Rome-Florence Direttissima represented all that was modern. In fact the speeds anticipated on the new line required the updating of signalling equipment and all fixed installations. This was to conform with the vast process of modernisation and technological improvements then planned for the rolling stock and fixed installations through the whole network.

Growing demand in the wake of the oil crisis of 1973 imposed a certain rationalisation on the railway enterprise but it had nevertheless recorded its worst ever post-war deficit in 1970.

The Pendolino

On October 11 1971, a prototype electric train called the Y0160 travelled the line between Turin and Asti under observation as a travelling laboratory. Because this particular stretch is full of curves it was regarded as ideal, for this was the first trial run of the new electric train that was to play a decisive part in the history of high speed in Italy. The prototype had been manufactured by Fiat. It was conceived as far back as 1960 and had taken ten years to build.

Four years later, during which adjustments had been made, Fiat delivered the first of four models ordered by the state railways. The great novelty of the train was that the casing, that is the body of the carriage, had variable trim, which allowed it to tilt towards the inside of the curve whenever high speeds were reached. The casing was made of a light alloy rather than steel, thus considerably reducing both weight and corrosion. Moreover, the motors were attached to the casing, something that was completely new. The first example of a Pendolino with variable trim entered service on the stretch between Ancona and Rome on July 2 1976. It could travel at a maximum speed of 250kph with 171 passengers on board.

The Pendolino is based on pendular principles which spare the passenger the effects of centrifugal forces experienced on bends, even when the train is travelling at speeds higher than those permitted on normal trains. The bogies remain firmly attached to the rails while the body of the carriage tilts, and so compensates for centrifugal force. The system of oscillating casing, or variable trim, allows the train to take curves with an elevation greater than that of the outer rail, thus providing greater compensation for centrifugal acceleration and allowing the train to travel at speeds between 20 per cent and 30 per cent higher than those of normal trains.

The principle of tilting is not new; the innovation is the gyroscope which forms the effective mechanism. The gyroscope is able to pick up variations in the geometry of the rails, announcing the approach of a curve and transmitting the announcement to the hydraulic pistons which actuate the tilting of the casing gradually and comfortably. For this reason the casing is slightly smaller than normal, well-rounded, and all the seats face forwards, as in an aeroplane, so as to avoid adding to the effects

The ETR 401 Pendolino, **above**, and the ETR 450

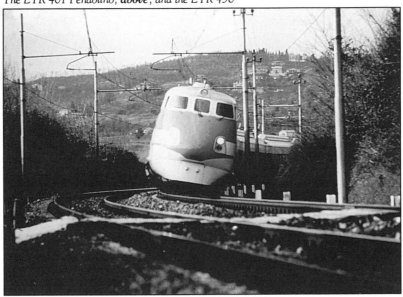

ETR 450 at Milan Central Station

of tilting, the negative effects of facing a direction opposite to that of the train's movement. At railway termini all the seats can be automatically turned around.

The facility for tilting on curves allows the train to reach high speeds even over the most tortuous stretches, without recourse to costly and sometimes impossible modifications to the track. The pendular motion is, of course, the origin of the name given to the electric train.

The introduction of the first Pendolino coincided with the relaunching of the general transport plan; something that was not so much due to a change of attitude on the part of the Italian government as to the oil crisis and its repercussions. In the same year that the new electric train made its first journey, a long-term plan was presented, aimed at restoring Italian railways to the standards established some years before by the UIC. High speed, considered to be a factor in European integration, was also on the plan's agenda. Following the oil crisis, there was an increase in demand for rail transport and it was in this period that a new environmental awareness began to emerge.

Another plan followed, but at the same time the state railways decided not to build any more trains due to lack of funds available for high speed. The first Pendolino thus remained an isolated example — an omission representing an enormous strategic error on the part of the railway authorities — and in effect the idea of high speed was sent into hibernation for 15 years. There is no comparable U-turn to be found in the entire history of Italian railway rolling-stock[7].

[7] Koenig, G K. Oltre il Pendolino. Alta velocita' e assetto variabile negli elettrotreni italiani; Valerio Levi, Rome, 1986, p99

Like France's TGV, the ETR 500 runs at its maximum speed on new track

There was a new wave of excitement in 1985 when a multi-disciplinary working group was formed under the auspices of the state railways. It was made up of more than 200 people and charged with studying all the essential aspects of a high speed system. The following year the feasibility study was completed.

As a result, the series of ETR 450s were removed to the workshops where they were modified. Changes were made to their electrical equipment and to the bogies and the variable trim was corrected. On November 13 1985, one of these modified trains completed the journey between Rome and Milan in four hours 45 minutes. Two and a half years later, in May 1988, the 450 was introduced on the same stretch and since then has regularly travelled on Italian lines, linking a number of cities and with varying results.

TWO GENERATIONS: the ETR 500 alongside the tilting ETR 450

The ETR 500

The future of high speed in Italy lies in the ETR 500, considered to be the progenitor of the future series of high speed trains. It can reach a speed of 300kph and consists of a block of ten carriages between two power units at front and back.

It differs from the previous model in a number of ways. The main difference is that the ETR 500 will only travel on purpose-built tracks, made up of long sequences of straight stretches, linked by very broad curves, which allow the train to reach and maintain 270kph almost everywhere, with peaks of 300kph. The unique tilting casing will disappear too, since the new tracks make it unnecessary. Finally the architecture of the new ETR 500 is very different from that of the 450. All the power of the new fast train is concentrated at the ends; a factor which allows a much more robust configuration and easier maintenance. By contrast the 450, which has motors mounted on each of the bogies, needs a long time for readjustments, even between one journey and the next. A not unimportant advance is the addition of a second-class section: thus the ETR 500 heralds the advent of high speed travel for the masses.

References

D'Angelo, A. 1988. I treni del futuro. Saranno Veloci, in Berenbgo Gardin, P (ed). Ferrovie Italiane. Editori Riuniti, Rome

Bortolotti, L. 1985. Viabilita' e sistemi infrastrutturali, in De Seta, C (ed). Storia d'Italia. Annali 8. Insediamenti e Territorio. Einaudi, Torino

Di Giafrancesco, M. 1972. Politica dei Trasporti e Sviluppo Economico Regionale: Aspetti Storici del Disequilibrio Italiano, in "Rivista di Politica Economica," a. LXII, 1972, n3, pp1537-1538

Giuntini, A. 1984. I Giganti della Montagna. Storia della Ferrovia Direttissima Bologna-Firenze 1845-1934. Olschki, Florence

Koenig, G K. 1986. Oltre il Pendolino. Alta Velocita' e Assetto Variabile negli Elettrotreni Italiani. Valerio Levi, Rome

Minoletti, G. 1953. Estetica dell'Allestimento Interno, in "Ingegneria Ferroviaria," a. VIII, 1953, n7-8 p535

7.

America's lost opportunity

Maury Klein, Professor of History, University of Rhode Island, Kingston

FOR A BRIEF time in the 1930s the United States held centre stage in the development of high speed trains. This supremacy survived World War II only by default and faded fast over the following decades until today the United States ranks far behind other nations in the field. The intriguing question is why this decline occurred. How did the nation with the largest and most highly developed rail system in the world lose this clear superiority?

This complex story can be told only in outline here. It begins properly with some of the factors that separate the American rail experience from that of most other nations. To serve a growing population expanding rapidly over a large continent, most early American railroads were built hastily and flimsily. The object was to create not a few good lines, but many adequate ones to serve its sprawling domain. By 1900 the United States had 1,224 operating railroads with 192,556 miles (310,074 kms) of track, yet the country's industrial economy had undergone such spectacular growth that it threatened to overwhelm even this huge system[1].

Shortly before 1900 the Age of Construction gave way to the Age of Reconstruction as Americans literally rebuilt their major rail arteries from the ground up. The entrepreneurs who undertook this gigantic task, led by the redoubtable E H Harriman, understood the domino effect wrought by railroad technology — namely, that one major improvement could not be attempted without undertaking several others at the same time. Bigger payloads required more powerful engines and larger cars, which in turn demanded heavier rails, more ballast, reduced grades and curvature, stronger bridges, improved signals, more durable ties, and an upgrading of other facilities[2].

The staggering cost of this transformation was made possible by a flood of traffic that poured onto the rail system after 1898, and by a capital market that cheerfully absorbed one enormous issue of new securities after another. It is important to remember that most American roads were originally built with private and/or state funds. The national (federal) government played little part, beyond offering land grants and providing loans, in the form of bonds for the first transcontinental railroad completed in 1869. Even this modest role soon faded; the Age of Reconstruction was

---

[1] Historical Statistics of the United States, Colonial Times to 1970. Washington, D C, 1975, Part 1, 728

[2] Harriman's role in this process is depicted in Maury Klein. 1990. Union Pacific: The Rebirth, 1894-1969. New York, pp48-181. It will be expanded in my forthcoming biography of Harriman.

underwritten entirely by the private sector[3].

Thus did the American experience produce not a cooperative partnership to develop this largest and most vital industry, but an adversarial relationship between business and government. Between 1900 and 1916 a public clamour arose to curb the immense power accumulating in the hands of corporations, and the entrepreneurs and bankers who controlled them. The result was a flood of legislation that put in place the regulatory apparatus that still characterises the American system[4].

The railroads had always been under intense public scrutiny and were subject from early times to regulation by the state governments. With the passage of the Interstate Commerce Act in 1887, they became the first industry to be regulated by the federal government. While the scope of this regulation was weak at first, it was greatly extended during the 1900s. During World War I the rail system was nationalised briefly, then returned to private ownership under a new regulatory framework imposed by the Transportation Act of 1920[5].

The events of this crucial period left a deep and lasting imprint on the destiny of American railroads in the 20th century. They imposed a straitjacket of regulation that transformed the carriers into a captive industry unable to control either its pricing or its major costs, such as labour. Unable to compete by offering lower rates, roads could only outdo competitors by providing better service. Yet even here they were limited in their scope of action and subject to regulatory strictures that left little room for initiative or innovation.

The timing of this change could not have been worse. The railroads came under severe restraints just when they were in urgent need of working capital to continue their modernisation. Rising costs combined with strict regulation of rates slashed the return on capital enough to make many, if not most, roads unprofitable and unable to float new security issues. If that were not enough, the Act of 1920 bound the railroads in regulatory knots just as they were falling victim to a technological revolution.

For 70 years railroads had dominated the transport industry because no new forms had risen to challenge them. After 1920, however, the automobile, truck, bus, and aeroplane appeared on the scene, while older forms like water transport and pipelines were reinvigorated. A lively contest for traffic arose among modes of transport competing less with each other than with other modes. The depression intensified this struggle as all sides vied for their share of a dwindling business[6].

---

[3] The complex, often adversarial relationship between private interests and the federal government in the building of the first transcontinental road is depicted in Maury Klein. 1988. Union Pacific: The Birth, 1862-1893. New York

[4] Maury Klein. 1990 "The Turning Point in American Railroad History," paper given at Coloquio Internacional sobre Transporte e Industrializacion siglos XIX y XX, Madrid, January 1990; Albro Martin. 1971. Enterprise Denied: Origins of the Decline of American Railroads, 1897-1917. New York

[5] Maury Klein. 1990. "Competition and Regulation: The Railroad Model," article in Business History Review, Summer 1990; Ari and Olive Hoogenboom. 1976. A History of the ICC: From Panacea to Palliative. New York; Walker D. Hines. 1928. War History of American Railroads. New Haven

[6] For more detail see Klein, Union Pacific: The Rebirth, 258-78

In these clashes the railroads found it impossible to compete against newer, more flexible modes unshackled by regulation. Many major systems tried to redefine themselves as transportation companies by adding truck, bus, and even air services, but every attempt at innovation ran up against the barrier of whether regulation would permit it. One area offering a loophole around regulation was technology itself. Despite the limited capital resources at their disposal, the railroads never ceased trying to improve their efficiency and upgrade their facilities. It was one such effort that produced America's shining hour in the realm of high speed trains.

By the 1930s automobiles and buses had already swept away much of the railroad's short-haul passenger business, but aeroplanes had yet to make inroads on the long-haul traffic. Although passenger travel was the smallest and least profitable area of railroad business, it had an important market value to both shippers and the public, whose contact with the carriers was as travellers. Unable to hold their short-haul business against the automobile, the railroads undertook a bold campaign to preserve their long-haul business by developing a new form of high speed train.

Known popularly as the streamliner, the new train borrowed its technology from rival modes. Advances in two critical areas made it possible to conceive this new mode of travel: improvements in the internal combustion engine (most notably the diesel), and research in aerodynamics and lightweight metal alloys spurred by the rise of aviation. Two railroads, the Union Pacific and the Chicago, Burlington & Quincy, pioneered in this work and separately unveiled the first streamliners in the spring of 1934[7].

Except for riding on rails, the new trains departed entirely from tradition. The revolutionary new diesel engine, by eliminating stops for fuel and water, could go 12 times the distance of a conventional train using coal. The sleek metallic cars cut both weight and wind resistance. The trains had new braking systems, sealed windows, climate control, improved lighting, adjustable seats with attached trays, and a host of other innovations. Even the crockery used modern materials that reduced its weight by more than half. The design and decor were striking, like nothing ever seen in a passenger train.

The streamliners went into service on long-haul routes, where they showed to the best advantage. Prior to May 1934 no locomotive had ever travelled more than 775 miles (1,248kms) non-stop. That month the Burlington's Zephyr raced from Denver to Chicago, 1,017 miles (1,638kms), in little over 13 hours, or half the usual schedule time, reaching a top speed of nearly 113 miles (182kms) per hour. As more companies ordered new trains, the setting of new speed records became commonplace by 1936. The Union Pacific cut a full day off travel time between Chicago and the West Coast, making the trip in 39 ³/₄ hours[8].

Public response to the streamliners surpassed all expectations. Nearly 700,000

---

[7] For details on each prototype see Klein, Union Pacific: The Rebirth, 295-308, and Richard C. Overton. 1965. Burlington Route. Lincoln, Neb, 393-406. The original versions had two major differences. The Burlington began with a diesel engine while the Union Pacific first used a Winton distillate engine before switching to a diesel. Where the Union Pacific's first cars were built of aluminium, the Burlington used stainless steel

[8] Overton, Burlington Route, 396-97, 400

Streamliner City of Portland at Boston during a national exhibition tour

people lined up to inspect the Union Pacific and Burlington trains in the cities where they were put on display. Thousands more gathered alongside tracks to watch them whizz by. The streamliner aroused wild enthusiasm, not only because it offered fast, luxurious travel but because it was a dazzling blend of old and familiar associations, with futuristic technology. Where the aeroplane was something new out of the blue, the streamliner was stunningly new in a familiar setting, where the leap of progress from its predecessors could be measured by one's own experience. The streamliner was not merely fast, though speed was one of its prime appeals. In this first age of chic it was sleek, glamorous, and thoroughly modern[9].

[9] Klein, Union Pacific: The Rebirth, 307-8

For an old and stodgy industry like the railroad, these were potent selling points. A funny thing had happened on the way to the future: the iron horse was no longer iron, or a horse. The hot breath of steam and the galloping surge of power that had always been a part of the romance of railroading had been put on the road to extinction. With these first high speed trains the railroads made their greatest break ever with the past.

In retrospect, the development of the streamliner seems a remarkable act of faith. During the throes of the Great Depression, when railroads were no less starved for capital than other businesses, many of them risked large investments in an area of traffic that had always been the least profitable (in fact unprofitable) for them. While there were plenty of people willing and eager to ride the new trains, the carriers were not responding to any pent-up demand. Why then did they sink money so desperately needed elsewhere into an area that promised little return?

The answer boils down to two related factors: image and regulation. The railroads were prisoners of the regulatory system, which put them at the mercy of the politicians. For this reason their public image mattered greatly, and most of the public knew the carriers as travellers rather than as shippers. One provision of the Transportation Act of 1920 forbade roads from dropping passenger services on any route without approval from the Interstate Commerce Commission. This obliged carriers to continue passenger operations on routes that ran heavy deficits. Most attempts to abandon service encountered stiff resistance and took much time[10].

Although streamliners might be a losing proposition financially — a question still hotly debated — they were important as a public relations device to boost the railroads' image. Given a choice, most companies would have preferred to go out of the passenger business altogether, but the law did not permit this option. The alternative was to spruce up passenger travel and try to make at least the long-haul service pay for itself.

By 1940 most major systems had installed streamliners and improved their passenger service in other ways. Public response remained enthusiastic and patronage high. While many problems still plagued the industry, the passenger puzzle seemed well on the road to solution. Then came World War II, which rendered a devastating blow to railroads in general and to the passenger service in particular.

Here was another turn of events that no-one could have foreseen. The crushing demands of war ran railroad plant and equipment into the ground. Wartime scarcity of labour and materials severely curtailed maintenance. The shiny new streamliners simply wore themselves out hauling record numbers of passengers and troops. At the same time, the war spurred technical developments in aviation that gave rise to radically improved passenger air service after the war. Full employment, coupled with consumer shortages, raised savings to record levels, creating a pent-up consumer demand that fuelled a postwar boom in the automobile industry[11].

In 1946 the rail industry confronted a situation riddled with irony. It emerged from the war fattened by the huge load of business but physically exhausted and in need of

---

[10] For the 1920 act see I L Sharfman. The Interstate Commerce Commission: A Study in Administrative Law and Procedure. New York, 1931-1937, 5 vols, 1:177-244

[11] Klein, Union Pacific: The Rebirth, 402-45

huge capital outlays for improvements. To rebuild its passenger fleet meant starting almost from scratch with another giant investment in new equipment. Most major systems undertook this task, even though they were aware of swimming against the tide of events. They invested in new equipment because they saw no alternative. If the ICC would not let them get out of the passenger business, they had to do what they could to attract customers to their trains.

Unfortunately, the post-war environment could not have been worse for their efforts. The economy soared into a prolonged upward climb, keeping employment and consumer spending high. Automobile sales climbed to record heights as the American love affair with cars turned into a raging passion. As housing starts reached unprecedented levels, suburbs sprang up like mushrooms and with them new highway systems. On one side the railroads surrendered the last remnants of short-haul passenger business; on the other, they saw the long-haul business relentlessly whittled away by a growing fleet of new jet aeroplanes[12].

By 1960 it was obvious to even the most incorrigible optimist that the railroads' massive post-war investment in new passenger equipment had been in vain. If the industry had been operating in a neutral environment, it might have taken the initiative to redefine its passenger mission in some positive manner and redirect its energies to capturing the traffic most available to it, by developing new equipment and marketing tactics. Instead it remained bound by an archaic regulatory system that had dulled initiative and created a pervasive atmosphere of negativism.

Far from developing new approaches to the passenger traffic, therefore, the railroads looked to get out of the business altogether. Instead of seeking positive and imaginative ways to stimulate the carriers in this field, public policy continued to hold the roads prisoner to unprofitable routes and to play the same old game the same old way. The result was a downward spiral into financial disaster that swept once proud systems into bankruptcy or mergers with other lines. The shocking collapse of the Penn Central, an ill-fated amalgam of what had once been the two proudest and most powerful railroads in the nation, finally spurred a long overdue shift in public policy[13].

A series of legislative enactments, culminating with the Staggers Act of 1980, gave the railroads a freedom of action they had not possessed in decades. For passengers, the key act was the formation in 1971 of a federal corporation, Amtrak, to take over the passenger service. This was an historic moment in the rail industry: after 130 years of service, the private carriers abandoned the passenger business to a government agency. The American rail industry became a collection of freight carriers with no interest in any other aspect of the business.

This evolution of function, along with the story behind it, explains how and why the United States not only fell rapidly from its leadership role in rail service but also lost interest in maintaining its primacy in the passenger field. The history of Amtrak has been one of constant struggle for survival, which makes all the more remarkable the achievements it has managed in 20 years. Moreover, it occupies the anomalous

---

[12] For details on this loss of business see James C Nelson. 1959. Railroad Transportation and Public Policy. Washington, D C; and U. S. Senate. 1961. National Transportation Policy. Sen. Report No. 445, 57 Cong., 1st Sess. Washington, D C, 385-424. The latter is better known as the Doyle Report

[13] For the collapse of Penn Central see Stephen Salsbury. 1982. No Way to Run a Railroad. New York

General Motors' Aerotrain, City of Las Vegas, pictured in 1956

position of being a public corporation serving a field where innovation and funding has traditionally come from the private sector.

Where, then, does high speed rail travel in the United States stand now? Ironically, rail passenger service seems to have come full circle. The American passion for the automobile has begun to turn sour in the fumes and traffic jams of freeways choked with traffic. Despite rapid expansion, the highway system has never managed to keep pace with the explosion of cars pouring onto it, and the need to refurbish this infrastructure grows at an alarming rate. Air travel too finds itself snarled in a form of gridlock that has made flying increasingly hectic and obnoxious.

This deteriorating state of travel has breathed some new life into high speed trains in recent years. In 1956 the much heralded Aerotrain, an American lightweight train built by General Motors, made its debut on the Pennsylvania Railroad and later the Union Pacific. Despite high hopes, the new train flopped. Nearly a decade later, as part of an attempt to revive the bankrupt New York, New Haven & Hartford Railroad, federal support was given for a high speed experiment called the Turbotrain. Unfortunately, the prototype was rushed into revenue service too quickly and proved a failure[14].

The fall of the New Haven in 1960 made it difficult for the government to ignore the commuter problem in the congested Northeast Corridor. In 1965 Congress passed the High Speed Ground Transportation Act, which contained three major provisions. It funded research and development on high speed ground transportation of all types, authorised work on a demonstration project that spurred creation of both the Turbotrain and the Metroliner, and launched the planning process for what ultimately became the Northeast Corridor Improvement Project[15].

Two years later a new cabinet position, the Department of Transportation, was created, and under it a new agency called the Federal Railroad Administration. The FRA took charge of research into high speed trains and oversaw development of the Turbotrain. From its efforts evolved the Northeast Corridor project, a high profile attempt to develop a modern rail transportation system in the most crowded area of the country. If successful, the project could serve as a model for similar efforts elsewhere[16].

Between 1976 and 1986 the government poured $2.3 billion into the Corridor project. Most of the money was used to rehabilitate the line while coping with as many as 1,000 train movements a day. Apart from this remedial work, some funds went to developing a new train called the Metroliner for high speed service on the run between Boston and Washington. Despite heroic efforts, the Corridor project produced only half a loaf. The Metroliner went into service only between New York and Washington at 125 miles (201kms) an hour, leaving the New York-Boston run with conventional service. Today the Metroliner remains the only high speed train in actual service in the United States[17].

Why was the Corridor project left uncompleted? The reason was primarily financial. In the end the government balked at tackling two expensive obstacles: reducing curvature on the Boston route to permit high speed runs, and electrifying the line from New Haven to Boston. The route from Washington to New Haven had been electrified as early as 1933, just before the advent of diesel power scuttled a growing movement toward conversion to electric lines. Although part of the original plan, electrification was dropped because of its cost. Today a traveller on the New York-Boston route still sits for ten or 15 minutes in New Haven while the railroad shifts from diesel to electric power or vice versa[18].

Recently Amtrak revived the Corridor project in a modest way by announcing plans to put a high speed train into service on the Boston-New York route by 1998. Using the Swedish X2000, largely because it holds curves well, the proposed train would

[14] Klein, Union Pacific: The Rebirth, 487, 489; "Tax Exempt Bonds for High Speed Rail Projects", Hearing before the Committee on Finance, 100 Cong., 2d Sess., Sen. Hrg. 100-674, Mar. 24, 1988, 41-42

[15] Interview with Arrigo Mongini of the Federal Railroad Administration, May 29, 1990. I am grateful to Mr. Mongini for his cooperation in this project

[16] "Advanced Transportation Systems," Hearing before the Subcommittee on Surface Transportation, 100 Cong., 1st Sess., Sen. Hrg. 101-369, Oct. 17, 1989, 8

[17] "Advanced Transportation Systems", 8, 14, 34-35; "Tax Exempt Bonds," 41-42. The Corridor project involved track utilised by three freight and five commuter lines, some private and some public

[18] Transportation Research Board of the National Academy of Sciences. 1977. Railroad Electrification: The Issues, Special Report 180. Washington, DC, 6, 8

travel up to 125mph and cut the schedule between the two cities from more than four to less than three hours. Under the plan, the entire route would be electrified but utilise the existing roadbed[19].

Irony abounds in this glacial coming of electric power to the Corridor. In 1900 the United States was the world leader in electrified roads; as late as 1930 it owned 20 per cent of the world's total. After World War II, when Europe had to rebuild its railroads, the decision was made to electrify. By contrast, American roads pursued a policy, begun about 1937, of investing heavily in oil-powered diesels. That choice, however rational at the time, has come back to haunt us in an age where both oil and labour costs have gone through the ceiling. It also cost us a potential power source for new high-speed trains[20].

One solution to this dilemma would be the creation of an entirely new technology. The work of two American scientists on one form of magnetic levitation helped prompt the FRA, which was underwriting research on linear induction motors, to produce a scale model demonstration of maglev as well, but the latter project was terminated in 1976. From this episode arose the half truth that Americans originated maglev only to see others develop it. "The Japanese and Germans took the ideas and theories of our scientists and turned them into working machines," complained Senator Harry Reid of Nevada. "We have the pride of authorship, but no longer the pride of ownership."[21]

This sort of grumbling over wounded national pride permeates much of the recent American discussion over developing high speed trains, but in truth the United States has only itself to blame for falling so far behind. Apart from the Metroliner, there is today no high speed American train in service, or even under testing. One knowledgeable authority believes that we are seven to ten years behind in developing high speed technology[22].

The final irony is that all the live projects in the realm of high speed trains today are being promoted by private interests with some help from individual states.

Except for the incomplete Corridor project, the federal government has at every critical juncture ducked responsibility for developing a coherent transportation system. Ours is a government that traditionally does not lead, but rather responds to crisis. Transportation policy has provided a glaring example of this truth.

None of the current projects has reached construction stage, and all rely on foreign technology. Two of them are in Florida, one of the fastest growing states. After six years of study, a consortium of interests is preparing to award a franchise in 1991 for a high speed electrified railroad using a modified version of the Swedish X-2 train that will ultimately connect Tampa, Orlando, and Miami, a distance of about 300 miles (483kms). A second group hopes to construct a high-profile maglev line from Orlando airport to a spot near several entertainment centres. Although this line will be only

[19] Providence Journal, March 27, 1992

[20] *Ibid*, 13-15

[21] "Advanced Transportation Systems", 4, 8, 14-15; Mongini interview, May 29, 1990. This myth that Americans created Mag-Lev overlooks the pioneering work of Hermann Kemper in Germany during the 1930s and after

[22] *Ibid*, 26, 53

Amtrak's story has been one of struggle in the face of lack of funds and political will

14 miles (23kms) long, it hopes to attain speeds of 250 miles (403kms) an hour. The technology here will be a German Transrapid model, the financing largely Japanese. Despite much talk, however, these projects remain in limbo[23].

Another consortium has for some years been working with the states of Nevada and California to design and build a high speed line from Las Vegas to the Los Angeles area. No decision has yet been made on whether to use maglev or some form of TGV system, and no franchise has yet been awarded. In Texas a state agency was formed to solicit proposals for a high speed line to link the "Texas Triangle" cities of Houston, Dallas, and Fort Worth. This project took a major leap forward in May 1992 with the decision by Texas to award a contract to Texas TGV, a French-American consortium of 24 companies, headed by Morrison-Knudsen, for a TGV system connecting the state's five leading cities. The 590-mile double-tracked system, projected to cost $5.8 billion, would connect Dallas, Houston, Fort Worth, Austin, and San Antonio by the century's end[24].

Two other projects deserve brief mention for the contrast they offer. The state of Ohio has taken the first steps toward feasibility studies for a high speed line connecting Cleveland, Cincinnati, and Columbus. On the other hand, Pennsylvania has withdrawn funding from its state agency on high speed transportation, thereby dashing hopes of building a high speed line between Philadelphia and Pittsburgh. However, there is activity of a related sort in Pittsburgh, where the Carnegie-Mellon group, which has long been involved in maglev research, wants to bring together a collection of firms to create an industrial centre capable of producing maglev technology[25].

These efforts were galvanised in November 1991 when Congress passed a $151 billion Surface Transportation Act that included $800 million for research into high speed train technology. One provision allotted $55 million for "steel-wheel technology studies that include the feasibility of guideway or track design, safety and reliability, environmental impact, land-use impact, energy and power consumption, signalling and control systems, and integration of high speed rail with other modes of transportation". Although the act contained a loan guarantee programme, it stopped short of permitting the issuance of tax-exempt bonds to finance rail projects[26].

This brief survey constitutes the sum of American work in high speed trains. It is not an impressive record. While the FRA has provided seed money for feasibility studies and is completing a study on the commercial viability of maglev in the United States, the federal government continues to dawdle. On May 2, 1990, a forum was held in Washington to explore ways of using federal money for research to help private industry develop an operational maglev system with technology designed and manufactured in the United States. The Surface Transportation Act provided an important boost but is hardly a ringing endorsement. The refusal of Congress to make bonds used for high speed rail projects exempt from federal taxes, which was deemed critical to financing them, remains a stiff obstacle[27].

In a curious way, Americans have gone back to their roots in dealing with high speed railroads. Although many analysts insist that federal aid is crucial, especially in the areas of research and development, we continue to rely largely on private entrepreneurs with some modest help from individual states. This approach worked well 150 years ago; whether it will be successful in today's very different world remains to be seen.

Bibliography

Hines, Walker D. 1928. War History of American Railroads. New Haven

Hoogenboom, Ari and Olive. 1976. A History of the ICC: From Panacea to Palliative. New York

Klein, Maury. 1988. Union Pacific: The Birth, 1862-1893. New York

Klein, Maury. 1990. Union Pacific: The Rebirth, 1894-1969. New York

Klein, Maury. 1990. "The Turning Point in American Railroad History," paper given at Coloquio Internacional sobre Transporte e Industrializacion siglos XIX y XX, Madrid, January 1990

Klein, Maury. 1990. "Competition and Regulation: the Railroad Model," Business History Review, Summer 1990, 64:2, 311-325

Martin, Albro. 1971. Enterprise Denied: Origins of the Decline of American Railroads, 1897-1917. New York

Nelson, James C. 1959. Railroad Transportation and Public Policy. Washington DC

Overton, Richard C. 1965. Burlington Route. Lincoln, Neb

Sharfman, I. L. 1931-1937. The Interstate Commerce Commission: A Study in Administrative Law and Procedure. New York, 5 vol

Transportation Research Board of the National Academy of Sciences. 1977. Railroad Electrification: The Issues, Special Report 180. Washington, D C

United States Congress. 1989. "Advanced Transportation Systems," Hearing before the Subcommittee on Surface Transportation, 100 Cong, 1st Sess, Senate Hearing 101-369, Oct. 17

United States Congress. 1988. "Tax Exempt Bonds for High Speed Rail Projects," Hearing before the Committee on Finance, 100 Cong, 2nd Sess, Senate Hearing 100-674, Mar. 24

United States Senate. 1961. National Transportation Policy, Sen Report No 445, 57 Cong, 1st Sess. Washington, DC

---

[23] *Ibid*, 37-38; "Tax Exempt Bonds," 42-45, 49-52, 80-82; Mongini interview, May 29, 1990

[24] Providence Journal, March 27, 1992

[25] Mongini interview, May 29, 1990

[26] *Ibid*

[27] Galen J. Reser to Senator Claiborne Pell, April 12, 1990. I am grateful to Todd G. Andrews of Senator Pell's office for providing me a copy of this letter and a press release on the forum. For the argument in favour of the bonds see the testimony in "Tax Exempt Bonds"

8.

BR's tale of two trains

Professor Christopher A Nash, Institute for Transport Studies, University of Leeds

THE HISTORY of high speed rail services in Britain has been essentially a tale of two trains — the Advanced Passenger Train and the diesel-electric powered High Speed Train (or InterCity 125).

The former was intended for use on the West Coast Main Line, which was electrified from London to Crewe, Manchester and Liverpool in 1966. Electrification of the route via Birmingham was completed in the following year. Trains heading north from Crewe still had to change to diesel traction until electrification through to Glasgow was completed in 1974.

None of this route would really qualify as a high speed line by today's standards. Initially, electric traction was limited to a top speed of 160kph; later this was raised to 180kph for locomotives equipped with high speed pantographs. Nevertheless, the combination of speed and frequency introduced with the new traction was hitherto unparalleled in Britain, with 25 per cent reductions in journey time being typical.

It was on this route, with its numerous curves and gradients — particularly north of Preston — that it was intended to raise speeds further by the use of the 250kph Advanced Passenger Train (APT), the tilting coaches of which would be permitted to run at higher speeds than those of conventional rolling stock, especially on curves. Although prototype trains of this type made a few runs in service in 1981, they did not achieve the required degree of reliability, and the project was subsequently scrapped[1]. With the failure of this train to enter regular service, no major improvement in speeds has yet been achieved on the West Coast route.

The history of the other group of main lines to London has been very different. Operated by diesel traction, they saw incremental improvement until the introduction of the 200kph high speed diesel train in the mid 1970s. This is a more conventional non-tilting train, more appropriate to routes with few curves, or where more money has been spent on straightening them out. It was first introduced on the routes from London to Bristol and Swansea in 1976, and was phased in on the East Coast Main Line from London to Leeds, Newcastle and Edinburgh during 1978 and 1979. The same rolling stock has since been introduced on other routes, although, as the infrastructure was generally not improved to permit speeds in excess of 160kph, the resultant improvement in journey time has been much less significant. Thus most of the evidence discussed here regarding high speed services in Britain relates to the introduction of this train.

[1] Potter, 1987

Effects of high speed on rail patronage

The first real opportunity to measure the change in patronage resulting from a major acceleration of services in post-war Britain was provided by a before-and-after study of the West Coast Main Line electrification in 1966[2].

This was based on one-day surveys of traffic conducted on all modes — not an entirely satisfactory approach given the large day-to-day variation in patronage, although it had the merit of allowing estimates to be made as to whether the additional patronage had swapped to rail from other modes, or was wholly new business. Generally traffic rose by some 25-50 per cent, with the percentage increase in traffic exceeding the percentage time saving. A regression of the percentage change in traffic on the percentage change in journey time produced an elasticity of -1.3; that is to say that, on average, a one per cent reduction in journey time had produced a 1.3 per cent rise in traffic.

Examination of the other modes suggested that there had been a substantial diversion of business traffic from air, but little diversion of business or leisure traffic from road. Presumably, then, most of the additional rail leisure traffic consisted of journeys which would not otherwise have been made by any mode. A subsequent study undertaken at Leeds University, which concentrated explicitly on the choice between rail and air, suggested that, if rail could achieve comparable door-to-door journey times, and at a lower price, then air would retain little traffic other than those feeding into other air services[3].

In other words, in terms of other features of service quality, rail was rated at least as good as air. Given the long journeys required to and from airports for the majority of air passengers, this suggested that particular rewards would come from reducing rail journey times below a threshold of about three hours, as was indeed achieved in the case of the main stations involved in this scheme.

When the time came to forecast the increase in patronage that would result from introduction of the diesel-powered High Speed Train, it was thought prudent to assume a rather lower level of extra traffic than was implied by the earlier work, partly because traffic was starting from a higher base, and it seemed likely that the relevant elasticity would fall as traffic grew. So it proved. Initial monitoring work within BR concentrated on use of the "control flow" technique. Under this method, no attempt was made to explain actual changes in patronage over time. Rather, each route on which services had been improved was compared with one or more unimproved routes which had displayed a similar path in traffic over time up to the time of improvement of the first route[4].

More recently, application has been made of time series regression analysis in two studies at Leeds University. The first used annual data on flows between all major conurbations over a ten-year period — a total of some 45 flows[5]. In a pooled time series/cross-section model, year-on-year percentage changes in traffic were regressed on a

[2] Evans, 1969

[3] Leake, 1971

[4] Shilton, 1982

[5] Fowkes, Nash and Whiteing, 1985

variety of explanatory variables, including fares, average earnings and car ownership. The effects of major service changes were estimated by use of dummy variables. This procedure combines some of the features of control flow analysis with regression analysis. Important variables are introduced explicitly, but any systematic unexplained growth in traffic applying both to improved and unimproved routes will also be disallowed when estimating the effect of service variations.

The mean effect of the High Speed Train on traffic was found to be of the order of 15 per cent growth in traffic over the course of two years; that of the extension of the West Coast Main Line electrification to Glasgow was slightly higher.

In the most recent study, time series regression has been applied to individual origin-destination pairs, using four-weekly data[6]. The wide range of results obtained for the effects of the High Speed Train is illustrated in Table 8.1.

	First Class	Standard Class	Total
Table 8.1 **Percent increase in traffic due to high speed train** **on selected routes to/from London** **Time Series Regression Results**			
Bath	84	43	54
Swindon	112	30	42
Cardiff	57	27	34
Bristol	55	26	28
York	22	17	23
Leeds	28	15	19
Plymouth	0	0	0
Median of 12 flows	32	16	23
Source: Owen and Phillips (1987)			

The biggest effects were found at Bath and Swindon, which, as well as enjoying the greatest improvement in service, are the closest stations in the sample to London. The increase in traffic may therefore include some commuting from areas which were previously thought to be outside the London commuter belt. Increases on the East Coast route to York and Leeds are rather lower, while to Plymouth (a route dominated by leisure traffic, and over which the full speed potential could only be realised for a short distance) no significant effect could be found.

It is interesting to note the degree to which increases were greater in First Class traffic than in second; this of course implies that the total increase in revenue will be considerably greater than the increases in traffic.

The overall impression created by the studies of the High Speed Train was of a journey time elasticity of the order of -0.8. That is, a one per cent rise in speed was

---

[6] Owen and Phillips, 1987

A TALE OF TWO TRAINS: *The High Speed Train,* **above**, *helped achieve a 15 per cent growth in patronage over two years.* **Below:** *The ill-fated APT never entered regular service*

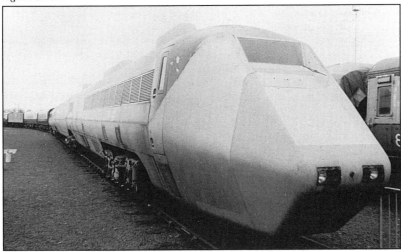

accompanied by a 0.8 per cent rise in traffic. However, there was some sign (not borne out by the Plymouth example) that traffic increased by a certain amount when the High Speed Train was introduced regardless of the extent of the time saving produced; conversely the increase in traffic was found to be less in the small number of cases where a major speed improvement had been introduced without new rolling stock.

This led to an alternative hypothesis that something like half of the increased traffic was due to the improved comfort and "image" of the new rolling stock, with a true journey time elasticity of around -0.4.[7] This hypothesis will be further discussed in the light of the "stated preference" results outlined in the next section.

Benefits of time savings to users of high speed rail services

In this section, we shall consider the benefits of high speed rail services in terms of time savings to rail travellers. In the next section, we consider a wider range of issues. In a road investment appraisal in Britain, time savings by travellers would be directly taken into account as a major social benefit. However, in Britain, main line rail improvement schemes are evaluated on purely commercial criteria. Thus the key question for British Rail is how far such benefits may be converted into additional revenue.

Most recent British work on the value passengers place on time savings has used so-called "stated preference" techniques. Starting with a study of the importance of frequency of service and the need to change trains undertaken by Steer and Willumsen (1981), there has been widespread use of these techniques for studying rail demand in recent years. There are many variants of the approach, but what they have in common is a reliance on the responses of interviewees to questions as to their preferences between hypothetical alternatives.

Table 8.2 shows an example from the study, from which two alternative hypothetical combinations are presented of timetable, fare, journey time and reliability. The respondents are asked to indicate their preference between alternatives A and B by ticking a box to show whether they "definitely" or "probably" prefer A or B, or like or dislike both equally. Because each interviewee may be given a number of these questions, and because the values may be carefully designed to ensure that they will reveal the information that is being sought, the result is that information at a high level of disaggregation can be obtained at very much less cost than by studying actual choices (the "revealed preference" approach).

A recent study sponsored by the Department of Transport with support from British Rail made extensive use of these methods to study what leisure travellers would be willing to pay to save travel time[8]. We undertook both the part of this study which dealt with long distance rail leisure travel, and a parallel project financed by the Science and Engineering Research Council, which studied business travel[9]. The results of these two projects will now be discussed.

In the study of leisure travel, passengers were interviewed on trains between London and Manchester, Birmingham and Manchester and Bristol and London. The resulting data were used to calibrate a discrete choice model, from which the value

[7] Shilton, 1982
[8] MVA Consultancy, University of Leeds and University of Oxford, 1987
[9] Marks, Fowkes and Nash, 1986

Table 8.2

Stated Preference Question

Respondents are given two different timetables, fares and levels of reliability and asked to stated whether they:

	Definitely Prefer A	Probably Prefer A	Like A and B Equally	Probably Prefer B	Definitely Prefer B
			A		
LONDON, dep.	2.50	3.20	3.50	4.20	4.50
Stockport...	5.10	5.40	6.10	6.40	7.10
Manchester, arr.	5.20	5.50	6.20	6.50	7.20
	Fares: One way £12, Return £24 Scheduled Journey Time: 2hrs 30mins Up to 10mins late				
			B		
LONDON, dep.	2.50	.	3.50	.	4.50
Stockport...	5.40	.	6.40	.	7.50
Manchester, arr.	5.50	.	6.50	.	7.50
	Fares: One way £10, Return £20 Schedule Journey Time: 3hrs Up to 30mins late				

passengers placed on savings in travel time could be estimated. As expected, there was a strong — though less than proportional — relationship between values of time savings and income, with the upper income group according a value twice that of the lowest. There was also some variation according to exact journey purpose, with an overall average of 5.9p per minute in 1985 prices. Results are given in Table 8.3.

For business travellers, the issues are more complicated. Typically, business travellers choose themselves between the alternative modes their employers will permit them to use. Since their employers pay the costs, one might expect them always to use the highest quality mode permitted, although this does not actually appear to be the case. Ultimately, then, what a business traveller is willing to pay to save time is the product of what the employer is willing to pay for, as well as the choice the employee makes. There are other relevant considerations. For example, long distance rail journeys typically start and end outside the normal working day, so that time savings are often converted into leisure time rather than devoted to additional work. Also, time spent on the train can be usefully employed, for work or for eating a meal.

These factors might lead to an expectation that the value employers place upon saving time for their workforce might be somewhat below the conventional British Department of Transport assumption that this equates to the wage rate plus a markup for the overhead costs of employing labour.

We thus undertook studies of the preferences of both a sample of employers regarding overall travel policy, and a sample of employees with respect to specific long distance journeys. In the stated preference exercise with the latter, it was made clear that the employee would be given a fixed expenses budget, and would be entitled to keep any unspent surplus. Thus the employees' willingness to pay represents a willingness to pay out of their own pocket. By contrast, the employer's willingness to pay represents a willingness to pay out of the funds of the organisation in question.

Table 8.3 shows the two values, together with the results of applying the standard method of valuing business travel time used by the British Department of Transport. In a situation where some of any time savings would be devoted to leisure and some to work, we would expect the appropriate valuation of travel time savings to lie somewhere between the employers' and the employees' valuation. Thus the standard Department of Transport assumption appears to lead to a reasonable estimate of what might be a typical valuation in practice, although one might of course still doubt whether such a high value — representing in part at least a benefit in terms of extra leisure time to a particularly well-paid sector of the community — should be taken as an appropriate valuation from the point of view of society as a whole.

Table 8.3
Values of long distance travel time savings (p/min)

(a) Leisure	
Visiting friends and relatives	6.6
Holiday	4.8
Returning home	4.6
Other	6.6
Overall	5.9
(b) Business	
Employee's willingness to pay	12.0p/min
Current Department of Transport assumptions	16.0p/min
Employer's willingness to pay	23.0p/min

Source: (a) Marks (1985)
             (b) Marks, Fowkes and Nash (1986)

In summary, then, the best evidence we have suggests values of travel time savings of the order of 6p per minute for leisure travellers and 16p per minute for business. If this is true, then there are very large benefits to users arising from the introduction of high speed trains. For instance, on the East Coast Main Line, a route carrying some ten million passengers per year at the time of the introduction of the high speed train. Given that about 25 per cent of these would be travelling on business, a 30-minute time saving per journey (probably an underestimate) would lead to an annual benefit of some £25m.

We may also use these values of travel time savings as the basis for a further estimate of the travel time elasticity of demand for rail travel. We approach this question by asking what increase in traffic the time saving would lead to if fares remained unchanged. We already have (from the time series regressions referred to earlier) a fairly precise and robust estimate of the sensitivity of traffic levels to fares, as being an elasticity of the order of -1.0. If we assume that the leisure travel elasticity is about -1.25, with a somewhat lower elasticity of, say, -0.5 for business travel, we may estimate the corresponding journey time elasticities from a knowledge of the value of time savings, and of fares and journey times.

Obviously, the latter will vary from route to route, and according to the type of ticket bought. In 1985, British Rail InterCity receipts averaged about 4.3p per kilometre, but with variations from 10p per kilometre for First Class travel on prime business routes, to bargain fares as low as 2.5p. Suppose we assume that, on average, business travellers pay 50 per cent more than leisure travellers and that business travel accounts for 25 per cent of travel. A reasonable mean speed to assume, including schedule delay, would be about 16kms per minute.

This would lead to typical journey time elasticities in the leisure market of the order of -0.8, while for business travel a typical value would be about -0.6. These results would suggest an average journey time elasticity very close to the value of -0.8 given by the High Speed Train monitoring studies, lending support to the view that the extra traffic was produced largely by the journey time reductions, with only a modest effect exerted by other quality of service variables.

Assuming this sort of level of generated traffic (which accords with the evidence quoted earlier) there is little doubt that the introduction of the high speed train on the East Coast Main Line was financially very profitable for BR. The total cost of 28 high speed sets was some £50m at 1978 prices, but since it released modern air conditioned stock for service elsewhere it avoided a similar expenditure on conventional rolling stock. Only some £15m (1978 prices) was spent on upgrading track and signalling. Estimates by one of our students suggest, on an incremental cost and revenue basis, an internal rate of return of 19-22 per cent, rising to 56-61 per cent when time savings to users are added in[10], in comparison with continuing to run the existing service.

Other costs and benefits

Let us now turn to the question of the broader costs and benefits of high speed rail services. Regarding costs, the principal consideration is the question of the effects on the environment. Higher speeds typically mean higher energy consumption and, consequently, higher emissions, either directly from diesel traction or at the power station if the traction is electric. Higher speeds also typically mean higher noise levels, other things being equal, although improvements in other aspects of design mean that the British high speed train at 200kph is no noisier than its predecessor at 160kph.

The biggest environmental objections come, however, where inadequacy of existing infrastructure, in terms of either speed or capacity, means that new infrastructure is required, leading to severance, the destruction of property and the spreading of noise and visual intrusion into new areas. To the extent that higher speeds encourage wholly new journeys to be made, all the adverse environmental effects are of course multiplied.

[10] Mafurirano, 1983

On the other hand, high speed rail services do attract traffic from other modes. We have seen already that there is better evidence of diversion from air than from road; but there is little doubt also that a considerable proportion of the extra traffic attracted to rail — particularly business traffic — has come from road. A study undertaken on behalf of the Department of Transport in 1984 considered that the best estimate was that, on a route unaffected by air competition, some 50 per cent of the extra traffic would have diverted from road. Recent estimates suggest that in terms of energy consumption and emissions, high speed rail is very much preferable to air or car, although not to express road coach (Table 8.4).

Table 8.4 Petroleum use by transport mode (litres per hundred passenger km)	
Commuting car	9.2
Aircraft	9.0
Off-peak car	4.2
High speed train	2.0
Express coach	0.9
Source: Earth Resources Research: Atmospheric Emissions from the Use of Transport in the UK (1989)	

Also, the amount of land taken is substantially less than for a new motorway of equivalent capacity, and the ability to contain the noise nuisance by measures such as tunnelling, noise baffles and other design features are much greater than in the case of an airport. If there has to be new transport capacity, there is good reason on environmental grounds for preferring rail.

In the absence of major new road capacity, a further obvious benefit of high speed rail is relief of congestion. Britain is already facing acute and worsening congestion, not just in cities, but also on some interurban motorways and trunk roads. The same study as referred to in the previous paragraph examined the degree to which removing traffic from various categories of road would yield benefits in terms of reductions in travel time and accidents for remaining road users. Both congestion and accident benefits were significant and related to the extra revenue generated by faster speeds even in the 1984 study. This was partly offset when the loss of revenue to the exchequer, from a reduction in taxed road transport in favour of untaxed rail, was taken into account.

Much is often made of the effect of high speed rail services in promoting economic growth and development, and there does appear to be good evidence that the fast link to Paris has had development effects in Lyon. There appears to be very little evidence of such an effect in Britain, although it is true that many of the cities served by high speed trains (Bristol, York, Leeds) have enjoyed a high degree of commercial development in recent years.

Most British studies of trunk road investment have concluded that, at most, it has led to minor reallocation of activity which would have taken place anyway[11]. What is clearer is that high speed rail services have led to a rise in long distance commuting into London from cities more than 100kms away, such as Swindon and Peterborough. Whether this is a desirable development is questionable, but it can be constrained by appropriate fares policies, as indeed British Rail is now seeking to do in its own commercial interest.

The future for high speed rail in Britain

Prospects for further major improvements in rail speeds in Britain may be divided into two categories: domestic, and Channel Tunnel services. Both are heavily conditioned by the continued insistence of the Government that any investment in improved InterCity rail infrastructure must be justified in narrow commercial terms.

This, plus the fact that the major InterCity routes in Britain are reasonably high quality and uncongested, means that the prospects for new domestic high speed routes are not good. While the East Coast Main Line became fully electrified in 1991, and the new fleet of electric locomotives built for it are capable of 225kph, there are currently no plans for upgrading the signalling to permit speeds in excess of the current maximum of 200kph.

On the West Coast Main Line, consideration is being given to measures to allow higher speeds on the southern part of the route, so that the prime business services between London and Manchester, Preston and Liverpool can be accelerated.

The position regarding the Channel Tunnel is rather different. When the Tunnel opens in 1993, the High Speed train sets will run on existing tracks between the tunnel portals and Waterloo Station in London, with a maximum speed of 150kph and numerous speed restrictions. The result is that the journey time for this section of the route will be 70 minutes.

By the turn of the century, it is generally agreed that this route will be heavily congested, and that extra track and terminal capacity will be needed (indeed some authorities argue that Channel Tunnel traffic has been underestimated, and that this, plus growth in domestic traffic, means that problems will be incurred long before this). In 1988, British Rail published a set of alternative proposals for a new high speed line between the Tunnel and both Waterloo and a new Channel Tunnel terminal at Kings Cross.

The favoured route would save some 22 minutes of journey time, which could be very significant given that journey times between London and both Paris and Brussels are likely to be around the three-hour threshold identified earlier. However, opposition to the new line on environmental grounds led BR to redesign it, with slightly reduced top speeds and a much greater distance in tunnel. The result was, however, to take the costs above what could be justified on the strictly commercial basis imposed by the government. After further studies, the Government announced that an alternative route, crossing the River Thames and entering London from the east, via Stratford, would be adopted. However, the current recession has led to a financial crisis in which BR is unable to finance any new investment projects, so it is unclear when this, or the West Coast Main Line upgrading, will go ahead.

---

[11] Parkinson, 1981

Conclusions

The modest steps towards higher rail speeds that have been taken in Britain so far (with the exception of the abortive investment in the Advanced Passenger Train) seem to have paid rich rewards both commercially and in terms of broader social benefits. If rail infrastructure were to be appraised on the same cost-benefit basis as new roads, there is little doubt that a new route from the Channel Tunnel to London, and further upgrading of domestic main lines, would be justified. Although high speed rail has some environmental disadvantages, it is probably preferable to further development of road or air transport. A key issue on which evidence is currently inadequate in the case of Britain is how far it diverts traffic from these modes, as opposed to generating wholly new traffic.

Bibliography

Earth Resources Research,1989. Atmospheric Emissions from the Use of Transport in the UK

Evans, A W, 1969. Inter City Travel and the London Midland Electrification. Journal of Transport Economics and Policy, Vol.III, 69-95

Fowkes, A S; Nash, C A; and Whiteing, A E, 1985. Understanding Trends in Inter-City Rail Traffic in Great Britain. Transportation Planning and Technology. Vol.10, 65-80

Leake, G R. 1971. Inter City Modal Split in Great Britain — Air versus Rail. Centre for Transport Studies, University of Leeds

Mafurirano, D. 1983. A Comparison of Cost-Benefit and Financial Rates of Return of an Inter City Rail Improvement Project (unpublished MSc Dissertation, University of Leeds)

Marks, P; Fowkes, A S; and Nash, C A. 1986. Valuing Long Distance Business Travel Time Savings for Evaluation: A Methodological Review and Application. Proceedings of the Planning and Transportation Research and Computation Summer Annual Meeting

MVA Consultancy; Institute for Transport Studies, University of Leeds; Transport Studies Unit, University of Oxford, 1987. The Value of Travel Time Savings, Policy Journals

Owen, A D, and Phillips, G D A. 1987. The Characteristics of Railway Passenger Demand: An Econometric Investigation. Journal of Transport Economics and Policy. Vol.XXI, 231-253

Parkinson, M. 1981. The Effect of Road Investment on Economic Development in the UK (Department of Transport, Government Economic Service, Working Paper No.43)

Potter, S. 1987. On the Right Lines? The Limits of Technological Innovation. Frances Pinter, London

Shilton, D. 1982. Modelling the Demand for High Speed Train Services. Journal of the Operational Research Society, Vol.33, 713-722

Steer, J K, and Willumsen, L. 1981. An Investigation of Passenger Preference Structures. Proceedings of the Planning and Transportation Research and Computation Summer Annual Meeting

9.
The Swedish high speed train project

Torbjörn Flink and Staffan Hultén, Stockholm School of Economics

"A HYPOTHESIS which one would like to verify is the following: under certain conditions railways are capable of competing successfully with domestic air traffic over longer, as well as shorter, distances. These conditions ought to be looked into and stated with respect to future technological prospects for both air and railway transport."[1]

THESE WORDS were written in January 1964 by the director of the newly created research and development department[2] at the Swedish state railways (SJ). He argued that the railway should be capable of giving the same travel time between Stockholm and Göteborg as the airlines. With minimal adjustments to the infrastructure and a

[1] Karsberg, Å, 1964, p. 1.
[2] Utvecklings och planerings avdelningen[3]

89

timing of slightly more than three hours it was concluded that the top speed of the train would have to be about 200kph.

These ideas were, in fact, not very far from those that guided the development of a Swedish high speed train through nearly three decades to its realisation when the first commercial runs were made in September 1990.

In this chapter we shall discuss the history of the Swedish high speed train project seen as an innovation process. Our main interest is in providing an answer to why it took so long to develop and introduce a high speed service. We begin with some remarks on the transformation of infrastructure systems in general, followed by a discussion of models of, and strategies for, innovation. The case presents some of the important features of the development process and the introduction of the project. Our analysis, containing structural as well as procedural variables, is able to give a fairly straightforward explanation.

On the transformation of infrastructure systems

In the 1960s the increased competition from road and air transport put both the Swedish railways and their suppliers under pressure to innovate in general, and to develop a high speed train, in particular. An imbalance was created due to the inability to respond to the demand for high speed trains in the short term. Not only were the railways and their suppliers forced to develop new trains and improve the fixed infrastructure, but they also had to fight for their existence against the pervasive "gales of creative destruction" manifested in the general pessimism about the future of railways.

But a forecast of increasing demand for fast and reliable passenger transport produced a market opportunity for high speed trains. This situation resembles what Dahmén has conceptualised as a "structural tension". A structural tension is an imbalance which might[3] stimulate entrepreneurial activity that in turn can start a chain reaction: "a development block" (see Dahmén's chapter (2) in this volume).

However, the introduction of innovations in infrastructure systems is restricted by the existence of interdependencies between system components and sub-systems. Nevertheless, incremental innovations are relatively easy to introduce because the overall system normally allows for small changes in one system component, so long as the innovation conforms to the system's standards. In contrast, when a radical innovation is introduced to an infrastructure system, it requires subsequent changes in the overall system structure. Therefore, radical innovations in infrastructure systems are brought in in local sectors of the system where it is less expensive and less complicated to introduce the innovation. For instance, the Swedish railway system gradually incorporated radical innovations such as the electrification in the 1930s and Automatic Train Control (ATC) in the 1970s.

Also, the life-cycle of the infrastructure system influences the direction and magnitude of innovative activity. In the formative stage of an infrastructure system,

---

[3] In Schumpeter's view, the response can be of two principal kinds: creative or adaptive. A creative response involves innovative action, creating something new, while an adaptive response means an unchanged pattern of action, for example producing more, or less, of the same as before. See Schumpeter, J A, 1947 and Dahmén, E, 1988.

when the initial system innovation is made, system components and technical solutions are assembled from established industries. The invention of the system is in fact a new combination of available technological solutions.

This was the case when the first railways were constructed by combining the rail system used for horse-drawn mine trolleys with the technology of steam engines originally constructed for other uses[4]. The first system innovation is followed by new ones that aim at overcoming limitations in the infrastructure system's performance. These secondary innovations often produce technical, economic and institutional problems of a much larger size than the problems they originally aimed to solve. Hughes has conceptualised such dilemmas in the evolution of infrastructure systems as "reverse salients".

"Reverse salients are components in the system that have fallen behind or are out of phase with the others."[5]

The correction of reverse salients requires the development of new ideas, new knowledge and innovations. These may later turn out to be valuable for firms in other industries or for system-builders in other infrastructure systems. Consequently the infrastructure system shifts from primarily borrowing ideas invented in other industries to producing ideas that are then made generally available.

We have noted earlier that the first railways consisted of a merger of available system components. Later on the railways in their turn produced a large number of inventions that proved to be valuable to other industries. One example is the Swedish railways' demand in the first decades of the 20th century for ball bearings, which proved to be a vital stimulus to the development of roller bearings by SKF (Svenska Kullagerfabriken). Infrastructure innovation is, therefore, in a complex way influenced by the technological interdependencies of the railway system's components, the infrastructure and the supplying industry. These influences were decisive for all high speed train projects that started in the late 1960s.

Innovative activity in long-term R&D projects

We said that we would view the development and introduction of the Swedish high speed train as an innovation process. In this section we search for some patterns of conduct that have relevance to project lead-time.

Models of innovation

The literature on R & D projects includes several models describing hypothetical patterns of the innovation process, the most basic and simple one being the linear model. According to this model an innovation passes through a sequence of phases, going from research and development, through testing to production, and finally marketing. Since the phases correspond to different functional departments of an organisation, the project passes through it like the baton in a relay race. Three principal anomalies, with corresponding corrections, can be identified in relation to this model.

---

[4] Vincent, H, 1980.
[5] Hughes, T P, 1987.

To begin with, it is in fact quite rare that pure research initiates innovations — it is more often the case that market needs stimulate the search for new solutions. In the industrial market, progressive users may be of vital importance for technological advancements.[6] A simple solution to this problem would be to include a feedback loop in the linear model. But this does not change the basic notion of a sequential procedure. Other types of feedback links, between the different phases, are very frequent in reality, leading to a more complex pattern.[7] For example, before a new product becomes marketable, several redesigns normally take place, thus incorporating people from the R & D, production and marketing department.

The second anomaly asserts that an innovation project does not take place in a vacuum — many factors outside the control of the project team intervene in the process and might change its preconditions. For instance, the state or stock of scientific and technological knowledge, as well as the general socio-economic situation, are not fixed, especially not when the project lead-time is long.[8] Conversely, the project may produce new knowledge, thus contributing to the stock of knowledge, as well as changing peoples' perceptions and beliefs. The overall intervention from the environment can be either positive or negative depending on the project's technological fit with the environment. If the project is connected to a slowly advancing technological trajectory then the single project has to find solutions to a proportionally larger number of problems, compared with the case when the project is connected to a rapidly advancing technological trajectory.[9]

The third anomaly stems from the more or less explicit assumption behind the linear model, that an innovation process is confined to a single organisation. All industrial organisations have exchange relationships with other organisations, the most obvious being a buyer-seller relationship. These are often long-term, stable and the basis for change. In an innovation process, an organisation is often dependent on knowledge and other resources controlled by other organisations — a situation stimulating a cooperative effort.[10]

Innovation strategies

Eliminating structural tensions by bringing complementary factors into balance can be approached in various ways, depending on the life-cycle stage of the system and the competencies, interests, resources and commitments of the actors participating in the innovation process.

The two approaches discussed by Nelson[11]— the parallel and the sequential —

[6] See Carlsson, B and Jacobsson, S, 1990.

[7] Kline, S J and Rosenberg, N, 1986.

[8] Abetti, P A and Stuart, R W, 1985, p199, present a model that has a two-way communication between the central chain of innovation, being similar to the linear model, and the environment represented by factors at four levels: socio-economic, market needs, technology and science.

[9] See Dosi, G, 1982 and Hughes, T P, 1987, p77.

[10] "Network firms emerge as the result of efforts to internalise selectively the variety of factors necessary to master the process of innovation", Antonelli, C, 1992, p21. See also Mattsson, L -G, 1978 and Johansson, J and Mattsson, L -G, 1992.

[11] Nelson, R R, 1961.

and the "rugby" model proposed by Takeuchi and Nonaka[12], discuss the impact of project strategy on lead-time. Nelson argues that the simultaneous investigation of several possible paths to the solution of an R & D problem saves time but demands more initial input of resources. Clearly, a competitive factor is also introduced, conducive to shorter lead-time. This strategy should be preferred when the initial uncertainty is high and the desired technical advances are large.

On the other hand, a sequential approach means that a variety of potential paths are tried out one at a time, until a satisfactory solution is found.[13] In this case we would expect a longer lead-time, exposing the project to more external information. It is possible to view the linear model as a sequential approach too, where different kinds of interrelated problems are solved one after the other. Apart from a longer lead-time, there is a clear risk in this case that solutions chosen at an early stage might become obsolete, leading to costly and time-consuming redesigns.[14] To regard this an over-lapping or "rugby" approach has been proposed, where all departments, with varying intensity over time, take part in the project from start to finish.[15] It is argued that this will both enhance quality and reduce lead-time.

As we stated earlier, in order successfully to change a product or process in an industrial system it is often necessary to activate and coordinate several actors. In the network approach, turning to your established supplier(s) means that you get access to the resources in the network.[16] However, this does not imply that you get access to all relevant information and resources, but rather that you get access to specific and path- dependent network capabilities. This should nevertheless produce a shorter lead-time compared with an intra-organisational approach.

The picture of an innovation process outlined above shows that we are dealing with a complex phenomenon. We do not intend to mould the different elements together into a distinct model — rather we see this set of factors as a loosely defined framework for analysis in this particular case. In the case below we have tried to extract the most important facts and events and to categorise them into four complementary problem areas: technical, organisational, political and economical.

A Swedish high speed train[17]

SETTING THE SCENE

Some preliminary tests with higher speeds, undertaken by electrical laboratory staff, were initiated in 1962. The purpose was to find out the limits of the existing power

[12] Hirotaka, T and Nonaka, I, 1986. A similar form of project organisation goes under the name of "simultaneous engineering".

[13] The difference in lead-time is defined in terms of the probability of finding a satisfactory solution in each period.

[14] Sometimes changed conditions can be of an opportunity character, leading to a better solution. On the other hand, better solutions will always come around sooner or later and can therefore be traded for lost market shares and revenues.

[15] Hirotaka, T and Nonaka, I, 1986.

[16] Easton, G, 1992, p9.

[17] This history of the Swedish high speed train project draws on the following publications: SJ Centralförvaltning; 1969, 1980 and annual reports. Flink, T and Hultén, S, 1990.

supply system. These tests led to three major developments.

● An improved contact wire arrangement was developed and introduced on a section of the Stockholm-Göteborg main line, thus increasing the speed limit from 130 to 160kph.

● The pantograph also had to be refined, and a new construction called "the double top" soon became standard on most electric locomotives. During the tests a speed record was set at 199kph.

● At the same time it was concluded that existing rolling stock was not suited for these speeds, since comfort became poor due to inaccurate dynamic qualities of the bogies and excessive lateral forces in the curves.

After study trips to Britain, Germany, Italy and France, the R & D department at SJ proposed a study of the technical requirements for a Swedish high speed train. The General Director agreed and the study was conducted during 1968 and 1969 in cooperation with some Swedish industrial companies. It is worth noting that Asea[18], the most important rolling stock producer, did not take part in this investigation.

The main conclusions of the study were:

● Since the high speed service had to include most main lines in Sweden, building new track, as in Japan, would be much too expensive.

● Rolling stock capable of overcoming the comfort problem at higher speeds was technically possible. A motor-coach train with tilting coaches, improved bogies and a top speed of 220kph would cut travel time by 40-50 per cent.

● It was important to start running as soon as possible and 1975 was set as the deadline. A train developed and manufactured solely in Sweden was considered out of the question, but it was still important that Swedish industry and SJ could take part in the development.[19] Hence, the two possibilities were a) to manufacture a foreign train under licence or b) to buy some components from abroad and develop the rest in Sweden.

● Some key data of the proposed technical characteristics are shown in Table 9.2.

When the report was presented in 1969 the newly appointed General Director questioned its beneficial economic effects for SJ. Consequently a new study was initiated, in which most departments were consulted for cost-benefit estimates. The results presented in 1973 showed a favourable net effect.

The content of this economic report is unofficial but we can point out some of the relevant preconditions. The evolution of the market for air and railway traffic is shown in Figure 9.1.

The threat from air traffic became very real in the 1970s and even more so in the 1980s. Road traffic had shown an enormous increase, from 5.6 billion passenger-kms in 1950, to 63.0 in 1968. The upsurges in railway traffic in 1973-74 and 1978-79 both coincided with oil crises and discount campaigns. In an article written by one of the members of the high speed train group the following elasticities were given:

---

[18] Today Asea Brown Boveri, or ABB.

[19] It was noted that Sweden in any case had to strengthen its research capabilities, both within SJ and in the universities.

Figure 9.1. Billions of passenger-kms produced by air and railway traffic in Sweden from 1951 to 1991.

	1951	1961	1971	1981	1991
Domestic air traffic	0.02	0.21	0.70	1.60	2.80
Domestic railway traffic	6.20	5.20	4.00	6.90	5.60

Sources: Statistics from the Swedish State Railway and the Swedish civil aviation authority.

Table 9.1. Demand elasticities for travel-time, price and frequency of departures.

	Elasticity
Travel time	-1.00 to -3.44
Price	-0.33 to -1.18
Frequency of departures	-0.14 to -0.60

Source: Knall, G., 1974, p. 23.

These figures show that a significant innovation (in travel time) can have a much larger effect in stimulating demand than more gradual changes.

DEVELOPING A HIGH SPEED TRAIN

A series of tests was started in 1970 by SJ's Mechanical Department, in cooperation with Asea, whose managers had presumably changed their minds.[20] The two principal objectives were to gain insights into the construction of a tilting mechanism and of a bogie generating small dynamic forces. A derailed commuter train was rebuilt and, following the German solution, equipped with flexible airbags to achieve the tilting. The trials were evaluated in 1973 but, since the technique was considered to be in doubt, further work was required. A contract for further tests was signed with Asea, and another agreement was reached with an independent Swedish inventor who had patented various tilting devices since 1934.

The new trainset, named X15, was constructed from the coach bodies of an old trainset, using the bogies and an improved pneumatic tilting mechanism from the former experimental trainset. An intensive testing programme was conducted in 1975, in which the Swedish speed record was raised to 238kph. However, the pneumatic tilting mechanism did not perform well enough and it was exchanged for a hydraulic system. The coach body was now mounted on hydrostatic bearings, a

---

[20] ASJ (Allmänna Svenska Järnvägsverkstäderna), which participated in the 1969 investigation, had a division that produced railcars. This division was soon acquired by Asea which then practically monopolised the market for powered rolling stock in Sweden.

The X15 experimental vehicle was used as a testbed between 1975 and 1986

solution that had to be changed later to a bolster-beam arrangement. This solution resembled the solution chosen by English and Italian engineers in the late 1960s. The latter reconstruction was not tested until 1982, when Asea built a prototype coach which was integrated in and tested on the old X15 train set. An important part of the test runs concerned the development of a soft, radially self-steered bogie. A computer model was developed in parallel, to simulate the dynamics of the wheel/rail interaction. The new bogie was adopted on commuter trains and normal coaches, as well as on the high speed train. It is interesting to note its effect on the maximum permitted axle load, which was raised from 11 to 17.5 tonnes (see Table 9.2).

THE PROJECT ORGANISATION

The project was initiated by the R & D department, where the theoretical work continued after the 1969 report, in cooperation with firms like Saab Aviation. Most of the field work was done by the engineering department and Asea, the latter doing research at the theoretical level as well. Still, formal responsibility for the project was held by the R & D Department, although it is evident that the design of the train was dominated by Asea and the Engineering Department. For example, the Director of the R & D department at SJ declared in 1969 that a pneumatic tilting mechanism would not work due to its slow response function. In general, the people in SJ's organisation were said to be sceptical about the technical and commercial potential of the project,

Table 9.2

Some characteristics of the Swedish high-speed train, years 1968, 1980 (proposed solution) and 1987 (final position).

	1968	1980	1987
Train type	railcar	railcar	trainset (1 power-unit)
Nr of passengers	150-250	330	288*
Total weight	125-175 tonnes	308 tonnes	343 tonnes
Length	90-120 metres	152 metres	140 metres
Nr of coaches	4-6	6	5 and 1 power-unit
Max. axle-load	9-11 tonnes	15 tonnes	17.5 tonnes
Max. speed	220 kph	160 or 200 kph	200 kph
Coach body	not specified	aluminium	stainless steel
Tilting	yes, 9-12°	yes, 6.5°	yes, 6.5°
Traction	gas turbine or electric mono-phase	electric mono-phase	electric three-phase
Brakes	mechanical, electric/mechanical hydrostatic	mechanical, electric	mechanical, electric
Max. power	3000 kW	2800 kW	3260 kW
Stockholm-Göteborg in	2h 26min	2h 57min	2h 59min
Commercial introduction	1975	1986 - 1989**	1990-92

Later changed to 243 in 1990, and 200 in 1992

**Gradual introduction of three prototype trains from 1986, full scale introduction 1989.*

Sources: SJ Centralförvaltning Utvecklingsavdelningen, 1969; Asea Journal, 1987.

among them the General Director. The small group of people directly involved in the high speed train project was well aware of the scepticism and, as soon as the operation of the experimental train X15 was reliable enough, people from SJ and the Swedish Department of Transport and Communications were invited to the trials.

The direct costs of the project during the 1970s, estimated at SEK20-40 million, were shared by SJ and Asea. Because the project had no budget of its own, the costs had to be absorbed by the respective departments within their normal activities. These figures suggest that the project was not considered one of the most important for SJ. Other projects demanded more resources, for example the development and introduction of ATC (Automatic Train Control).

In 1978 a new GD was appointed who agreed to the request for a second high speed train investigation. The state of the art in Sweden had to be assessed, probably with some international comparisons and an estimation of the costs and benefits involved. An official version of the report was published in 1980 and distributed to many important decision-makers. The purpose was to clear the way for a financial solution to the project.

In the reorganisation of SJ in 1982, the R & D Department was scrapped and responsibility for the high speed train project was taken over by a project group called S200. Personnel from the most important departments were engaged on a full-time basis. The purpose of the group was to clear the way for the realisation of the high speed train project, a task that included ensuring appropriate resources, managing the acquisition of the trains, scanning the environment for new information, and efforts to market the project both internally and externally. This kind of project organisation was new to SJ and produced some friction at the beginning. Later it became a well accepted model for project management.

THE POLITICIANS

Politicians in Sweden were not unaware of the rapid development within the railway sector, both domestically and internationally. In 1973 a Bill was introduced in the Riksdag (Parliament) enabling actions to raise the competitiveness of the railways, including high speed train services in Sweden in accordance with the 1969 report. This was followed by several other Bills, and in 1975 decisions were taken in favour of a speedy introduction of high speed trains.

Despite this favourable situation, no immediate action was taken by SJ or by the Swedish Department of Transport and Communications to secure overall finance for the project. The 1980 report was followed by a request from SJ for the financing of the acquisition of a fleet of high speed trains. By this time the political support was not immediately available, but after some negotiations about the socio-economic effects, a decision was reached in the autumn of 1981. One particular issue was the extent of the availability of the high speed services to the population of Sweden. Estimates by SJ showed that about 75 per cent of the Swedish population would enjoy such benefits.

THE BIDDING PROCESS

The positive political decision posed a new problem for SJ: should it give the order to Asea or were there better alternatives elsewhere? It was decided that the building of the trains should be put out to tender.

More than ten possible suppliers were given detailed specifications and invited to bid in 1982. SJ demanded that the offers should include a Life Cycle Cost Analysis, a novelty that forced the suppliers carefully to consider all costs for maintenance and so on occurring throughout the economic life of the train.

Offers were submitted by a dozen companies, but none of them could fulfil the requirements, particularly those associated with maximum axle-load and noise-level.

The X2000: product of many years of development

The restrictions were somewhat modified and new specifications sent out in 1984. The bids were still not satisfactory, and a third request went out in 1985. Some restrictions in the specification had been further relaxed, notably the maximum axle-load which was raised from 15 to 17.5 tonnes. This was possible after Banavdelningen (Department for Infrastructure) had been convinced that the dynamic forces transmitted from the wheel to the rail could be kept low with the use of modern bogies. However, several of the suppliers had now lost interest in the project.

In Spring 1986 the remaining suppliers sent in their bids. This time they all presented a new type of traction equipment: GTO tyristors permitting efficient use of the light and robust three-phase asynchronous motors. These newly developed power-electronic components made it easier to fulfil SJ's requirements for axle-load. Finally, Asea was given the order and production of the trains was started at KVAB, Sweden's largest supplier of coach bodies. The plan had been to order three prototype trains for testing and, later, 17 train sets with an option for another 32. Now it was decided to order the first 20 train sets at a cost of SEK1.6 billion.

THE INFRASTRUCTURE

The upgrading of the main lines to 160kph that began in 1968 did not continue. Priority was given to the development and implementation of the ATC and other security systems, but work on welded rails, improved power supply and the elimination of level crossings also continued. The improvement of the infrastructure went slowly because financial resources were sparse. Some of these changes also served the high speed trains, but they were far from sufficient to allow high speeds on the Swedish railway network.

The situation did not change until 1986, despite the decision to introduce high speed trains that was taken in 1981. For instance, the number of level-crossings between Stockholm and Göteborg decreased from 558 in 1963 to 300 in 1985 and was brought down to 90 in 1992. The upgrading of the Stockholm-Göteborg line now includes the adoption of glass fibre cables for signalling and improvement of the power supply system.

The result of all these delays was that the planned travel-time of less than three hours between Stockholm and Göteborg could not be realised before late 1992. However, the first train commenced operation in September 1990, between Stockholm and Göteborg. Subsequently the number of high speed departures has progressively increased, but notably not the total number of departures. The high speed service was extended to Karlstad in August 1992, and will later include Linköping, Malmö and Sundsvall.

The impact of high-speed trains in Sweden

This section gives a brief account of some of the industrial and commercial effects of the development and introduction of the Swedish high speed train. Most certainly the project has given both SJ and its suppliers a good knowledge-base for further developments. For ABB, the train has a substantial export potential thanks to its compatibility with existing infrastructure. Promotional activities are carried out in the USA, Portugal, Germany and Australia.[21]

When interpreting the effects on the transport market we should keep the following in mind. The introduction has so far been carried out gradually on only one line and is not yet completed. The travel time target of less than three hours was not achieved until August 1992. Furthermore, the recession and the introduction of value added tax on air and railway fares have initiated a general decrease in travelling (see Figure 9.1). Also, the market for domestic air travel was deregulated in 1992 leading to dramatic price reductions on some lines.

---

[21] In spring 1992 ABB lost an order from the Finnish state railways for tilting high speed trains in competition with the Italian Pendolino train.

Table 9.3

Some data about and effects of the introduction of the high-speed rail service between Stockholm and Göteborg.

Load factor X2000	60% (35-40% on ordinary trains)
Punctuality of X2000	90-97% within 5 minutes (better than ordinary trains)
New passengers	67% (60% from air, 7% from road)
Ticket price X2000	989 SEK (1,180 by air. Full fare unchanged, several special offers with 30-40% discount introduced)
Rail market share	Slightly up (about 7-8 %)
Capacity	No increase so far

Sources: *Swedish State Railway: Marketing Department and Dagens Industri, 1991.*

A negative effect of the substitution of X2000 for ordinary trains is that there are fewer intermediate stops. On the positive side is the improved image of the railways in general, possibly increasing the chances for the construction of new lines.

Analysis and conclusions

When the Swedish high speed train project was initiated in 1968, with the high speed train investigation, few of those involved in the project imagined that it would take more than 20 years to develop a Swedish high speed train. Why did the original 1975 plan not come to fruition? One explanation was hinted at in the 1969 report, in which the lead-time for developing an all-Swedish train was estimated to be at least ten years. But this leaves another ten years to be accounted for.

In the early 1970s economic restrictions, together with institutional rigidities, forced the high speed train group to advance slowly. The original idea of connecting the Swedish project to similar ones in other countries was also abandoned. Instead, the high speed train tests were conducted by Asea and SJ in cooperation. The formalisation of the project after the economic report was presented in 1973 confirmed the well established national user-producer relationship between Asea and SJ.

The national industrial project group successfully solved some salient technical problems but other important problems were left unsolved for more than ten years. A successful solution for the high speed train bogie was found within a couple of years. The tilting mechanism on the other hand proved to be much harder to construct. A sequence of different concepts were tested between 1970 and 1982 before a satisfactory one was developed. In general, much of the problem-solving throughout the project was conducted sequentially, both within and among the different problem areas, and several solutions became obsolete, demanding renewed attention.[22]

---

[22] The important changes in some vital technical dimensions shown in Table 9.2 is a good illustration to this point. It can be noted that the first version of the Italian Pendolino train, the ETR 401, put in service in 1976, met almost all demands outlined in the 1969 report.

When SJ presented the second high speed report in 1980 the earlier political and economic solutions were reconsidered. At the same time doubts had emerged about Swedish technical competence, resulting in a bidding process. This turnaround marked an important change in strategy. The dependence on the national network was broken and the bidding process that followed can be seen as an example of the parallel approach to solve an R & D problem. For the first time the Swedish supplier was put under competitive pressure. SJ also reorganised internally. The anatomy of the S200 group was quite similar to that of the "rugby" model. Despite this, the upgrading of the infrastructure came to lag behind the building of the rolling stock.

Our overall conclusion is that the delay was caused by the sum of an interrelated set of technical, institutional and economic factors. The initial state of these factors, that is the institutional rigidity, technical uncertainty, financial restrictions and the strength of existing relationships, biased the national project towards a slowly advancing search process, characterised by sequential problem-solving. This situation later stimulated SJ, having secured the financial means, to open up for competition. The elimination of the remaining tensions, that is producing a viable train, and the subsequent adjusting of the infrastructure, finally shifted the structural tensions from the railway system to other parts of the transport system.

The case shows that an enlarged analytical framework, including both system structure and process variables, is conducive to a deeper understanding of innovative activities. External conditioning, feed-back loops and inter-organisational coordination are important features of long-term research and development processes. However, the need to enlarge the framework must be confronted with the demand for clarity and transparency — a trade-off to which we have no definite solution.

In relation to what is stated above two questions come to mind:

● **"Why did we get a Swedish high-speed train at all?"**

● **"Was the delay all negative?"**

Here we will briefly outline some tentative explanations. The project group in Sweden had few, but competent and progressive, technicians. Some of them worked continuously for 20 years on the project, while the turnover in personnel was much higher among key decision-makers. This is an outstanding feature in both the Swedish and the Italian project, whereas the failed English APT project showed greater turbulence.[23] Asea was also able to catch up with developments at the technological frontier, especially during the 1980s.

From an economic point of view the new product or process should be on the market as soon as possible. We have seen how domestic air traffic gained market share and momentum during the 1970s and '80s, while SJ lost potential revenues. On the other hand, the risk of a technical failure would certainly have been higher if the introduction had been made in 1975. The train is, at least technically, more advanced than would have been the case in 1975.[24]

It is interesting to see that much of the new technology came from other sectors, such as the GTO-Tyristor. We might then hypothetically state that when an infrastructure system is revitalised it tends to repeat the pattern from its early stages, of combining existing technologies to something new.

Bibliography

Abetti, P A and Stuart, R W. "Entrepreneurship and technology transfer. Key factors in the innovation process" in Sexton, D L and Smilor, R W, (eds), The art and science of entrepreneurship, Ballinger Cambridge, Massachusetts, 1985

Antonelli, C, "The economic theory of information networks", in Antonelli, C (ed) The economics of information networks, North-Holland, Amsterdam, 1992

Asea Journal, 2, 1987

Carlsson, B and Jacobsson, S "What makes the automation industry strategic?", paper presented at the EARIE conference, Lisbon, Portugal, December 1990

Dagens industri, October 22 1991

Dahmén, E, "Development Blocks in Industrial Economics", Scandinavian Economic History Review, 1988

Dosi, G, "Technological paradigms and technological trajectories. A suggested interpretation of the determinants and directions of technical change", Research Policy, vol. 11, 1982

Easton, G, "Why networks?", in Axelsson, B. and Easton, G. (eds.), Industrial networks. A new view of reality., Routledge, London, 1992

Flink, T and Hultén, S, Det svenska snabbtågsprojektet - de första 20 åren, EFI Research Report, 1990

Hughes, T P, "The Evolution of Large Technical Systems", in Bijker, Hughes and Pinch (eds), The Social Construction of Technological Systems, The MIT Press, Cambridge, Mass, 1987

Håkansson, H, Industrial Technological Development, Croom Helm, London, 1987

Johansson, J and Mattsson, L -G, "Network positions and strategic action — an analytical framework" in Axelsson, B and Easton, G (eds), Industrial networks. A new view of reality., Routledge, London, 1992

Karsberg, Å, "Högre hastigheter i SJ persontrafik?", internal memo, January 1964

Knall, G, "Snabbtågen halverar dagens restider", Teknisk Tidskrift, March 1974

Mattsson, L -G, "Impact of stability in supplier-buyer relations on innovative behaviour of industrial markets", in Fisk, Arndt and Gronhaug (eds) Future directions for marketing, Marketing Science Institute, 1978

Nelson, R R, "Uncertainty, learning and the economics of parallel research and development efforts", The Review of Economics and Statistics, November 1961

Potter, S, On the right lines?, Frances Pinter, London, 1987

Schumpeter, J A, "The creative response in economic history", The Journal of Economic History, November 1947.

SJ Centralförvaltning Utvecklingsavdelning, "Höga hastigheter i SJ persontrafik, tekniska förutsättningar" 1969

SJ Centralförvaltning, "SJ snabbtågsprojekt — utredning 1980", 1980

SJ Centralförvaltning, Annual reports from 1963 to 1990

Takeuchi, H and Nonaka, I "The new new product development game", Harvard Business Review, January-February 1986.

Vincent, H, L'age du Chemin de fer, Paris, 1980

---

[23] See Potter, S, 1987, p137, and his chapter in this volume (14).

[24] It can be argued, of course, that if the introduction had been successful we would have a second generation high speed train today, and possibly also some new lines.

10.
High speed train development in Germany

Professor G Aberle, University of Giessen, Germany

Difficult decision making

IN GERMANY three main factors have contributed to the building of new railway lines for high speed traffic:

● At the beginning of the 1970s approximately 350 million tonnes of freight were carried by train and further sizeable increases were predicted for 1990 and 2000. If the anticipated bottlenecks were to be avoided, new railway line construction would be needed. In fact there was a noticeable drop in rail freight transport, and in 1989 Deutsche Bundesbahn (German Railways) carried only 288 million tonnes.

● The great success of high speed train development in Japan, and later in France, provided an incentive to reach considerably higher speeds in Germany as well. But to do this, new lines would have to be built.

● In the light of a significant decline in rail passenger transport, the railway enterprise reviewed its strategy for competing with the private car and air travel, making the claim that rail was "twice as fast as the car and half as fast as the plane". To substantiate this claim, the railway needed high speed traffic.

At first the German high speed rail programme concentrated on building new lines (Neubaustrecken). High speed trains were not really considered before the early 1980s. This was the crucial difference between Germany and France, where the TGV was designed and presented to the public as a complete high speed railway system, right from the beginning.

In the late 1960s, Deutsche Bundesbahn presented its conversion programme, *Ausbauprogram 1970*; it included 3,550kms of Neubau- und Ausbaustrecken, that is construction of new lines and conversion of existing lines to cater for high speeds. A maximum speed of about 300kph was planned for the new lines. In 1973 construction began on the new line from Hannover to Würzburg (327kms). Two years later the original design speed of 300kph was reduced to 200kph. The first high speed lines did not come into operation until nearly 18 years later.

June 2 1991: the start of high speed rail operation

There was considerable opposition to the first Neubaustrecken, from Hannover to

Würzburg and Mannheim to Stuttgart. Criticism came from both conservationists and from those people who lived near the new lines — but where there would be no railway station. Lengthy litigation followed, leading to a substantial increase in construction costs. About 15 billion DM had to be invested to build 425kms of new line.

Contrary to initial plans, both Neubaustrecken are of only minor importance for freight transport. This is not due to any lack of freight volume, but to technical problems in mixing passenger and freight traffic on the new lines. Since the maximum speed of freight trains is only 160kph, passing loops had to be built along the high speed lines to allow the faster passenger trains to overtake.

The first high speed train, the InterCity Experimental (ICE), and the prototype of the InterCity Express (ICE) was not finished until 1985. On June 2 1991, 21 InterCity Express units were ready for use. These high speed trains were very expensive since their design had to be started from scratch. While it was estimated in 1985 that the cost of one high speed train (ICE) would be 35 million DM, the final price rose to 50 million DM per train unit, comprising 12 cars with 615 seats, and including a restaurant car.

Despite some teething troubles, the ICE high speed traffic in Germany got off to a good start. However, because the number of available trains is still limited, only the Hamburg-Hannover-Kassel-Frankfurt/Main-Stuttgart-München route was operating at the time of writing. This route has a regular hourly service and, on the newly-built sections, (Hamburg-Fulda, Mannheim-Stuttgart) the maximum speed is 250kph. The main bottleneck on this route is the section between Stuttgart and Ulm (Gieslinger Steige) where difficult terrain means speed is limited to 80kph.

With the introduction of ICE high speed passenger traffic, considerable reductions in travelling time were possible:

Hannover-Frankfurt: 57 minutes (30 per cent)

Hannover-Stuttgart: 109 minutes (32 per cent)

Mannheim-Stuttgart: 37 minutes (48 per cent)

Frankfurt-Stuttgart: 49 minutes (37 per cent)

Freight journey times were also reduced.

ICE passenger traffic had already exceeded forecast levels in 1991. Two main factors account for this success: the saving of time and improved comfort while travelling. With a high occupancy (47.3 per cent), a high proportion of first class passengers and a special pricing system, ICE revenues are 1.7 times higher than the average revenues of long-distance passenger trains. However, a final statement as to the running costs of the ICE could not yet be made at the time of writing, as maintenance expenses were not yet known.

Problems and first experiences

The building costs of the first two Neubaustrecken were very high, compared with other international projects, because they were designed to cater for heavy freight as well as passenger transport. This demanded appropriate track design, with gentle gradients and large-radius curves. Consequently, more than 30 per cent of both tracks have to run through tunnels.

In actual fact the capacity for freight is limited, because high speed passenger trains and conventional freight trains can not run through a tunnel at the same time. Hence only a few high speed freight trains (160kph freight expresses) with purpose-built wagons can be integrated into a daily mixed-traffic schedule.

For this reason the economic efficiency of the new railway lines is at risk. Because preliminary calculations were based on both passenger and freight transport, there is now a danger that, in view of the high investments in the rail network and track vehicles, the economic performance of Deutsche Bundesbahn will deteriorate rather than improve. Subsequent high speed rail projects have thus been restricted to passenger traffic.

Due to incompatibility of particular design features, like different electricity supply systems, heavier motive power units and wagons 12cms broader (3.02 metres) than those in other countries, the ICE can only be used in Germany and parts of Switzerland. The dead weight of the ICE, at 906 tonnes, produces considerably higher energy consumption than conventional or InterCity trains. For international high speed traffic, multi-system vehicles and redesigned wagons are required. In addition, it is going to be necessary to build special trains to use the Channel Tunnel, because of the narrower British loading gauge. All this will increase costs. Lack of international cooperation in building high speed trains can be blamed partly on the railway industry in different countries acting to protect its own special interests.

Further plans for high speed traffic in Germany

There are plans to increase the number of ICE trains from 41 to 150 by 1995, and to order 20 multi-power train units for international high speed traffic, at a total capital outlay of more than 6 billion DM.

The main new high speed lines, designed for a maximum speed of 300kph, but carrying only passenger traffic, are:

Köln-Frankfurt/Main (completion by 2000)

Hannover-Stendal-Berlin (completion by 1997)

Stuttgart-Ulm (completion date not yet known due to planning difficulties)

The existing lines intended for conversion into high speed lines (Ausbaustrecken with a maximum speed up to 200kph) are:

Dortmund-Kassel (completion by 1994)

Kassel-Erfurt-Leipzig-Dresden (completion by 1997)

Hannover-Magdeburg (completion by 1993)

Karlsruhe-Basel (completion by 1994)

Nürnberg-München (completion by 1997)

Köln-Aachen (completion by 1996)

A network of 2,500kms of high speed railway line is planned for the year 2000, but with timing and funding complications, completion can not be guaranteed at all. Moreover, the extremely high investment in infrastructure for high speed traffic is

Above: *An InterCity Express under test on the new line from Hannover to Würzburg. The new trains are considerably heavier and use more energy than conventional trains, such as the Lufthansa Airport Express, pictured,* **below,** *at Bacharach, on the line between Frankfurt and Düsseldorf*

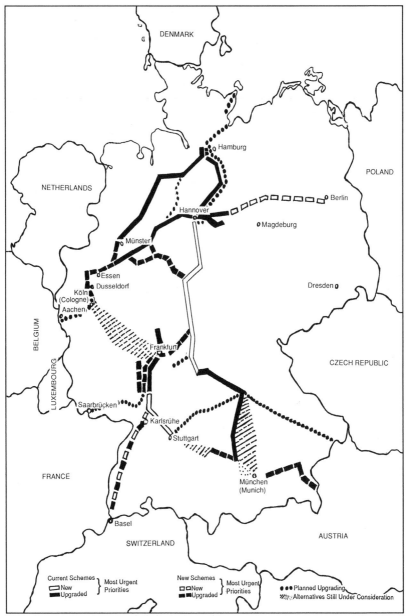

Map showing Deutsche Bundesbahn high speed investment aspirations

increasingly criticised and, in addition to ecological and spatial concerns, its economic viability is questioned.

In addition to high speed traffic running on rails, discussions have been underway in Germany about building the first magnetic high speed railway (maglev transit system), called the Transrapid. So far, 1.6 billion DM have been provided from public funds for the development of the maglev technique. In December 1991 the development of Transrapid technology was officially completed. Now construction of the first maglev line between Hamburg and Berlin (about 250km) is due to be included in the federal transport plan, the cost of building the line being estimated at about 8 billion DM. The decision is based more on industrial policy criteria than economic ones, for it is said that if Germany wants to export the Transrapid system, a demonstration line will first have to be built in Germany.

However, critics of the Transrapid argue as follows: On the relatively short distance between Hamburg and Berlin, where stations are very close together, the potential for gaining time in comparison with the ICE is negligible. The advantage gained in travelling time does not justify such high investment.

At high speeds, the Transrapid causes and unacceptable level of noise pollution. Hence, given the very high population density in Germany, speeds of 400-500kph can hardly ever be reached. The track can not be taken into heavily built-up city centres because it is built on special concrete pillars. Stations therefore have to be located on the outskirts of the city. Then, to change transport mode makes things even more complicated and time-consuming, so time gains become further eroded. In Hamburg and Berlin particularly, these are very serious problems, to which solutions have yet to be found. Nor have the additional — probably very high — costs of such urban integration been included in the above estimate of 8 billion DM.

The Transrapid is technically isolated and integration into the existing transportation system seems hardly possible, given the difficulties of providing suitable points of contact between the magnetic railway system and the existing rail network. As well as the transportation aspects, there are technical, economic, urban planning, ecological and safety considerations to be taken into account, not to mention the gaining of public acceptability.

With urgent investment needed in East Germany and capital resources already short, an additional demand for an 8 billion DM investment (or more) does not come at an opportune time — and this is the case with private finance too. It is doubtful whether the Transrapid can operate without financial loss. There is no guarantee that the projected revenues will cover the operating costs, let alone contribute to capital cost recovery.

Since the Hamburg-Berlin route is also linked by Neu- and Ausbaustrecken of Deutsche Bundesbahn, it is feared that the revenues gained by the Transrapid will, for the most part, be abstracted from Deutsche Bundesbahn. Deutsche Bundesbahn will consequently incur greater losses and public expenditure will come under more pressure than ever.

High speed merits questioned

At the moment, the enthusiasm for new railway lines is discernibly waning. These high speed lines are very expensive and their planning and construction can take

ICE — Restaurant car interior

anything from ten to 20 years. Moreover, the economic efficiency of these very substantial investments, further increased by environmental requirements, can by no means be guaranteed.

In view of increasing bottlenecks in the road network, and a predicted increase of 100 per cent in road freight traffic and 50 per cent in rail freight traffic by the year 2010, rail transport capacity has to increase. Recent investigations show that railway capacity could be increased by 30 per cent, using advanced electronics in infrastructure and locomotives. The financial implications for Germany (both West and East) would amount to approximately 6 billion DM (three billion ECUs). The investment programme could be implemented gradually and might be concluded by 1998 or 2000. The economic advantages of such a strategy are obvious.

New plans for special high speed railway lines are therefore not likely to be implemented. High speed is no longer a primary consideration — performance standards, reliability and economic efficiency appear much more important. This is particularly true considering the needs of the former DDR, where more than 100 billion DM of new investment is necessary to modernise the railway system.

11.
Shinkansen: the Japanese dream

Masatake Matsuda, Executive Vice-President, East Japan Railway Company

THE TOHOKU Shinkansen and the Joetsu Shinkansen were extended to Tokyo Station on June 20 1991. Tohoku and Joetsu Shinkansen trains, in cream and green, now stand at platforms 13 and 14, side by side with the white and blue Shinkansen trains. This means that Japan's four Shinkansen lines, totalling 2,040kms have been joined together, 27 years after the 1964 opening of the Tokaido Shinkansen, between Tokyo and Osaka.

In 1989, the four Shinkansen carried 236 million passengers more than 93 million train-kilometres. The Joetsu Shinkansen achieves the fastest track speed of 275kph, while the fastest station-to-station speed is 210.6kph, between Sendai and Morioka on the Tohoku Shinkansen.

From July 1992, the Tohoku Shinkansen has also served Yamagata, using an older line widened to standard gauge for through operation. The Shinkansen construction plan to expand the network, which had been temporarily suspended, has been resumed on some sections of these routes.

Decisions on the Tohoku-Joetsu construction plan

The Tokaido Shinkansen began service between Tokyo and Osaka on October 1 1964. By July 1967 it had carried 100 million passengers; by March 1969, 200 million; and by July 1970, 300 million, when, for the first time ever, it was competing successfully with air transport. The social and economic impact of the Shinkansen was so great that demand grew for a nationwide Shinkansen network that would reduce inter-regional time-distances, allow efficient redistribution of population and industries, and reduce regional inequalities. The National Shinkansen Improvement Law was passed in 1970, leading to approval, in October 1971, for the construction plan for the Joetsu Shinkansen and for the Tohoku Shinkansen as far as Morioka.

Existing conventional lines had been improved in the 1960s. The Tohoku Main Line electrification was completed in 1968; on the Joetsu Line the New Shimizu Tunnel was finished; and the whole line was double-tracked in 1967. Thus, both lines were able to cope with ever increasing traffic demand caused by growing industrialisation and the development of tourism. In the 1970s, however, the Tokyo metropolitan area spread rapidly and the population along rail corridors increased apace. Because of the greater numbers of commuter trains, it was impossible to run more long-distance expresses. Increased transport capacity was clearly needed.

Routes and facilities of the Tohoku and Joetsu Shinkansen

Most of the route of the Tohoku Shinkansen runs parallel to the older Tohoku Main Line. Fourteen stations were planned between Ueno and Morioka, while the total distance was reduced by 38.8kms from a previous length of 531.7kms. The route of the Joetsu Shinkansen follows the older Takasaki, Joetsu and Shinetsu Lines. Since the route passes through the mountains which form the spine of the Japanese archipelago, long tunnels were unavoidable; and since it also passes through areas of high snowfall, appropriate measures had to be taken to cope with the snow. Seven stations were planned between the junction at Omiya and the Niigata terminal. The original distance of 303.6kms was reduced by 34.1kms.

Both lines were designed for a maximum speed of 260kph, just as on the Sanyo Shinkansen, rather than the 210kph of the Tokaido. The maximum gradient was limited to 15 per cent, instead of the 20 per cent of the Tokaido Shinkansen, and the minimum curve radius was eased from the Tokaido's 2,500 to 4,000 metres. Based on the Sanyo Shinkansen construction standards, substantial improvements were made in measures against noise, vibration and snow. Structures were designed to resist earthquakes. Some 24 per cent of the Tohoku Shinkansen runs through tunnels, 55 per cent on viaducts and 16 per cent on bridges.

The corresponding numbers for the Joetsu Shinkansen are: tunnels 40 per cent, viaducts 40 per cent and bridges 11 per cent. There are relatively few embankments and cuttings. Viaducts were deliberately chosen for much of the route to facilitate standardisation in design and construction and to minimise maintenance. Furthermore, continuous vertical separation ensured reduced impact on cities and towns en route, and any future urban development need not be restricted.

The Tokaido Shinkansen used crushed rock for ballast and the Sanyo Shinkansen is partly on slab track. On the Tohoku and Joetsu Shinkansen an improved anti-vibration slab track was used, with a slab mat underneath as an anti-noise, anti-vibration measure on most sections. Although the slab track construction was a little more expensive than traditional ballast, its use cuts maintenance costs by more than 80 per cent, good track condition can be maintained and it offers better running stability and a smooth ride at high speed.

The composite-compound catenary developed for the Tokaido Shinkansen was

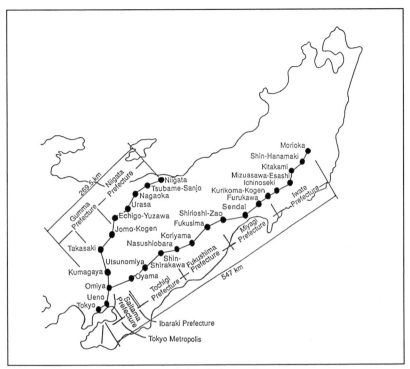

Above: Location of the Joetsu and Tohoku Shinkansen lines

Below: Profile of the Joetsu line

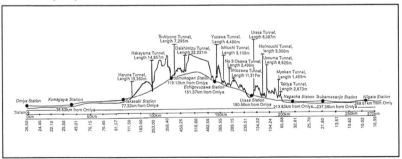

further improved for the Tohoku and Joetsu. It became a heavy compound system with its trolley-wire tension increased and the wire suspension strengthened to prevent the catenary from changing position. For radio communication between train and ground the leakage coaxial cable was installed the length of the line. The Automatic Train Control and cab signal system is similar to that of the Tokaido and Sanyo Shinkansen.

113

Niigata prefecture, through which the Joetsu Shinkansen runs, is an area with very heavy snowfall. In the Echigo-Yuzawa district, which has the highest snowfall on the line, the maximum depth of snow reaches 271cms in a normal year and the maximum daily snowfall is 91cms. Since snow on roads can be melted efficiently by water sprinklers, an automatic snow-melting system was installed on 78kms of track between Jomokogen and Niigata. When snowfall above a specified level is detected, the system is automatically activated to sprinkle warm water over the tracks.

*Snow is a frequent problem in Japanese winters, as, **left**, on the Tohuku Shinkansen. The diagram shows snow-removal equipment on the Series 200 Shinkansen. On the facing page, the diagram illustrates the on-track snow clearance system on the Joetsu Shinkansen*

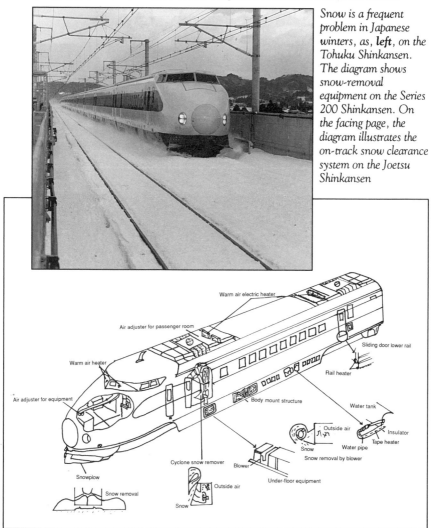

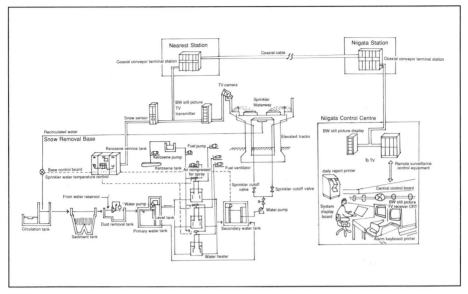

Rolling stock for commercial operation

The 200-series electric trains for the Tohoku and Joetsu Shinkansen are similar to those of the Tokaido in their electric traction system, with each axle having a motor. Motor output was increased from the 180kW of the Tokaido Shinkansen to 230kW because the Joetsu trains have to run on long continuous gradients and, on the Tohoku, where there are no snow-melting sprinklers, the train must be able to plough its way through snow-covered sections of line. Power supply is 25kV-50Hz, and the control system is thyristor phase control with rheostatic braking. The maximum speed was initially set at 210kph. Under-floor equipment is covered by a "body mount" system to protect it from snow. A cyclone separator removes moisture and snow from the air conditioner and equipment cooler. The car body is aluminium alloy, and axle loads do not exceed 17 tonnes.

Each 12-car train has one Green Car (first class) with 52 seats, a total seating capacity of 833 in second class cars and a half-car buffet. There were 57 train sets ready for operation when the lines opened.

Construction work and initial opening north of Omiya

Construction work was started on the Tohoku and Joetsu Shinkansen in November 1971, with a view to opening in 1976. Japanese National Railways undertook construction of the Tohoku, while Japan Railway Construction Public Corporation built the Joetsu. The original plan for the Tohoku Shinkansen was that construction work should go ahead along the entire length of the line, from Tokyo to Morioka; but since negotiations with local people and governments proved difficult, only the section between Omiya and Morioka could initially be opened.

Throughout the construction work numerous problems arose, including sudden price increases on construction materials as a result of the oil crisis, and curbs on public spending under national government policy. Nevertheless the project progressed and engineering work was completed in December 1981, even on the Ageo-Ina section where land purchase was delayed until the last minute. In January 1982, the tracks from Omiya to Morioka were joined. Trial runs started in March between Omiya and Morioka, and on June 23 1982 the Tohoku Shinkansen began operation.

A 43kms section near Oyama, where work had already been completed, was used for various tests, ranging from environmental considerations such as noise and vibration, to assessment of rolling-stock and facilities. During the trials a 961-series electric train reached a record speed of 319kph.

The Joetsu Shinkansen also suffered as a result of the two oil crises, and there were other problems too. Long tunnels had to be excavated to take the line across the Mikuni mountains. These included the Dai-Shimizu, Haruna and Nakayama tunnels, ranging from 15kms to 22kms in length. The work was hampered by adverse geological conditions and high-pressure spring water, particularly in the Haruna and Nakayama tunnels. These difficulties were eventually overcome by employing ground-strengthening emulsion-injection technology, developed for the Seikan Undersea Tunnel, and "NATM" technology which consists mainly of supporting the ground with rock bolts. It was in Japan that these technologies were first fully developed and successfully employed.

As far as bridge technology is concerned, Akayagawa Bridge is the longest concrete-arch railway bridge in the world, and Agatsumagawa Bridge, constructed with the latest technology, is the longest cantilever bridge in Japan.

Nakayama Tunnel had to be realigned for part of the route to avoid soft ground, due to repeated problems with spring water. Consequently, the opening of the Joetsu Shinkansen between Omiya and Niigata was delayed until November 15 1982, four months after the opening of the Tohoku Shinkansen.

Successes following the opening of the line north of Omiya

The Tohoku Shinkansen reduced the travelling time between Omiya and Morioka to three hours 17 minutes, from the previous six hours 23 minutes. When the Tohoku Shinkansen opened in June, ten trains ran each way daily; this was increased to 30 trains in November when the Joetsu Shinkansen opened.

On the Joetsu Shinkansen the travelling time between Omiya and Niigata was reduced to one hour 45 minutes, and 21 trains ran in each direction daily. Traffic volume in the first year was 17.98 million on the Tohoku, and 12.85 million on the Joetsu, compared with 23.33 million on the Tokaido Shinkansen in its first year. To provide Shinkansen connections from Tokyo, special Shinkansen Relay Trains operated between Ueno and Omiya on the existing line. The total traffic in the first month of Shinkansen service on the Shinkansen and the parallel older lines was about 17 per cent above the previous year for both the Tohoku and the Joetsu, while passenger traffic on competing airlines fell sharply and the number of private cars on motorways decreased as well.

Extension to Ueno

Originally the Tohoku and Joetsu Shinkansen were planned to run from Tokyo Station: none were to run from Ueno. The government of Tokyo's Taito ward, however, demanded a Ueno Shinkansen station. As the number of trains on the Tokaido Shinkansen increased, Tokyo Station did not have enough platforms for Tohoku and Joetsu trains. Therefore a decision was made to construct a Shinkansen station four levels below Ueno Station to supplement Tokyo Station. This change of plan was approved in 1977 and construction work started the following year.

The work between Ueno and Omiya was near densely populated urban districts, some of it close to, directly under, or above existing railway lines. Work, therefore, had to proceed with great care, and the construction time was strictly limited. Under these conditions, Ueno No2 Tunnel was excavated to 12.7m outside diameter by the shield-driving method. This was one of the largest tunnel sections in the world to be built by this method. The Ueno-Omiya section was finally opened on March 14 1985, and the long-awaited through operation into Tokyo was accomplished.

The speed of the fastest trains of the Tohoku Shinkansen between Ueno and Morioka was increased to 240kph and the fastest travel time reduced to two hours 45 minutes. The number of trains operating per day reached a total of 94 each way.

The maximum speed of the Joetsu Shinkansen trains between Ueno and Niigata was 210kph and the fastest travel time, one hour 53 minutes, with 62 trains a day. After the Ueno Station opened, passenger traffic volume reached 31 million in the first year on the Tohoku, 32 per cent up on the previous year, and on the Joetsu 16 million, an increase of 45 per cent.

By July 18 1985, 100 million passengers had been carried on Tohoku and Joetsu Shinkansen trains. By August the count was 200 million, by June 1989 300 million, and on February 20 1991 — eight years eight months after the Omiya opening — the total reached 400 million. In this time the total distance covered by train journeys reached 174 million train-kilometres, without a single passenger casualty. Delays averaged 0.1 minute per train, so we might reasonably claim that safe and reliable transport has been established.

From March 1990, the maximum speed of the Joetsu Shinkansen was increased to 275kph between Jomokogen and Urasa. In June of the same year, double-decker Green Cars were introduced on the Tohoku Shinkansen. December 1990 saw the opening of the Gala Yuzawa skiing ground, developed by the East Japan Railway Company, and skiers can now travel by Shinkansen direct to the slopes.

OPENING OF THE SERVICE TO TOKYO STATION

On June 20 1991, the 3.6kms Tokyo-Ueno section began operation, after completion of construction work in the densely populated centre of the capital. Tohoku Shinkansen construction work between Tokyo and Morioka, begun in November 1971, was completed nearly 20 years later. With the completion of this historic project, direct transfer is now possible between the Tokaido Shinkansen and the Tohoku or Joetsu Shinkansen at Tokyo Station, and it is no longer necessary to change trains at Ueno on trips between Tokyo and Morioka, or from Tokyo to Niigata. This saves about 20 minutes on trips between northern regional cities and Tokyo.

Shinkansen changes with privatisation of JNR

On April 1 1987, Japanese National Railways (JNR) was divided into six regional passenger railway companies and one nationwide freight company, and privatised. At that time the Tokaido Shinkansen was taken over by the Central Japan Railway Company, and the Tohoku and Joetsu Shinkansen by the East Japan Railway Company. However, the ground facilities of each Shinkansen were inherited by the Shinkansen Property Corporation, assets were valued at present replacement value, and each of the three passenger railway companies was to pay rental, including principal and interest, on an equal-payment 30-year amortisation. The rental was determined by assessing the asset value and earning power of each Shinkansen.

Later, the Government proposed to sell the Shinkansen facilities to these railway companies, with the intention of selling each Shinkansen to its operating railway in October 1991, at a price reflecting its value at the time of transfer, with payment by instalments.

Shinkansen-conventional line, through operation

As the track gauge of the Shinkansen differs from that of other JR lines, through operation is not possible. If, however, a conventional line is rebuilt to standard gauge, a Shinkansen train can run through on it, TGV-style, thus avoiding a troublesome transfer. Furthermore, by increasing train speed on the rebuilt line, travelling time can be reduced.

Work to alter the track gauge between Fukushima and Yamagata, on the Ou Line, was due for completion in July 1992. The Shinkansen cars for this through operation have the same body size as those on conventional lines, but the axle load will be lightened to 13 tonnes to enable through-running. Train speed on the Shinkansen is 240kph and on the rebuilt line 130kph. These changes mean a cut in travelling time between Tokyo and Yamagata from three hours ten minutes to about two hours 40 minutes.

THE SHINKANSEN FAMILY: *Facing page*, Series 300; **above,** *the new Series 400 on the Yamagata line;* **below, left**, *series 200; and,* **right**, *the original Type 0 alongside a new Type 100*

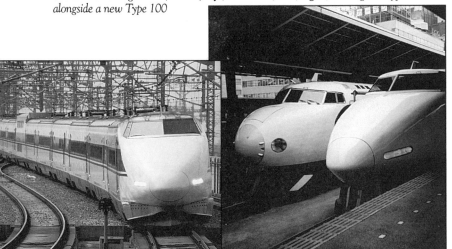

Speed-up plan

Lightweight, high speed Shinkansen test cars for speeds of 300kph to 350kph have been under development to connect Tokyo-Sendai and Tokyo-Niigata in one hour by spring 1992. The train consists of four bogie cars and five articulated-type cars, is 200 metres long and weighs a total of 256 tonnes, that is half the weight of the "traditional" Shinkansen. The car body is of aluminium alloy, the target weight being 55 per cent of the old Shinkansen.

The main circuit system uses PWM converter and VVVF inverter with regenerative braking. Total weight is reduced by the use of high-revolution induction, high-frequency main converter and high-density magnetic-flux iron-core main transformer.

Prior to production of this test train, the prototype 400-series Shinkansen cars for through operation on the Ou Line were tested for high speed running, and reached 366kph on the Joetsu Shinkansen in March 1991.

Conclusion

Following the success of the Tokaido Shinkansen, construction of the Tohoku and Joetsu Shinkansen was begun, with a view to providing a national Shinkansen network. Although work was delayed by investment limits due to oil crises and by environmental problems, both Shinkansen lines opened in 1982 and the traffic volume has been increasing. In June 1992, through operation to Tokyo station was achieved, as originally planned.

Now the annual traffic volume on the Tohoku Shinkansen stands at about 50 million and on the Joetsu, 20 million. Although these figures are not as large as the 120 million of the Tokaido, they are far greater than the 17 million of the French TGV-Southeast Line. As the ground facilities of the Tohoku and Joetsu Shinkansen have been designed and constructed to accommodate a 260kph operation, technological developments for higher speeds are being promoted, with full consideration of any future environmental problems.

Table 11.1: *Shinkansen traffic figures*

		1985	1986	1987	1988	1989
Passengers carried (millions)	Tokaido	133	135	102	112	117
	Sanyo			55	61	62
	Tohoku	31	31	45	49	51
	Joetsu	15	16	17	19	20
	Total	179	182	219	241	250
Passenger-kilometres (millions)	Tokaido	43,864	44,300	32,123	36,299	37,404
	Sanyo			13,153	14,792	15,002
	Tohoku	8,085	8,214	8,929	9,677	9,892
	Joetsu	3,474	3,429	3,209	3,583	3,666
	Total	55,423	55,943	57,414	64,351	65,964

Notes: Based on JNR Audit Report and data collected by Ministry of Transport. Figures for 1985 and 1986 are for JNR, and those for subsequent years, for JR Group companies. Tokaido and Sanyo Shinkansen figures, post-1970 are separated by operating company

Part Three: Thematic issues

12.
Introduction
By the Editors

WE SHALL now take a closer look at some of the aspects of high speed trains touched upon in the preceding part, namely public policy, project management, train design, stations and environmental problems. These issues are both general and specific in character.

They are general in the sense that they have an international and a timeless validity, and specific since they focus narrowly on some of the topics in the multifaceted context of high speed trains.

Railways are still an important part of a nation's transport system and are usually run by state monopolies. Consequently, major projects like high speed train services are of great public concern. We have seen that strong public support for these projects is almost a necessity, although not sufficient in itself as a condition for success.

Why is it that different states pursue different policy strategies towards the railways? And why is it that this pattern tends to be persistent over time? Dobbin puts forward a hypothesis that can account for the persistence of state strategies over time, even though the needs may change. Applied to the case of railways in the USA and France, he gives an explanation for the fact that state intervention follows the same pattern today as it did a century ago. The stability can be accounted for by the interacting concepts of institutional capacity and institutional culture.

The capacity can be said to designate the quantity and quality of the resources possessed by public entities and directed towards certain fields of activity.

The culture is the collective understanding of the nature of collective action and the locus of economic rationality. The elements of capacity and culture evolve over time in mutually reinforcing processes. Dobbin argues that, given the positive outcome of the state strategy pursued in one period, in this case the 19th century period of railway development, the probability of a repeated pattern of state action is high.

The British APT represents one of the most technically advanced projects in the history of high speed, and also the most costly failure. When describing and analysing this project, Potter draws our attention to its organisational aspects. He concludes that mismanagement of the innovation process was a major cause of the inability to solve the problems encountered. Even though serious technical problems did arise and politicians and unions sometimes obstructed the development, the basic failure was the less than adequate organisation of human resources.

121

Another interesting question is whether any dominant design of high speed lines has emerged from the past 30 years of research and development efforts. It is still a bit early to tell. The differing needs in terms of capacity and speed, as well as financial means, for different connections make such an evolution doubtful.

The Channel Tunnel project and the PBKA (Paris, Brussels, Köln, Amsterdam) network project have accentuated the problem of technical diversity. At the beginning of the railway era each operator chose technical standards according to, among other things, the needs of its traffic and the beliefs of the engineers.

The demand for internal compatibility when enlarging the network meant that the initial solutions became permanent. The evolution of the national high speed networks has often followed a similar logic. The incompatibility of national (high speed) railway networks imposes costs on all parts, and means that the technical designs of trains for international services fall below the optimum. Puffert discusses this problem and illustrates it with the ongoing work on an integrated European high speed train network.

The benefits of common standards are not only seen in the costs and quality of international services, but also in economies of scale in component and rolling stock production. The task of the UIC (international railway union) to unify standards is not an easy one. Gateway technologies may overcome some of the problems, but in many instances major modification has to be made to avoid the consequences of letting the lowest common denominator rule.

The chapter by Heskett provides an interesting historical overview of train designs. It is noted that whenever railways have been in a competitive situation, design has been important. As a consequence of both technical and strategic considerations, different streamlined shapes of trains appeared in several countries in the 1930s. This was during the first wave of high speed trains.

However, both the competitive and the technological context of railways change continuously, and hence put new demands on design. It is therefore interesting to note the Japanese strategy towards the design of the Shinkansen trains. Instead of deciding on the interior and exterior design of these trains once and for all, as part of a homogenous corporate image programme, an incremental strategy with continuous improvements was opted for. Equally interesting is the description of the British experience of HST (InterCity 125) design, showing the complex interdependencies between function and image, and how conventional concepts of design had to be reconsidered.

The introduction of high speed train lines is often accompanied by a modernisation of the railway stations. That a railway station is not just a place where trains stop becomes clear in the paper by Richards and McKenzie. Instead it can be seen as a centre for social and cultural activities. Historically, the stations were much more central to urban life than they are today, a fact which is vividly described in the first part of the chapter.

However, the expected revitalisation of railway stations with the introduction of high speed services poses both opportunities and problems for decision-makers. The array of new functions to be supplied, outlined in the second part of this contribution, often have to be incorporated into old cultural and architectural milieux. The advantage of supplying city centre-to-city centre transport is thus accompanied by delicate problems in terms of combining demands for efficient operation with the preservation of historical and cultural values.

High speed trains are frequently described as environmentally, economically and socially viable alternatives, or complements, to road and air transport. This is a common view on the effects of these trains, and indeed the dominant one in this book so far.

However, it is quite possible to find arguments that reverse the effects in all three categories. In the thought-provoking chapter by Whitelegg and Holzapfel we are confronted with a totally different perception of the effects of investments in faster transport. The time-saving benefit, for instance, is offset by the fact that people tend to devote a fairly constant amount of time to travelling. Thus, the result is just an augmented spatial mobility and increased use of energy. Fast, high-quality passenger transport serves only a small fraction of the population, and tends to increase the degree of inequality. Furthermore, the bulk of journeys in society are very short. It is therefore argued that a reallocation of the investments from inter-regional high speed links to regional and local transport systems would produce more environmentally, economically and socially justifiable effects.

13.
Vive la différence!

Public policy and the development of high speed trains in France and the USA[1]
Frank R Dobbin, Department of Sociology, Princeton University, New Jersey

Fired by the success of its first high speed train link between Paris and Lyon, the French government is thinking of more. *(The Economist 1984)*

A private group today announced a proposal to build what it hopes will be the nation's first high speed train... from Houston to Dallas. *(New York Times, Belkin, 1989)*

FRANCE AND the United States have pursued dramatically different policies to facilitate the growth of high speed rail transport. In France, central state planners have orchestrated the development of high speed train services, while in the United States that task has been left to entrepreneurs and state and local governments. This difference is surprising in the light of the fact that passenger rail transport is a state monopoly in both countries.

This chapter examines high speed train policy in the two countries, highlighting parallels in each, with the policies employed to promote railways during the 19th century. Why have the United States and France pursued such divergent high speed train (HST) policies, and why are their HST policies so strikingly similar to those adopted to promote steam railways? I argue that the answer lies in persisting organisational capacities and cultural representations of the French and American states.

In recent years institutionalists have pointed out that traditional interest group and rational choice approaches to the state simply do not explain the continuity over time in national policy strategies. Nation states pursue internally consistent problem-solving strategies over long periods of time, even as regimes with radically different political orientations take office. Pioneering work in this field comes from political scientists.

Stephen Krasner (1978) found in an historical study of American raw materials policy that, one after another, American administrations have pursued a single broad policy strategy, advocating market pricing and allocation — even when that policy disadvantaged domestic firms. John Zysman (1983) found in a comparative study of

[1] I am grateful to Keith Allum for research assistance, and to Princeton's University Committee on Research in the Humanities and Social Sciences for funding.

France, Britain, West Germany, the United States, and Japan, that nations tend to pursue internally consistent policies to promote diverse industries. Each country adopts policies that resemble its past policies.

The dilemma these studies pose for the predominant perspectives on policy formation is that they show policy shifts within nations — the usual focus of policy studies — to be relatively inconsequential in the light of persisting cross-national differences in policy.

The "New Institutionalism" in politics

Institutional theory locates policy continuity in state institutions. States repeat their previous policy strategies when faced with new problems because they have at their disposal the institutional capacities that were developed to effect previous policies. Stephen Krasner (1984) uses the analogy of "branching" to describe the process. Once a nation state has made a particular policy choice and "branched" in one direction by creating a certain set of policy institutions, it cannot easily branch in the opposite direction because prior choices constrain present options. Existing policy institutions facilitate similar policies, and they may disable dissimilar policies. Thus Skocpol and Finegold (1982) find that the presence of a federal agricultural agency at the outset of the Great Depression facilitated the job of Roosevelt's Agricultural Adjustment programme, while the virtual absence of an industrial agency doomed the efforts of the National Recovery Administration.

This perspective is intuitively appealing, for it suggests that if a new policy is predicated on the use of, say, a national bank, that policy is most likely to succeed in a nation that has such a bank.

A number of "institutional capacities" studies have examined cases of policy failure, in which novel policy strategies fail during implementation due to the absence of adequate administrative capacities. The National Recovery Administration is a case in point. However, in the vast majority of cases, prior policy strategies are replicated not because existing state capacities select out unusual policies, but because states initially choose new policies that resemble existing ones.

Much of the process of policy reproduction occurs at the stage of policy conceptualisation. Because policy-makers in different nations tend to envision mutually exclusive sets of policy alternatives, broad policy choices are actually made when alternatives are being formulated. Thus, when it came to building high speed railways, it virtually never occurred to Americans that Washington might plan and build a network. Equally, it never occurred to the French that private interests might take over these tasks.

Institutionalised cultural meaning

I want to suggest that institutionalised cultural meaning can explain these different ways of conceiving public problems and their solutions. Existing social structures offer models of how the world works to policymakers and to the public. They shape how we think about what is rational, what is fair, and what is possible (Dobbin forthcoming).

As Max Weber argued, notions of rationality are highly institutionalised in modern societies. Institutionalised rationality also varies considerably from one modern social system to the next. Recent social constructionist approaches to institutions offer some useful insights.

First, rationalised cultural meaning takes the form of means-ends designations which act as prescriptions for action (Douglas 1986; Meyer 1987).

Second, rationalised meaning is inherently falsifiable, and is constantly subjected to empirical validation. Commonly understood means-ends relationships can be falsified in much the way that scientific paradigms are falsified. Minor empirical inconsistencies may be incorporated into existing meaning systems, but major inconsistencies tend to elicit alternative explanatory frameworks (Wuthnow 1987).

Third, rationalised meaning is inherently collective, and this is how we can distinguish it from interest group ideologies. Rationalised meaning is comprised of the taken-for-granted understandings of the world that entire societies hold (Sewell 1985; Berger and Luckmann 1965).

Rationalised meaning appears in what Kenneth Dyson (1983) calls "industrial culture", which refers to the institutionalised logic of economic organisation in a nation. Industrial cultures are comprised of the customs of economic life and the logics that underlie those customs.

In schematic terms, the United States has an industrial culture that is market-oriented and France has an industrial culture that is oriented to state concertation of the economy. When we try to understand policy choices in these two countries we can identify state institutional capacities that contribute to particular choices. We can also identify predispositions to certain courses of action, which I attribute to institutionalised cultural meaning, that influence how problems are conceptualised.

Capacities and meaning in the French and American states

The social constructionist approach employed here treats instrumental social institutions as embodiments of culture, and as such it suggests that organisational and cultural aspects of social institutions are inextricable. Thus, when American citizens promoted early railways under the auspices of local governments in the 19th century, they did so in part because substantial organisational resources were situated at the local level, and in part because local government had been constructed as the appropriate locus of collective action. Empirically it is difficult to disentangle these two motivations, and the social constructionist approach suggests that the effort to disentangle the two is motivated by a false distinction between structure and culture that pervades modern social thought.

However, one important reason to try to distinguish the cultural from the structural is that a particular social structure may have diverse cultural meanings in different societies because culture is not a direct reflection of structure.

CAPACITIES

Institutional capacity refers to the administrative and technical configuration of the nation state. I will argue that state capacity is important, in part because it determines where decision-making and public action will be located, for example, in the central state or at the local level. Figure 13.1 outlines characteristics of state structure that proved salient to the formation of policies to promote railroads.

Figure 13.1

INSTITUTIONAL CAPACITIES	
FRANCE	UNITED STATES
Centralised state structure	Federal state structure
Professionalised bureaucracy	Amateur bureaucracy
State control of engineering	Private-sector control of engineering
State control of transport administration	Private-sector transport administration

STATE CENTRALISATION-FEDERALISM

By the early 19th century, the French state provided the West's benchmark of centralised authority. A series of French regimes had reorganised public authority to undermine the power of the local nobility and to concentrate military power in Paris (Anderson 1974). Local and provincial governments had no independent authority to speak of. That system has survived a series of revolutions in government (Hall 1986).

By contrast, political authority was deliberately decentralised in the blueprint for American government. The separate states were afforded extensive decision-making powers, and localities were granted wide powers of self-determination (Tocqueville 1945).

THE BUREAUCRACY

To extend political and military control over far flung feifdoms, early French monarchs built an elaborate Parisian bureaucracy, with tentacles in the provinces in the form of centrally appointed officials who carried out the King's will. Over several centuries a complex bureaucracy arose which was concerned with military matters, commerce, and transport (Fischer and Lundgreen 1975; Suleiman 1974). As Tocqueville (1955) insists, France's administrative structure was not drastically changed by the age of revolution.

By contrast, the American government had unusually meagre central administrative control. Weak bureaucracies existed for the mails and military, but in other areas federal administrative powers were minimal (Skowroneck 1982). It was not until the early 20th century that the federal government developed appreciable administrative powers, and the American bureaucracy has remained significantly weaker than its European counterparts.

CONTROL OF ENGINEERING

In France, civil engineering had long been a state monopoly, for the state built the nation's highways and canals. The state employed the lion's share of the nation's civil engineers, and trained those engineers in public academies. Of particular importance

127

was the Corps des Ponts et Chaussées (bridges and highways corps), which the King established in 1716 and to which he granted an independent école in 1775 (Fischer and Lundgreen 1975). Because the state undertook all major civil engineering tasks, engineering became part of the civil service.

By contrast, turnpikes and canals had, with few exceptions, been designed, built, and operated privately in the United States (Goodrich 1960, p21). Army-trained civil engineers often designed public transport projects, but they did so after leaving public service. Washington never attempted to monopolise the education of civil engineers in a public academy; instead private universities and institutes trained civil engineers. In the 20th century, as governments began building turnpikes, sea ports, and airports with public monies they turned to private-sector engineers for assistance. The growth of public accommodations, then, did not lead to the centralisation of control over engineering.

LOCATION OF TRANSPORT ADMINISTRATION

Well before the railway era, the French state operated turnpikes (royal roads) and canals. The Administration Générale des Ponts et Chaussées (Bridges and Highways Board) had the task of designing and operating inter-city roads in the 1830s, when railway technology first appeared in France (Price 1983).

Today most facilities for public transport are owned and operated by the state, including the SNCF, Air France, and domestic airlines. By contrast, American turnpikes and canals were built and operated by private interests in the 19th century. In the 20th century state and federal governments took over the administration of highways, and the federal government has reluctantly taken over inter-city passenger railways. Yet the air transport, bus, and trucking industries remain privately managed.

Culture

Rationalised cultural meaning is largely the result of everyday experience with social institutions, and it frequently takes the form of no-nonsense, demystified, means-ends designations oriented to instrumental ends (Swidler 1986). I argue that public institutions in France and the US contributed to substantially different notions of collective action, economic rationality, and the role of government in the economy. Figure 13.2 outlines those differences.

COLLECTIVE ACTORS

In different nations, social institutions produce different notions of the appropriate source of collective action in society, and those notions depend to a large extent on where legitimate collective authority is lodged. France's active state has contributed to the social construction of the central state as the corporate entity that embodies the interests of the nation (Hayward 1986; Zeldin 1979).

By contrast, American political institutions depict authority as emanating from below, and have contributed to the notion that unhindered citizens and regional governments can best represent and pursue the interests of the community and nation (Tocqueville 1945). In the American construction of collective action, the central state poses a potential threat to the legitimate authority of localities and private entities to pursue goals such as economic growth (Lipset 1963).

Figure 13.2

INSTITUTIONAL CULTURE	
FRANCE	UNITED STATES
Central state as collective actor	Localities and private interests as collective actors
State rationality	Market rationality
Government concertation of economy	Government incentives & market regulation

LOCATION OF ECONOMIC RATIONALITY

Social institutions also represent the driving force of economic growth variously across nations (cf Zysman 1983). In both countries, public notions of the logic of economic rationality have retained certain elements since the dawn of the railway age. France's military and political successes had long been attributed to the wisdom and power of the absolutist state, and the same logic was found in discussions of economic life. Since at least the time of Richelieu the French had thought of state concertation of the actions of individuals as an important component in economic growth; only the state could orchestrate the inchoate actions of individuals so as to achieve the collective goal of growth (Machin 1977; Hayward 1986).

By contrast, Americans had believed in the efficacy of private action and came to see market mechanisms as the only force that could rationalise the actions of individual citizens. In part this was the case because the writers of the Constitution had built in safeguards against the abuse of public power, which led Americans to think of public power as inherently corrupt and disruptive to private life.

One result of these differences is that the French have had relatively more confidence in the rationality of state concertation, and Americans have had relatively more confidence in the rationality of market mechanisms.

ROLE OF THE STATE IN THE ECONOMY

Political culture carried related notions of the exact role each state should play in its economy. French political culture identified state concertation of the economy as proper. State orchestration of economic life since the time of Louis XIV had led the French to view oversight and orchestration as the rightful role of the state.

By contrast, in the United States the central state had been constructed as a weak overarching framework that existed to facilitate the operation of political democracy and economic liberty at the local level. The role of the central state in the economy was at first limited to enabling states and localities to pursue their goals (Miller 1959). After a brief flirtation with a federal role oriented to providing positive incentives to private industry, public policies led Americans to believe that the federal government could best serve the public by stimulating market competition.

How did these state characteristics influence railway policy in these two countries?

Rail policies in France and the US

Figure 13.3 outlines the principal differences between the railway policies of France and the United States. It will be shown below that these differences characterised both 19th century steam railroad policies and 20th century high speed train policies.

Figure 13.3

POLICIES GOVERNING STEAM RAILROADS AND HIGH SPEED TRAINS	
FRANCE	**UNITED STATES**
Central state initiative	State and local initiative
Public orchestration of financing	Private and regional financing
Public route planning	Private route planning
Public choice of technology	Private choice of technology
Public orchestration of construction	Private orchestration of construction

France: The Grande Réseau and the TGV

The earliest French railways were private lines built to transport coal. Soon after the introduction of steam locomotives the French state assumed responsibility for railway planning and development. Fiscal constraints prevented the state from building and operating a rail network without private aid, but state engineers designed a centralised rail system that could be nationalised when circumstances allowed. Private companies provided partial financing, and in turn were given operating franchises (Doukas 1945; Guillamot 1899). In 1937 the French government nationalised the railway system under the Société National des Chemins de Fer (SNCF).

By the early 1970s the SNCF began to show interest in high speed rail technology. To accommodate rising demand on the Paris-Lyon railway the SNCF expected to have to build a second line. Instead, in 1974 the SNCF proposed to build a high speed passenger rail line, with electric-powered Trains à Grande Vitesse (TGV) that would travel at 270kph. Construction began in 1976, and service on the line commenced in 1981.

The line was an instant success, and in less than a decade more than a dozen new lines were under construction or on the drawing board. Today France has the most elaborate high speed rail network in the world, and the French have begun to export their technology and know-how.

PUBLIC INITIATIVE

Before private enterprise built a single important railway in France, the state assumed the initiative for designing and putting into place a truly national rail network. The network was centrally planned so as to achieve maximum efficiency and to best serve the needs of France. The Bridges and Highways Board initiated all railway projects, and while legislative approval was required for new lines, the efforts of private interests and local governments to initiate projects on their own, or even to sway the Board, were ignored (Lefranc 1930).

In the early 1970s the SNCF initiated the first TGV project for the route between Paris and Lyon. It was the SNCF's engineers and economists who, facing declining ridership and a contracting rail network in the mid-60s, saw in Japan's Shinkansen line between Tokyo and Osaka a means to reinvigorate the industry (Faujas 1991).

It was those SNCF engineers and economists, with substantial autonomy to pursue projects on their own initiative, who established a Research Department at the SNCF and undertook the studies that led to France's TGV system — just as it was the engineers at Ponts et Chaussées who initiated the studies that eventuated in France's huge centralised rail network in the 19th century.

PUBLIC ORCHESTRATION OF FINANCING

In the 19th century the state assumed responsibility for guaranteeing that the three major capital costs associated with railways — land, construction, and rolling stock — would be met. The state acquired the right of way for each line, and for most lines either laid the track itself or contributed toward the cost of construction (Kaufmann 1900). The private franchises were designed to attract private capital — especially from London money markets — to pay for rolling stock and to contribute to construction costs (Dobbin forthcoming).

The SNCF similarly arranged TGV financing to combine private and public sources of funds. As before, a capitalisation scheme was developed which could attract foreign capital, and as before the scheme was successful; one third of the capital for the first TGV line came from New York banks alone, and the SNCF went to international money markets again to fund subsequent lines (US House 1984, p26; Macdonald 1991). For the Paris-Atlantic line the state found fully 70 per cent of the 13 billion francs needed in private money markets (Economist 1984; Macdonald 1991).

Despite the remarkable financial success of the first two lines, the state continues to provide public aid for future progress on the TGV, including a total of about 66 million ECUs for the period 1990-1994 — largely to be used for the design of a third-generation TGV (European Information Service 1990).

More generally, the SNCF retains the authority to raise funds as it sees fit. For instance, it has financed rolling stock by selling new TGV train sets to a banking consortium and then leasing them back (Black 1991; Freeman 1991).

PUBLIC CHOICE OF ROUTES

The French state chose all major railway routes in the 19th century. In the early 1830s, when only short coal-carrying lines had been constructed, the state placed a moratorium on the granting of private charters until state engineers could develop a national route plan of their own. State engineers were given full authority to make route decisions, and they fastidiously refused to be influenced by local politicians who wanted rail services, arguing that if localities were allowed to influence route decisions the nation would end up with an incoherent rail system (Villedeuil 1903).

Likewise, state officials at the SNCF have been responsible for route and destination decisions for high speed trains. In the aftermath of the Paris-Lyon line's financial success, the government planned lines connecting Paris with Lille, Calais (and the Channel Tunnel), and Brussels to the north; with Le Mans, Tours, and eventually Bordeaux to the south-west; with Nancy and Strasbourg to the east; and with Marseille and Cannes to the south (Neher 1989).

As in the 19th century, state technocrats retain authority to plan new lines on objective technical grounds; nonetheless, when the SNCF last unveiled a plan, Mitterand's Government sent it back to the drawing board and called for a more ambitious and aggressive one (Black 1991). The new scheme, introduced in May 1991, called for 16 new TGV lines that would require 4,700kms of track to be laid at a cost of some 200 billion francs (Faujas 1991c). The SNCF's planners have largely ignored the concerns of localities and environmentalists who have sought to influence route decisions, insisting that, for the good of the nation, such decisions must be made by clear-minded technocrats, not by groups with partisan and regional demands.

PUBLIC DESIGN OF TECHNOLOGY

Engineers from the Bridges and Highways Board made all relevant engineering decisions for the nation's steam railways. They made decisions about bridge and tunnel construction, the circumference of curves, the incline of the track, and so on. When it came to rolling stock, the board established such strict technical specifications that, for all intents and purposes, they designed the carriages and locomotives themselves (Dunham 1941).

State engineers have similarly been central in the design of high speed train technology. They have established construction standards to ensure reliability and safety. They have also placed France at the technological vanguard of high speed rail transit by designing the TGV trains virtually from the ground up. The TGV's own rolling stock division — GEC-Altshom, a subsidiary of the Compagnie Générale d'Électricité — engineers the train sets. The TGV's research and development efforts have led to a series of technological advances that enable the French to market their trains internationally (Neher 1989). In 1991 GEC-Altshom led a consortium called the Texas TGV in a successful bid for a $5.8 billion contract for a high speed rail connection between Dallas and Houston, and the makers of the TGV are now bidding on contracts in Taiwan, South Korea, Canada, and elsewhere in the United States (Agence France Presse 1991).

PUBLIC CONSTRUCTION

The state built a number of France's early railways itself, and closely supervised those built by private contractors. Public officials reasoned that if France wanted well-built railways that would serve the nation, the state would do best to build them itself (Audiganne 1858). Private parties, the French reasoned, would build shoddy lines because they would try to minimise cost in order to maximise their own profits. By contrast, public construction would ensure that all funds were being used to maximise the quality of rail lines.

Likewise, on the Paris-Lyon line, the state never seriously considered franchising the route to a private concern for construction and operation, despite the fact that the line was projected to turn a profit, and therefore might have attracted private bids.

Proponents of the Paris-Atlantic line, which was likewise projected to turn a profit, did not advocate privatisation, even when Mitterand stalled the project owing to a fiscal crisis (Economist 1984).

The origins of French rail policies

We have argued that these outcomes may be traced to state capacities and institutionalised cultural meaning.

INSTITUTIONAL CAPACITIES

In the 20th century, as in the 19th, French state capacities facilitated public control of transport. The state has held the ability to take the lead in the railway industry, and private sector capacities in transport have remained undeveloped. A comparison of figures 13.1 and 13.2 suggests why this was the case.

First, the central state took the initiative for the development of both steam and high speed railways, in part because French state structure was centralised, which meant that provincial and local governments could not challenge the authority of Parisian bureaucrats to do so; and, importantly, could not effect rail plans of their own.

Second, the centralised state structure enabled Paris to orchestrate the financing of both 19th and 20th century rail networks, in part because it enabled the central state to make unilateral decisions about where to invest public monies. Of course, the ability of the central state to control public funds was key here, and that ability was a result of France's centralised revenue-gathering system. In addition, the state had significant prior experience in transport administration in both periods; the state had operated turnpikes and canals before the advent of steam railways, and air transport and conventional railways before the advent of high speed trains.

Third, state domination of engineering made the state the natural candidate to design the railway system, as well as the rolling stock. France's professionalised bureaucracy was also paramount here, because professional norms allowed technocrats to remain aloof from regional interests in their planning decisions. Just as the presence of extensive engineering expertise in the state was a necessary condition for public route planning, the absence of extensive private-sector civil engineering expertise made private route planning impracticable. France's minister of commerce and public works complained of the privately-drawn railway plans submitted to the state in the early 1830s:

> "Often... the Bridges and Highways Board is obliged to have the plans redrawn" (Moniteur Universel 1833, p1206).

Fourth, these same capacities led the French state to select track and rolling stock technologies in both centuries. The state has held the lion's share of the nation's expertise in transport engineering and administration since before the invention of the steam locomotive, and since 1937 has operated the nation's railways.

Finally, public orchestration of construction was facilitated by the fact that the state dominated administration of the canals and public highways in 19th century France, which meant that the state was better equipped than were private transport concerns to coordinate construction. While private barge and stage coach companies operated on canals and highways, the state had built and managed both sorts of facilities. By the 20th century the situation was little changed.

INSTITUTIONALISED CULTURAL MEANING

While institutional capacities clearly enabled the French state to influence the course of railway development, the policy agenda was predicated on the presumptions that the central state is an appropriate collective actor, that the state can be a source of rationality, and that concertation of economic life is an appropriate role for the state. The French took for granted that the state should coordinate railway development, and this more than anything shaped the course of railway policy.

The fact that the French state is recognised as an appropriate collective actor coloured railway policy in significant ways. As a result, in the words of *The Economist*:

> "For the French, railways were always an arm of the state and they... recognised their crucial strategic importance." (1985a p55).

In other words, because it was considered proper for the French state to take responsibility for achieving collective goals and to preclude private actors and local governments from doing so, the French assumed in both periods that the railways, and any other industries that were vital to the economy, could and should be governed by the state.

The notion that the state bureaucracy could achieve economic rationality through expert planning was found in debates surrounding route decisions in the 19th century, when railway supporters argued that state officials could best design a network that would serve the nation, and that the interference of private parties and local governments would undermine the overall rationality of the system (Audiganne 1858).

For the new high speed rail network, public officials and private parties agreed from the outset that state orchestration would eventuate in the most efficient service. Transport minister Paul Quiles reiterated those sentiments when he argued that privatisation would not render the project more efficient:

> "Our analysis shows there is no advantage to the community — privatisation is not on the agenda. Our aim is to have a railway in a sound financial state, meeting the demands of the community. Good management is in no way at odds with the concept of a public company." (Quoted in Black 1991).

As a result, neither private parties nor politicians have contended that private entrepreneurs should undertake high speed train developments.

The widespread understanding that the French state can, and should, orchestrate economic growth also played an important role in setting the policy agenda surrounding steam railways and high speed trains. Key here is the notion that state bureaucrats can and should do more than simply make mundane managerial decisions. As one frustrated British Rail official put it:

> "'The French ministry runs a transport policy, it doesn't try to manage the railways,' because the Ministry is, for the French, the proper place for the development of a comprehensive transport policy." (Economist 1985a, p60).

The ministry had such blanket authority to plan for the future that Paul Quiles has recently called for opening the decision process to the input of interested parties:

> "I would like (the Ministry) come out into the open... Debate, for me, is a method of political action." (Quoted in Faujas 1991b).

Quiles proposes that each new project should be presented in a public forum for debate, rather than, as in the past, proffered by the Ministry as a *fait accompli*.

In short, the same assumptions about the nature of collective action, the locus of economic rationality, and the appropriate role of the state that influenced steam railway policy continue to influence transport policy today. As a result, French policymakers and railway enthusiasts continue to presume the central state to be the proper actor to spur railway development, and continue to believe that central coordination of transport will eventuate in a more rational and effective rail system than will unbridled private interests and market forces.

The United States: Each town for itself

The earliest American railways were built by private entrepreneurs, frequently with the financial backing of state and local governments. State and city governments contributed to the costs of railways built westward from Philadelphia, New York, Baltimore, and Boston in competition to secure the first transport link to the West. Municipal governments in the East and Midwest competed with one another to attract railway services, and entrepreneurs competed to win franchises between major metropolitan centres (Fisher 1947).

Later, Congress provided land grants to trans-continental railway builders to stimulate development. However, graft and corruption at the local, state, and federal levels brought public aid to railroads to an end. By the late 1960s it had become clear that if Congress did not nationalise the passenger rail service and portions of the freight service, America's rail system would collapse, and Congress reluctantly did just that.

In the 1970s American state and local governments began to show interest in high speed rail transport to remedy problems of overcrowding on highways and in airports (Ekistics 1972). While passenger railway service was operated under a public monopoly in the United States, proposals for high speed trains came almost exclusively from private interests and local governments. Amtrak and Congressional leaders agreed that Washington would not initiate high speed rail transport. They argued that the federal government could not afford to build high speed railways, and that the most efficient system would be produced by market mechanisms. As a result, a number of states and localities have encouraged private groups to develop plans for high speed trains. As in the 19th century, states and localities have put together incentive packages including rights-of-way, promises of stock subscriptions, and financial assistance through public bond offerings. Next I examine these policies in more detail.

STATE AND LOCAL INITIATIVE

States and municipalities retained substantial decision authority after the Revolution. Local and regional governments used their powers, and funds, to build rail lines that would serve them. Few governments actually built railroads, but many initiated railway projects and offered incentives to lure railway entrepreneurs, usually in the form of government-backed bonds.

By 1861 state and local governments had provided roughly 30 per cent of the total capital costs of the railroads, exclusive of land grants (Goodrich 1960, p. 268-270). The federal government took the initiative to promote inter-state railways, at the behest of states, in a half-dozen cases.

In the 1980s initiative for high speed train projects has come from state and local governments. Florida's legislature established a High Speed Rail Commission in 1982 to design incentives that would attract private parties to bid for a 314-mile Miami-Orlando-Tampa franchise, which is estimated to cost between $2.2 and $4.6 billion[2] (Klein 1984, p34). State and local governments have likewise initiated studies for lines in California, Nevada, New York, Pennsylvania, Ohio, Michigan, Illinois, Texas, New Mexico, Oregon, and Washington (Cupper 1984, p30; Wiedrich 1989; Subcommittee on High-Speed Rail Systems 1985).

The same logic of "rivalistic state mercantilism" that characterised state and local debates about steam railroads can be found in the high speed train debates today (Bishop 1907; Hungerford 1928). In 1988 Florida House Speaker Jon Mills echoed the kind of boosterism that characterised steam railroad rhetoric:

> "We're going to have the most modern rail system in the world. We will be ahead of California, Massachusetts, Illinois and all of our technological competitors."
> (Quoted in Boston Globe 1988)

In addition, in both periods, governments sought to attract private developers to the plans they initiated by offering land grants. In the 19th century, state and federal governments provided grants of large tracts of land to railway builders, who used land grants to secure the capital needed to build the lines (Haney 1910; Henry 1945). Similarly, state officials in Florida and elsewhere have proposed offering land grants to high speed train developers, in addition to rights-of-way, which would enable them to attract capital in the same manner (Klein 1984, p34; Wiedrich 1989).

ABB, the international bidder that received a green light to proceed with plans in Florida, noted that the Florida plan was based on a public-private partnership "modelled on the approach which encouraged construction of railroads across the western United States and down Florida's peninsula" (quoted in Railway Age 1989).

PRIVATE AND REGIONAL FINANCING

For most 19th century railroads, state and local governments offered stock and bond subscriptions as incentives to private developers. After corruption and graft sullied the notion of public investment in railroads, most states outlawed future state and local aid. While Congress financed feasibility studies for trans-continental routes, in only one case did it provide financial assistance — in the form of a bond offering. In a half-dozen cases Congress offered land grants as incentives to inter-state railroads, but strict constitutional constructionists argued that even land grants exceeded the constitutional powers of Congress (Sanborn 1899).

Since the 1970s state and federal legislatures have financed feasibility studies for high speed rail systems, but have refused to underwrite the cost of construction.[3] After funding the first feasibility study in Florida, the legislature insisted that developers pay for future studies and pay the costs of the public hearing and approval process (Railway Age 1989).[4]

As in the 19th century Florida and other states have proposed the use of tax-exempt bonds to finance rail construction, and in 1984 federal legislation was introduced to allow governments to issue tax-exempt public bonds for high speed train projects (Cupper 1984, p39).

136

At the federal level the Senate allocated a million dollars to the Army Corps of Engineers, which did the feasibility studies for the trans-continental roads, for feasibility studies into magnetic levitation technology. The Department of Transportation allocated a similar sum for its own studies (Feder 1989). However, federal officials steadfastly refuse to consider public financing of construction. At a privately-organised conference on high speed trains in 1984 Federal Railroad Administrator John H Riley vowed "firmly and repeatedly, that no federal funding is available to finance the tremendous capital costs associated with systems" (Cupper 1984, p30). The succeeding head of the Federal Railroad Administration, Gilbert Carmichael, argued that only small federal sums would be available:

> "There will be Federal money, but it will go to the systems where we see big commitments from states and localities, industry and investors." (Quoted in Feder 1989).

PRIVATE ROUTE PLANNING

Railway entrepreneurs made key route and destination decisions for America's earliest railroads. State and federal governments were loath to dictate to private companies, but they did use incentives to encourage railway companies to build lines that would serve them. Because railway developers wrote their own charters, which were then approved by state legislatures, they retained control over route decisions; by contrast, in France, state bureaucrats designed lines and wrote charters for private firms. Even in the case of the trans-continental lines, Army engineers only undertook the initial feasibility studies and did not plan the actual routes (Dobbin forthcoming).

The Florida legislature, and its High-Speed Rail Commission, have insisted that private initiative and market forces should determine the outline of the rail system. Private franchise applicants have been directed to submit route and station plans as well as financing proposals (Railway Age 1989). In fact, in each of the thirteen regional high speed train studies initiated by 1985, state and local governments allocated planning and feasibility studies to the private sector, either by promising

---

[2] The Texas legislature likewise established the Texas High Speed Rail Authority to award franchises in 1988 (Boston Globe 1989). California and Nevada established the California-Nevada Super Speed Train Commission to attract a private entity to develop a Las Vegas-Los Angeles train (Miller 1989).

[3] The one exception to federal reluctance to get involved in high speed rail is on the Northeast Corridor. Amtrak has upgraded Boston-New York-Washington track so that trains can now run at 125mph on some segments of the route. Amtrak is now considering a $300 million plan to link Boston and New York by high speed train service, cutting the run to three hours or less which transportation experts believe would offer serious competition to the airline shuttle services (Chicago Tribune 1988b). Amtrak appears to be willing to take initiative on this route because it constitutes an upgrade of a line it inherited and because it involves so many states that no one state can be expected to take responsibility. The project has been jointly undertaken by Amtrak and the Coalition of Northeast Governors (Chicago Tribune 1988a).

[4] In Texas the German High Speed Consortium spent $1.2 million on a feasibility study for a Houston-Dallas line, and a firm called Texas Railroad Company spent a like amount (Engineering News Record 1985a). The latter company also contracted to buy a bankrupt railroad's half interest in a Dallas-Houston right-of-way for $17.5 million.

franchises to successful planners or by employing private firms to undertake studies (Subcommittee on High-Speed Rail Systems 1985).

PRIVATE CHOICE OF TECHNOLOGY

In the 19th century, American governments exercised virtually no control over railway technology. Neither Congress nor the states tried to standardise rail gauge, construction standards, or rolling stock technology. One result was that by 1861 half of America's total trackage was in some gauge other than the 4ft 8½ inches that would become standard, and by the end of the 1860s American railroads still used at least a dozen different gauges (Westbay 1934, p32; Poor 1871).

It was not until 1886 that railroads agreed among themselves to standardise track gauge. Another result was that railroads were not required to instal brakes on trains until near the end of the century.

A similar situation is developing in American high speed railway technology. By contrast with France, the American government has made no effort to influence the choice of technology, nor even to standardise technology. It is not unlikely that different American high speed rail systems will use incompatible roadbeds and propulsion systems, which have been developed in Sweden, France, Germany, Japan, or Canada (Boston Globe 1988; Armstrong 1989).

The one government foray into technology development took the form of federal funding for basic research at Massachusetts Institute of Technology in the early 1970s. That research, which first demonstrated the feasibility of magnetic levitation technology, lost funding in 1975 and since that time only German and Japanese government-backed consortiums have pursued the technology (Feder 1989).

PRIVATE ORCHESTRATION OF CONSTRUCTION

In the 19th century private railway firms organised construction with almost no public intervention. Railway entrepreneurs managed construction as they saw fit, often hiring foreign-born labourers and making route and technology decisions as they proceeded. While the United States has yet to see a completed high speed rail project, all of the proposed projects would be supervised by private parties subject to weak federal and state regulation.

The origins of American rail policies

INSTITUTIONAL CAPACITIES

In general, state capacities influenced policy in America by determining that decisions would be made, and action taken, locally. Local governments, state governments, and private entrepreneurs would act independently because state structure situated authority and decision-making power at the local level.

Firstly, state and local governments took the initiative in steam railroad development in large measure because the federal state structure afforded them the authority to do so, and seemed to deny Congress the power to undertake large-scale projects (Callender 1902). Of course, because state capacities in transport were underdeveloped at the federal level, it was unlikely that federal officials would spearhead the railway revolution. In both periods, land grants were promoted to attract private entrepreneurs to government-initiated projects, in part because, with the division of tax revenues across three levels of government, states had limited capital resources.

Secondly, state and local governments took the lead in organising financing for steam railroads and for high speed trains in part because their capacities to raise funds are great, relative to those of the federal government. Thirdly, private route planning in the United States came about in both periods largely because civil engineers were located in the private sector — a result of the fact that canals and turnpikes were built privately.

On the other hand, by the 20th century, most railway engineers were ostensibly federal employees because they worked for Amtrak and Conrail. In principle, then, the state had the capacity to plan routes and make decisions about rolling stock technology.

Fourthly, for the steam railroads the state left decisions about technology to the private sector in part because the state employed few technical experts and had little experience with transport administration, but again by the 20th century the federal government certainly had adequate technical expertise to take over these tasks.

Finally, the decision to leave construction up to the private sector in both centuries is in large measure a result of America's meagre professionalised bureaucracy and lack of experience in transport administration. Nonetheless, federal experience with the construction of airports and seaports certainly rendered Washington capable of orchestrating the construction of high speed train projects.

INSTITUTIONALISED CULTURAL MEANING

The problem of weak federal state capacities in the 19th century was largely resolved by the 1970s. While the federal government was arguably incapable of orchestrating steam railway development, it seems clear that Washington had the necessary administrative and technical resources to orchestrate high speed train development. I contend that the possibility never entered the political agenda because it was inconsistent with America's political culture.

Firstly, the American conception of states, local governments, and private actors as the appropriate pursuers of collective ends had a palpable effect on public policy in the 20th century, as in the 19th. In the 19th century Congress presumed that transport development was the duty of state and local governments, until the 1850s brought the prospect of trans-continental railroads which were beyond the scope of regional governments. Even then many in Congress challenged the federal government's legitimate authority to provide land grants to stimulate the construction of railroads.

When it came to high speed trains, politicians and federal officials believed in a minimal role for the federal government. Federal Railroad Administrator John Riley envisioned a federal role in which the FRA would merely be "a part in the process of enhancing credibility" of the concept of high speed rail — not the leader in designing and financing high speed trains (quoted in Cupper 1984, p31). In sharp contrast to the French experience, neither congressmen nor federal transport officials thought of the federal government as the appropriate locus of action.

Secondly, the American belief in private-sector rationality, and scepticism about the capacity of the public sector to effect rationality, clearly helped to produce rail policies that located decision authority — over routes, technology, and construction — in the private sector. Railway enthusiasts in both periods argued that market demand would ensure that lines were properly placed, and that entrepreneurs were better equipped, and motivated, to judge where demand warranted railways than were public officials (US Congress 1987). Moreover, local and private interests have disparaged the idea of federal leadership because they view the federal government as ineffective and cumbersome. As Paul Reistrup, associate chairman of the private High Speed Rail Association and a former Amtrak president, argued:

"There is room for some local and state governmental help, but keep the feds out. We don't need their help and we don't need their hindrance. All they do is study, study and study some more. And the whole purpose, of course, is not to do anything. I've been there, and I know." (Quoted in Wiedrich 1989)

Thirdly, the American belief that the state's proper role in the economy is to provide incentives to business and promote market competition has clearly influenced the decisions to allocate financial responsibility for railroads to the private sector. French analysts, such as TGV rolling stock division chief André Thinières, are perplexed by the American state's reluctance to provide direct aid to railroads:

"A key issue working against us in the US is the psychological bias against putting public money in trains. It's quite okay to invest public money in highways and airports, but not in trains." (Neher 1989)

Despite the fact that the organisational obstacles to providing state and federal aid to transportation projects has been overcome in the cases of sea ports, airports, and highways, Americans react suspiciously to all sorts of proposals to provide public assistance for putatively private projects.

Conclusion

I have been arguing that the dramatically different state strategies for the development of high speed trains found in the United States and France are reminiscent of the railway strategies pursued by 19th century governments in those two nations. While both France and the United States now have public inter-city rail networks, French high speed train development has been initiated, planned, financed, and carried out by the state, while US high speed train development has been relegated to the private sector.

I have suggested that there are two elements to an explanation of why these two countries are now replicating the strategies they used to develop steam railroads. Firstly, the French state has the administrative capacities, broadly defined, to carry out HST development on its own. The state has the fiscal power, the administrative might, the concentration of public authority, and the technical expertise to undertake high speed train development — as it did in the 19th century.

By contrast, in the United States the balance of public administrative might and technical competence favours state and local governments. More broadly, the private sector has had substantial experience in transportation and is thus well equipped to take on the task.

Secondly, and perhaps more importantly, we have seen that alternative strategies for promoting high speed trains never appeared on the political agendas in France or the United States. For all intents and purposes it never occurred to the French that

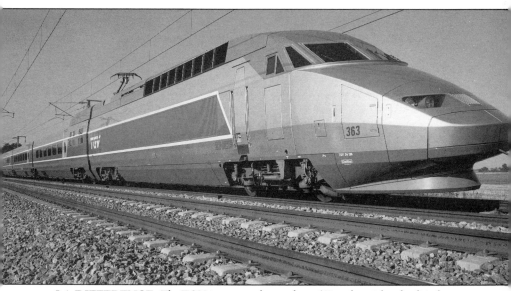

LA DIFFERENCE: *The TGV is very much a product of French social and political institutions*

they might allow entrepreneurs and markets to determine where and when high speed train systems would be built. Americans never seriously considered the possibility that the federal government might plan and build high speed train lines.

I have argued that this difference can be traced to the experiences of French and US citizens with their particular forms of government. The reality of French government is that the state serves as a collective actor and organises large segments of the economy. The reality is that public policy depicts private parties and state and local governments as the appropriate sources of collective action, and the state relegates decisions about the economy to entrepreneurs and markets. I have referred to those realities as aspects of institutionalised cultural meaning, for they embody national understandings of the nature of collective action, the locus of economic rationality, and the appropriate role of the state in the economy.

Institutionalised meaning tends to create self-fulfilling prophesies, which is one reason why it tends to persist. In the United States, where political culture depicts state intervention in the economy as inefficient, only bankrupt industries are put under state management (Amtrak and Conrail, for example). In turn those industries continue to lose money, fuelling the notion that state industrial management is inefficient.

By contrast, in France, where political culture depicts public industrial management as efficient, the state takes initiatives on new projects that are expected to be profitable, such as the TGV, and takes over successful industries to run them better, such as electronics. Successful experiences then reinforce those strategies.

The aim of this chapter has been to explore, in a preliminary way, the causes of policy continuity within countries. Why is it that American regimes of the 1830s and the 1980s pursued similar strategies for promoting steam railroads and high speed trains? Traditional interest group arguments clearly fail to explain these policy choices. Instead I have tried to sketch out the effects of institutional capacities on where public decision authority is located, and hence where public action is initiated. I have also tried to sketch out the effects of institutionalised cultural meaning on how problems and their solutions are conceptualised in the first place, to suggest that nations choose from among policy alternatives that are narrowly constrained by past experience.

References

Agence Presse France. 1991. "French Win 5.8 Billion Dollar Contract for High Speed Train." Agence Presse France. May 29

Almond, Gabriel, and Sidney Verba. 1963. The Civic Culture: Political Attitudes and Democracy in Five Nations. Princeton University Press, Princeton

Anderson, Perry. 1974. Lineages of the Absolutist State. New Left Books, London

Armstrong, Scott. 1989. "Plans for High-Speed Rail Pick Up." The Christian Science Monitor. 26 December, 6

Audiganne, Armand. 1858. Les Chemins de Fer Aujourd'hui et dans Cent Ans. Capelle-Librarie, Paris

Belkin, Lisa. 1989. "Group Proposes High-Speed Train for Texas." New York Times. 28 September, A22

Bell, Daniel. 1980. The Winding Passage. ABT Books, Cambridge, MA

Berger, Peter, and Thomas Luckmann, 1965. The Social Construction of Reality: A Treatise on the Sociology of Knowledge. Garden City: Doubleday

Bishop, Avard Longley. 1907. "The State Works of Pennsylvania." Transactions 8:147-297

Black, David. 1991. "Tracks to nowhere; The Government believes that privatisation is the cure for the ills of British Rail. The rest of the world disagrees." Independent. October 6

Bonnafous, A. 1987. "The Regional Impact of the TGV." Transportation 14:127-137

Boston Globe. 1988. "Florida Unveils 4 Plans for a High-Speed Train." 29 March, 38

Calender. G S. 1902. "The Early Transportation and Banking Enterprises of the States in Relation to the Growth of Corporations." Quarterly Journal of Economics 17:111-162

Chicago Tribune. 1988. "High-speed Train Tested in East." 23 October

Chicago Tribune. 1988. "High Speed Trains May

Gain U.S. Niche." 30 October

Cupper, Dan. 1984. "Enthusiasm Mounting in US for High Speed Ride into Third Century." Mass Transit. September, 30-42

Dobbin, Frank. Forthcoming. States and Industrial Cultures: Britain, France, and the United States in the Railway Age. Cambridge University Press, New York

Douglas, Mary. 1986. How Institutions Think. Syracuse University Press, Syracuse, NY

Doukas, Kimon A. 1945. The French Railroads and the State. Columbia University Press, New York

Dunham, Arthur L. 1941. "How the First French Railways Were Planned." Journal of Economic History 14: 12-25

Dunlavy, Colleen. Forthcoming. Politics and Industrialisation: Early Railroads in the United States and Prussia. Princeton University Press, Princeton

Dyson, Kenneth. 1983. "The Cultural, Ideological and Structural Context", pp26-66 in Industrial Crisis: A Comparative Study of the State and Industry. Kenneth Dyson and Stephen Wilks (Eds). Oxford: Martin Robinson

Economist. 1983. "Faster trains, Bigger Losses." 19 November, 76

Economist. 1984. "On a Rail and a Prayer." September, 49

Economist. 1985a. "Return Train." 24 August, 53-60

Economist. 1985b. "The World and its Railways: Redefining Their Role." 31 August, 25-32

Economist. 1985c. "The World and its Railways: Higher Speeds and Lower Costs." 7 September, 33-38

Economist. 1985d. "The World and its Railways: The Fast Track." 14 September, 25-28

Economist. 1988. "A Faster Route to Europe." 16 July, 53-54

Economist. 1989. "Faster and Still Faster." September, 52

Engineering News Record. 1986. "High-speed Rail Network Under Study in Europe." 6 March, 16

Engineering News Record. 1985. "High Speed Rail Line Feasible." 31 October, 14

European Information Service. 1990. "Commission Approves Aid to French High-speed Train." European Report 1607: 13

Faujas, Alain. 1991a. "Il y a Dix Ans Le TGV Paris-Lyon Sauve le Chemin de Fer." Le Monde. September 23

Faujas, Alain. 1991b. "Le Ministre de l'Équipement Partisan d'un 'vaste débat' sur les Projets d'Infrastructure." Le Monde. September 13

Faujas, Alain. 1991c. "Un Programme de 210 Milliards de francs Le Schema Directeur TGV Revoit la Construction de Seize Lignes Ferroviaires a Grande Vitesse." Le Monde. May 16

Feder, Barnaby J. 1989. "Building a 'Flying Train': U.S. Interest Grows but Others Are Ahead." New York Times. 13 December, D6

Fischer, Wolfram, and Peter Lundgreen. 1975. "The Recruitment and Training of Administrative Personnel", Pp456-561 in The Formation of National States in Western Europe (Ed Charles Tilly). Princeton, NJ: Princeton University Press

Fisher, Charles E. 1947. Whistler's Railroad: The Western Railroad of Massachusetts. Bulletin No. 69. Boston: The Railway and Locomotive Historical Society

Freeman, Len. 1991. "Foreign Trains Could Run on British Rail Tracks." The Press Association Newsfile. July 11

Frybourg, Michael. 1984. "The New Paris-Southeast Line and the High Speed Train." Ekistics 51:120-123

Geertz, Clifford. 1983. Local Knowledge: Further Essays in Interpretive Anthropology. Basic, New York

Goodrich, Carter. 1960. Government Promotion of American Canals and Railroads 1800-1890. Columbia University Press, New York

Guillamot, Georges. 1899. L'Organisation des Chemins de Fer en France. Arthur Rousseau, Paris

Gutis, Philip S. 1990. "Amtrak Presses Northeast Strategy But Riders and Rivals Seem Unfazed." New York Times. 16 January, A16

Habermas, Jurgen. 1984. The Theory of Communicative Action. Volume One. Reason and the Rationalisation of Society. Beacon, Boston

Hall, Peter. 1986. Governing the Economy: The Politics of State Intervention in Britain and France. Oxford University Press, New York

Hall, Peter. Forthcoming. "The Movement From Keynesianism to Monetarism: Institutional Analysis and British Economic Policy in the 1970s," in Svein Steinmo, Kathleen Thelen, and Frank Longstreth (Eds) Historical Institutionalism in Comparative

Politics: State, Society, and Economy. Cambridge University Press, New York

Haney, Lewis Henry. 1910. A Congressional History of Railways in the United States 1850 to 1887, University of Wisconsin Bulletin 342. University of Wisconsin Press, Madison

Hayward, Jack. 1974. The One and Indivisible French Republic. Norton, New York

Hayward, Jack. 1986. The State and the Market Economy: Industrial Patriotism and Economic Intervention in France. New York: New York University Press

Henry, Robert S. 1945. "The American Land Grant Legend in American History Texts." Mississippi Valley Historical Review, 32: 171-194

Hungerford, Edward. 1928. The Story of the B. & O. Railroad, Two Volumes. Putnam, New York

Inkeles, Alex, and David Smith. 1974. Becoming Modern. Harvard University Press, Cambridge, MA

Kariel, Henry S. 1961. The Decline of American Pluralism. Stanford University Press, Stanford

Kaufmann, Richard de. 1900. La Politique Française en Matière de Chemins de Fer. Librarie Polytechnique, Paris

Klein, Gil. 1984. "Florida at the Head of the High Speed Rail Pack." Mass Transit. September

Krasner, Stephen D. 1978. Defending the National Interest: Raw Materials Investments and U.S. Foreign Policy. Princeton University Press, Princeton

Krasner, Stephen D. 1984. "Approaches to the State: Alternative Conceptions and Historical Dynamics." Comparative Politics 223-246

Lancaster, G A, and C T. Taylor. 1988. "A Study of Diffusion of Innovations in Respect of the High Speed Trains." Journal of European Marketing 22:21-47

Lefranc, Georges. 1930. "The French Railroads, 1823-1842." Journal of Economic and Business History 299-331

Lipset, Seymour Martin. 1963. The First New Nation: The United States in Historical and Comparative Perspective. Norton, New York

Los Angeles Times. 1989. "Magnetic Train Plan Puts Disney on Troublesome Track in Florida." 5 June

Lowi, Theodore J. 1969. The End of Liberalism: Ideology, Policy and the Crisis of Public Authority. Norton, New York

Macdonald, Alastair. 1991. "French Railway Courts Investors at High Speed." The Reuter Library Report. October 10

Machin, Howard. 1977. The Prefect in French Public Administration. Croom Helm, London

Meyer, John W, John Boll and George Thomas, 1987. "Ontology and Rationalisation in the Western Cultural Account", pp 12-37 in Institutional Structure:

Constituting State, Society and the Individual. Eds George M Thomas, John W Meyer, Francisco C Ramirez and John Boli. Beverly Hills: Sage

Miller, John C. 1959. Origins of the American Revolution. Revised Edition. Stanford University Press, Stanford, CA

Miller, William G. 1989. "Europe High-Speed Rail Network Closer as Three Nations Agree on a New Link." Boston Globe. 14 August, 12

Miller, Alan C. 1989. "Panel To Consider Ambitious Plan for Network of High-Speed Trains." Los Angeles Times. 18 October, A24

Moniteur Universel. 1833. Moniteur Universel. Paris

Neher, Jacques. 1989. "French Hope U.S. Hears High-speed Train Whistle." Chicago Tribune 25 September

Nice, David C. 1989. "Consideration of High-Speed Rail Service in the United States." Transportation Research 23A:359-65

O'Connor, James. 1984. Accumulation Crisis. Blackwell, New York

O'Connor, James. 1973. The Fiscal Crisis of the State. St. Martin's New York

Poor, Henry V. 1871. Manual of the Railroads of the United States for 1871-1872. Poor, New York

Poulantzas, Nicos. 1972. "The Problem of the Capitalist State." In Ideology in the Social Sciences. Ed. Robin Blackburn. Pp. 238- 53. Fontana, London

Price, Roger. 1981. The Economic History of Modern France, 1730-1914. Macmillan, London

Price, Roger. 1983. The Modernisation of Rural France: Communications Networks and Agricultural Market Structure in Nineteenth-Century France. New York: St Martin's

Railway Age. 1989. "Florida: One Contender Left." December, 42- 43

Sanborn, John Bell. 1899. Congressional Grants of Land in Aid of Railways. University of Wisconsin Press, Madison

Sewell, William H., Jr. 1985. "Ideologies and Social Revolutions: Reflections on the French Case." Journal of Modern History 57: 57-85

Skocpol, Theda, and Kenneth Finegold. 1982. "State Capacity and Economic Intervention in the Early New Deal." Political Science Quarterly 97: 255-278

Skowroneck, Stephen. 1982. Building a New American State: The Expansion of National Administrative Capacities: 1877-1920. Cambridge University Press, New York

Subcommittee on High-Speed Rail Systems. 1985. "High-Speed Rail Systems in the United States." Journal of Transportation Engineering 2:79-94

Suleiman, Ezra. 1974. Politics, Power and Bureaucracy in France: The Administrative Elite. Princeton University Press, Princeton NJ

Swidler, Ann. 1986. "Culture in Action: Symbols and Strategies." American Sociological Review 51: 273-286

Taylor, Lawrence R. 1972. "South California Prospects for High Speed Interurban Transportation." Ekistics 33:13-17

Tocqueville, Alexis de. 1955 (reprint). The Old Regime and the French Revolution. Doubleday, Garden City

Tocqueville, Alexis de. 1945 (reprint). Democracy in America. Two Volumes. Henry Reeve and Phillips Bradley (trans.). Vintage, New York

Tuppen, J N. 1982. "France's Train a Grande Vitesse." Geography 67:343-44

US Congress. Senate. Committee on Commerce, Science, and Transportation. Hearing on Advanced Transportation Systems. 101st Cong., 1st sess., 1989

US Congress. House. Committee on Science and Technology. Report of the European Study Mission. 98th Cong., 1st sess., 1983. Serial 1

US Congress. House. Committee on the Judiciary. Hearing on High Speed Inter-city Rail Passenger Service. 98th Cong, 2nd sess, 1984. Serial no. 57

US Congress. House. Committee on Science, Space, and Technology. Hearing on High Speed Railroad Technology. 100th Cong., 1st sess, 1987. No. 11

US Congress. Senate. Committee on Finance. Hearing on Tax Exempt Bonds for High Speed Rail Projects. 100th Cong., 2nd sess., 1988

Villedeuil, Laurent de. 1903. Bibliographie des Chemins de Fer. Villedeuil, Paris

Westbay, JH 1934. "The Standardisation of the Track Gauge on American Railways." Railway and Local Historical Society Bulletin 34: 28-35

Wiedrich, Bob. 1989. "High-speed Trains: Next Stop the U.S." Chicago Tribune. 30 April

Wuthnow, Robert. 1987. Meaning and Moral Order: Explorations in Cultural Analysis. University of California Press, Berkeley

Yates, Ronald. 1989. "After 25 Years, Bullet Train is Still a Blast." Chicago Tribune. 6 October, 6

Zeldin, Theodore. 1977. France, 1848-1945: Intellect, Taste and Anxiety, Volume Two. Clarendon, Oxford

Zysman, John. 1983. Governments, Markets, and Growth: Financial Systems and the Politics of Industrial Change. Cornell University Press, Ithaca

Zysman, John. 1977. Political Strategies for Industrial Order: State, Market, and Industry in France. University of California Press, Berkeley.

14.

Managing high speed train projects

Dr Stephen Potter, Faculty of Technology, The Open University, Milton Keynes, UK

THE LAST 20 years have seen a revolution in high speed rail technology, with the development of a number of high speed passenger trains capable of 300kph and 400kph emerging as a realistic target. But there has also been a large number of failed projects. This chapter looks at Britain's experience of both successful and unsuccessful high speed train projects and examines the factors contributing to success and failure.

Conventional and radical high speed trains

In the 1960s a number of radical guided ground transport designs emerged to challenge conventional railways. One British project, which got as far as a research prototype, was the tracked hovercraft, powered by a linear induction motor. This government-funded project was cancelled in 1973 after £3.5 million had been spent.

By this time interest had shifted towards magnetic levitation (maglev), rather than an air cushion, for such linear induction-powered trains. A consortium of British Rail, GEC and Brush continued development, with the aim of producing a viable small-scale maglev system. This project led to the world's first public maglev line opened in 1984 to link Birmingham airport with the nearby Birmingham International railway station.

This very limited application of maglev can hardly be construed as challenging conventional railways as a strategic technology. High speed maglev developments in Germany and Japan are more in this vein, yet in practice they appear to have very limited scope for application. This is because of technological improvements in conventional railways. Operating speeds have been raised from a general maximum of 160kph in the early 1960s, to 210kph on Japan's first Shinkansen line in 1964, to 300kph on France's TGV Atlantique in 1989.

There is still a lot more speed potential to be obtained from conventional railway systems and maglev simply does not have a large enough speed or cost advantage for it to be a serious challenger. The development of superconductive materials could alter the running costs of maglev to some extent, but it is still hard to envisage a mass market for maglev systems like that enjoyed by rail or air today.

Conventional fast trains linked into existing comprehensive systems are highly competitive for journeys up to 600kms and air is equally competitive at distances beyond that, so the prospects for maglev look pretty limited.[1]

---

[1] See Potter. 1987. pp 180-83

The pioneering maglev at Birmingham airport continues to plough a lonely furrow

Approaches to high speed train development

There have been several alternative approaches worldwide to achieving high speeds on conventional railway lines. At one extreme is to be found a totally new, dedicated railway network combined with a dedicated but technically unsophisticated train, such as the original Shinkansen, while at the other extreme can be found a very technologically advanced train operating on existing track, such as Britain's Advanced Passenger Train and Sweden's X2000. Broadly speaking, the more new track you are able to build, the less technically complex the train needs to be.

These differing approaches beg a question. Are we in the middle of a time of experimentation with different technological mixes of track and rolling stock, out of which will emerge a dominant approach? Or rather, do these different mixes reflect a key underlying diversity in railway markets and politics between countries, so that we should have no expectation of one particular approach dominating?

The key to conventional rail operations at speeds above 160kph was a technological breakthrough in bogie design that was made in Britain in the early 1960s. Until then, train speeds had been limited by two main factors. One was that, above about 160kph, unstable vibration of the train's wheelsets ("hunting") occurred. The second was track damage caused by the sheer momentum of fast, heavy trains, particularly on curves. The only way then known to push train speeds to above 160kph was to build an entirely new line with gentle curves. This permitted the use of wheels that were less susceptible to hunting vibrations, but which could not take sharp bends. This is exactly what the Japanese did on their 210kph Shinkansen line.

Essentially, the Shinkansen represents an almost maglev-type approach, for it is a system that is totally separate from the rest of Japan's railways, even to the extent that the track is built to a wider gauge than the rest of the country's railways. The unique population geography of Japan's Pacific coastal belt made this an economic proposition. Along the first Shinkansen route, the Tokaido line, live 37 million people and 125 million passenger journeys per annum are made on the line. This is a transport corridor of a density unparalleled anywhere else in the world. The next busiest is the Paris-Lyon route, along which about 15 million passenger journeys per annum take place. Most other European lines carry considerably lower volumes.

The success of Japan's Shinkansen had a major impact on the thinking of railway management in many countries. In Britain, it helped British Rail to shrug off the negative Beeching era, and in France, Italy and Germany, the building of new lines began to be seriously considered. However, instead of simply imitating the Shinkansen, two countries sought to advance beyond it. In both Britain and France, research had been undertaken into the "hunting" problem and, by the mid-1960s, both had developed rail suspension for use in trains operating at over 200kph which could run on ordinary track.

In France, Italy and Germany, the construction of major sections of new track was economically and politically viable. What is often misunderstood is that the new lines in these countries have been built to upgrade a much larger network of existing lines. For example, the new high speed 412kms Paris-Lyon *Ligne à Grande Vitesse* (LGV line) permitted a major upgrading of services on more than 1,600kms of lines linked into it. Although the 270kph top speed of the TGV can only be achieved on the purpose-built LGV line, this fast core trunk route has transformed rail travel over the whole of southern France.

Indeed, the Japanese are now adopting this approach for the further development of the Shinkansen network. It is now recognised that further new lines are not economically viable and so existing lines are being linked to the Shinkansen network (with a third rail being laid to allow for mixed narrow/standard gauge traffic) and new, smaller, Shinkansen trains built that can run on these existing lines.

In Britain in the late 1960s, the construction of any new railway lines was politically out of the question, for a number of reasons. Firstly, the lack of state intervention in planning Britain's rail network in the 19th century had resulted in an overprovision of trunk lines. A key factor in favour of the Paris-Lyon LGV was the need for additional capacity along this corridor. No such argument could be mustered for any InterCity line in Britain (see Wickens, 1985).

Secondly, state support for Britain's railways has always been low by European standards (see Roberts et al, 1984). A comparison between state investment in rail and other transport projects in the period over which the Advanced Passenger Train (APT) was developed highlights this:

"From its beginning in 1967 to 1982, the APT project cost £47 million — under £3 million a year. Over the same period expenditure on new motorways and other trunk roads was £5,300 million (averaging £400 million a year) and the Concorde project alone cost £2,000 million to develop from 1962 to 1976 (£140 million a year). The Paris-Lyon TGV line and stock cost about £1,000 million."
(Potter, 1987, p58)

147

Above: *Prototype High Speed Train approaching Edinburgh Waverley station in 1975 and,* **facing page,** *the refined model, minus buffers, which eventually entered service*

This general situation forced British Rail into a position where, if it was to opt for a fast train (operating at more than 200kph), it would have to develop a technologically complex vehicle to operate on existing lines. This led to the basic design requirements of the Advanced Passenger Train (APT). It had to have a tilting body, otherwise it would rarely exploit its top speed, having to slow down when approaching curves. It would also need high-performance brakes to stop in the distance provided by the existing signalling system.

However, coupled with the development of the APT, British Rail wisely decided to build the less ambitious High Speed Train. This was a quickly-developed "low-tech" diesel-powered train that exploited the high-speed bogie design to raise operating speeds from a maximum of 160 to 200kph. Marketed as the InterCity 125, to emphasise the top speed of 125mph (200kph), a fleet of nearly 100 of these trains entered passenger service from 1976. It was, and still is, the world's fastest diesel train.

Managing the development of the Advanced Passenger Train

The first stage of the APT project saw the assembly of a project team within British Rail's Research Department. This initial stage, authorised in 1968, was to build an experimental train to test the feasibility of the APT concept. Initially, progress was rapid; the experimental gas turbine-powered APT-E train was completed in 1972 and, from then til 1976, undertook a series of impressive trials, raising the British speed record for rail to 245.4kph in the process.

However, the purpose of BR's Research Department was to undertake basic scientific research which, when proven, would be applied in the appropriate engineer-

ing departments of the railway and built by BR's manufacturing wing, British Rail Engineering Ltd (BREL). However, nothing as big or as technologically complex as the APT had previously emerged from BR Research. So, when the project was handed over to the Chief Mechanical and Electrical Engineer's (CM & EE) Traction and Rolling Stock Design Department, the core of the APT Project Team transferred across as well.

Its remit was to build three electric-powered prototype passenger trains (APT-P), with the intention that these would enter passenger trials on the London-Glasgow route from 1977, followed by production APTs from 1980.

The core of the APT Project Team that was transferred into the CM & EE Department numbered 30 people. This group eventually grew to between 70 and 80, plus 40 outside contractors. However, the concept of a project team was totally alien to the way in which the CM & EE Department was organised. This was structured on a "functional" basis, that is according to the broad engineering divisions of the railway.

Thus, the Traction and Rolling Stock Design Department had separate offices for locomotives and carriage design, containing specialist engineers for electrical equipment, power equipment, brakes, air conditioning, and so on. Work was allocated to Traction and Rolling Stock Engineers who had to co-ordinate all the specialist jobs in their section. They would be responsible for several design and development jobs at any one time.

There was no concept of allocating people exclusively to one project or to grouping people into multi-disciplinary project teams. Work on a project was handed on between individuals or groups in different engineering disciplines. However, the APT was organised on a multi-discipline project team basis. The APT project team contained specialists with skills in all the design areas necessary for the train's development. These specialists duplicated the engineers already in the CM & EE

149

APT TEST RUNS: Above, *northbound at Low Gill, Cumbria, March 1986 and —* **below** — *southbound in the Lune gorge, Cumbria, May 1987*

Department, and in many cases this was resented by the established engineers who felt that the APT team members were poaching on their territory.

Secondly, there were several senior engineers within CM & EE who were sceptical about the whole APT concept. They had just seen through the rapid and successful development of the High Speed Train and viewed the APT as an impractical high-tech irrelevance.

The danger of retaining a project team structure for the APT's development had been recognised, but it was felt that any problems could be dealt with. Problems of managing a radical project in an organisation geared to routine or evolutionary operations are not, of course, unique to British Rail. They face any large organisation attempting major innovatory projects. Consequently the structural factors that affect an organisation's ability to innovate have received considerable attention from management scientists. Oakley (1984) for example, discusses why departments which have a functional structure (in order to efficiently carry out routine tasks) tend to be mechanistic and unsuited to activities like innovative design, which require a more flexible "organic" structure. Francis and Winstanley (1988) similarly point out the problems of work flow and organisation in functionally-organised engineering companies.

Development problems with the APT

The construction of the APT-P prototypes was undertaken under the direction of the APT Project Group by some 30 sub-contracting companies. BREL made the train bodies and bogies, and the engines and traction equipment were manufactured by the Swedish firm, ASEA. The trains were assembled in the BREL workshops in Derby.

A government delay in authorising the construction of the prototypes, combined with manufacturing delays at BREL, resulted in the programme slipping. It was not until February 1979 that the first prototype electric train was ready, with proving trials commencing in May. In December 1979, this train set another UK speed record, at 260kph. Although the three prototype trains were able to make a series of very fast runs on ordinary, curved lines, there were considerable problems with tilt failures, binding tread brakes and on the gearboxes.

The lack of passenger trials became a source of embarrassment to BR and increasing pressure was applied to the APT project team to get the trains into service. The government would only authorise a production run of APTs once the prototypes had proved themselves in actual passenger use.

Finally, on December 7 1981, a single APT-P entered passenger service. The first journey from Glasgow to London was completed on time without hitch, but the glory was short-lived. On the return trip a fault developed, shutting down the tilting mechanism. The train had to slow down for curves and so ran late. This was repaired and two more attempts were made to run the train.

But in addition to the APT's technical problems, the train was hit by the worst winter conditions for 30 years and a combination of these problems ensured that neither run was successful. Unwilling to see such a prestigious train operate unreliably, BR withdrew the APT from passenger service. One train was briefly used in 1984-5 as an unadvertised relief train, but never again did the APT see scheduled service.

Why did the APT fail?

What was really behind the APT's problems? Were the technical failures alone an adequate explanation, or were they merely symptoms of a much deeper problem of managing a complex, innovative project within a large organisation?

TECHNICAL PROBLEMS

Clearly there were technical problems, and perhaps the best way to tackle this question is to begin by looking at these. The main problems were:

● Tilting mechanism jamming or failing

● Tread brakes binding and overheating

● Hydrokinetic brake problems causing axle failure

● Poor ride of articulated bogies

● Gearbox failures

The problems with the tilting mechanism were experienced early in the development of the APT-P and persisted throughout the project. One early problem was that the tilt response was found to be rather late and jerky. The sensor activating the tilt was therefore relocated on the preceding coach. Each coach in the train then "anticipated" curves and so was tilting as it entered into them.

The APT had two types of brakes: the innovative water-turbine "hydrokinetic" brakes for use at high speed, and conventional tread brakes for use at under 80kph. The main reason for the tread brakes binding was that the clearance with the wheels was too small and it only required a very small error in manufacturing, assembly or maintenance to result in the brakes constantly dragging. The friction of dragging brakes would cause the hub of the wheel to become hot and this could pull the hub and wheel out of fit and loosen the wheel on the axle. This problem was eventually overcome, but it was accepted that for any production trains a less sensitive design would be necessary.

The most serious technical problem encountered by the APT-P related to the hydrokinetic brakes and axle. A bearing failure in one brake had led to an axle nearly shearing apart. As with the tread brakes, this was another example of one failure setting off a series of major unanticipated effects. As the bearing collapsed, its case became loose and rotated against the casing of the brake. This friction heated up the central part of the axle and the brake flange. When these cooled, the bolt holding the brake and axle was loosened, potentially risking a serious accident. Replacing the aluminium flange with one made of steel cured this problem, but with such a potentially dangerous situation arising from a simple bearing failure, trial running of the trains was virtually halted.

The gearbox problem related to a lubrication weakness. If oil became contaminated, lubrication was ineffective, causing bearings to fail. There were also problems of oil leakage through seals. The failures were quite frequent and so held up the general development of the train. The problem was solved by both improving maintenance to reduce contamination and fitting oil coolers.

MANUFACTURING PROBLEMS

The most disturbing problems on the APT-P trains did not relate to design and technical problems, but to the quality of manufacture and assembly. In April 1980 one APT-P suffered a derailment while travelling at 200kph. The cause of this was found to be a collapsed wheelset. A ring of bolts securing the axle to the hydrokinetic brake housing had simply not been tightened during assembly. The bolts had fractured and the wheelset fell apart.

The breakdown during the APT's third run in public service in 1981 was also caused by poor assembly. A rubber grommet had not been fitted over a wire which, in consequence, had chafed through, causing a short circuit which then shorted out the whole train control system, which had been incorrectly wired up.

What was behind the poor standard of manufacture and assembly of the APT-P trains? In the case of the dragging tread brakes it was a design problem. The specification was higher than could realistically be expected from a railway workshop. Equally, the design of the gearboxes required maintenance standards higher than generally found in operational BR depots. These two examples raise the question as to whether the designers of the APT were out of touch with the realities of railway manufacturing and maintenance facilities. Oakley (1984) emphasises this danger in engineering design:

> "Many designers have practical experience of production and fully understand the limitations and capabilities that they must work within. Unfortunately, there are also many who do not have this experience and, quite simply, do not appreciate the systems that they are supposed to be designing for" (Oakley, 1984, Ch 6)

But in the case of the APT, although there were some instances of such design faults, these were isolated lapses rather than a general design malaise. Overall, the APT design did not require any more special attention in manufacture than other new train project.

A separate, but related, explanation concerns the workshop "culture" of the rail industry. Was it that the APT did not require higher production standards, but rather a different style of production? In older, "medium"-technology industries, like the railways, there is a tradition that the shop floor can modify and amend design details. The experience of the shop floor employees is almost like a final check on the designer. This tradition, rooted in the "craft building" of rail trades, did lead to problems, for a number of design details of the APT-Ps were changed without telling the design office. In some cases people on the shop floor simply did not believe that the lightweight APT designs would work because they were so different from familiar traditional designs.

Although this problem of "culture" was very real, it only accounted for a few of the problems on the APT-P and none of the really serious ones. This brings us on to other explanations — were the standards of construction of the APT particularly poor? If so, then why?

ORGANISATIONAL STRUCTURE AND PROJECT MANAGEMENT

The individual technical difficulties experienced by the APT reflected a basic problem of innovation management and organisation. As noted above, there were technical problems and there were some problems arising from the difference in engineering standards and culture between the APT's designers and the train's assemblers in the BREL workshops. But these were not of a sufficiently large magnitude to cause the scale of problems that were experienced. It was in the management of the APT project that the true seeds of failure lay.

As mentioned above, the management structure adopted to develop the APT-P prototypes was to move the APT Project Group from BR Research into the functionally-organised CM & EE Department. The APT Project Group found itself very isolated. The Chief Mechanical and Electrical Engineer was very supportive, but a number of key engineers viewed the whole approach of the APT as a threat to their professional reputation, status and method of working. To them, the APT was a distraction of valuable staff time which could be better used working on "real" trains.

So, while senior management of the CM & EE Department was sympathetic to the APT, at a day-to-day working level, the Project Group received little support. APT work got shunted down to the lowest level of priority and it would take days or weeks for even the most minor of modifications to be done.

The practical effects of this antagonism filtered through to other parts of the railway. At this time, the links between CM & EE and BREL, which built most of BR's rolling stock, were very strong. Just as in the case of the CM & EE Department, the senior management of BREL was supportive of the APT, but enormous problems arose if an individual workshop manager viewed the APT-P as a low priority "experimental" job. Such an attitude held up both the construction and modifications on the APT-Ps and also had an enormous effect upon quality control. There were significant differences in the quality of work between workshops where the manager was enthusiastic about the APT and those where the manager was not. Many of the problems of reliability with the APT-Ps were a direct result of such attitudes leading to poor quality control.

Once running trials began, problems of lack of commitment to the APT in other parts of British Rail became apparent. The commissioning team and the APT-Ps were based at an operational depot, working with staff maintaining and servicing existing InterCity trains. They also had to fit their exacting 200kph (or faster) test schedules into the daily pattern of much slower services along the busy West Coast Main Line. The image of the APT as a "distracting high-tech irrelevance" did not help the commissioning team to undertake their work.

The development, testing and modifications to the APT-Ps thus became a very protracted process. Behind this was the crucial problem of a divided attitude within the whole railway as to the credibility of the APT project. Added to this was a weakness in the nature of the APT project group itself which made bridging the credibility gap that much harder. The group consisted of highly capable engineers, but they were not strong on management skills. Designing a high-performance train is one thing, but having the ability to win the support of a large number of departments and key individuals in order to smooth the development and testing process is another.

The APT Project Group lacked the guidance and general support of the CM & EE Department and its accumulated railway experience. Hence, particularly when other parts of the BR organisation were involved, the APT team learnt only from its own mistakes. It had very little access to the practical experience of others. The isolation of the APT group within CM & EE resulted in a lack of such support and mistakes occurred which simply should never have happened.

REORGANISATION

Given this situation, the progress that was achieved on the APT-Ps was remarkable. But, three years after the start of the development work, just as the APT project was beginning to win the enthusiasm of others within CM & EE and trials were starting with the prototypes, a new managerial factor came into play that virtually halted any real progress. This was the total reorganisation of the Mechanical and Electrical Engineering Department. Starting in 1976, this reorganisation took four years to complete.

The objective of the reorganisation was to produce a department that related closely to the main business markets of British Rail. From the late 1970s, a radical restructuring of British Rail had been underway to produce an organisation that focused on rail's markets, rather than its operations. These major markets sectors are InterCity, Network SouthEast (London suburban services), Regional Railways (non-London local and inter-regional passenger services), Freight and European Passenger Services. CM & EE was the first BR department to adopt "sector management", but the reorganisation continued through other parts of the railway and has only recently reached its conclusion, with most staff allocated to the business sectors.

The sector-based reorganisation of CM & EE resulted in traction and rolling stock functions being combined under one Engineer and the division being restructured into three product groups (Freight, InterCity and Suburban). Essentially it remained functionally organised, but focused on three broad business sectors. All staff, including the APT project group, were reallocated within this new structure. So, from being a tightly-knit project group, development work on the APT came to be managed in the same linear progression-type manner as the rest of the department.

The incorporation of the APT project group into the new Traction and Rolling Stock Department not only broke up the cohesion of the team approach, but resulted in many APT engineers finding that their new bosses were the very people who had despised and ridiculed the APT. Not surprisingly many people left for posts which did not involve such uncomfortable circumstances.

This rapidly drained the APT project of its most capable and skilled people, just as the APT was entering the crucial testing and "debugging" phase. At the very point when the project required the strongest focus and greatest resources, those resources were dissipated or lost.

REORGANISING THE APT PROJECT

In 1982, realising that something was seriously wrong with the APT project, the BR Board appointed the engineering consultancy firm of Ford and Dain Ltd to undertake an assessment of the technology and management of the APT project. The consultants considered the technology to be basically sound, but were very concerned about the way in which the work on the APT had become isolated within CM & EE and the fact that some engineers were undertaking work in areas in which they were very inexperienced. The fact that the APT had been a project slotted into a department organised on divisional lines (first functional and then sector/functionally based) was of particular concern. It was felt that the only way to implement a project such as the APT in a large industry like BR was to have a "product champion"[2] with access to a well-backed, strong engineering team. This would involve:

● The appointment of a project manager who had total technical and financial responsibility for the project.

● That project manager would report directly to senior management

● A committed team would be allocated work by the project manager.

Ford and Dain very much supported the project team approach. However, their concept of a project team was somewhat different to the one that had previously existed for the APT. Theirs was one that was compatible with the restructured organisation of CM & EE.

MANAGING INNOVATIVE PROJECTS

In 1982, while Ford and Dain's report was being completed, a new project manager was appointed for the APT. His role was to co-ordinate work on the project by people now in various different sections of M & EE and other BR departments. They were not removed from their sectors to work exclusively on the APT, but the project manager was given the authority and backing to ensure that his work was done. This sort of project management is usually referred to as a matrix organisation. In a matrix organisation, the members of the project team are responsible operationally to their project manager, but they also remain members of their functional department, being responsible to their head of department for the quality of their work and career development.

Using this type of project team overcame the main drawbacks of the original APT project team structure. One main problem with the APT's original project organisation was that, because people were exclusively appointed to the APT Project Group, the skill in that team remained static. The sort of skills needed for different phases of a project change all the time. At the beginning of the APT project, the bulk of the work was in engineering design, but very different skills were needed for testing and debugging. What happened with the APT Group was that the skills that were the strength of the team in the earlier stages of the project became less relevant later on. Most of the APT Project Group had little management experience outside the project itself, so although their engineering experience was extensive, they lacked many of the abilities needed to cope with the development and testing phases of the APT, which called for the cooperation and coordination of people from many different parts of British Rail.

By not creating an isolated team, but drawing people as necessary from within the sectors of M & EE, it was possible to change the skills in the project team to match the differing needs of work as it progressed. Equally, from a staff point of view, this matrix structure provided a settled situation, with none of the disturbances associated with the break-up of a team once the project ended.

Hence, this sort of project team does not have the problem of key people getting out once the end of a project is in sight. As researchers have documented, the matrix

---

[2] The importance of a "product champion" role is a key conclusion in Rothwell. 1977

approach facilitates the gradual development of a project, from research and design through production, without the discontinuity of formally transferring projects from department to department[3]. Overall, the aim of the new management structure for the APT was to combine the experience and continuity of a functional department with the direction and cohesion of a project team. Interestingly, this is virtually the exact management structure used for all major projects by SNCF in France, including the TGV.

As to why the 200kph High Speed Train did not encounter the same problems as the APT, this appears to be because it was technically a much simpler project whose technology fitted in with how the CM & EE department worked. There was a strong, undivided commitment to the HST at all levels in the department and the crucial development and testing stages were over by the time the disruptive effects of the 1976-80 reorganisation of CM & EE began to bite. By that time the HSTs were in series production.

But the HST did suffer from a number of technical bugs which had to be tackled with the trains in passenger service. In particular they suffered from gearbox failures and internal coolant leaks.

The successors to the APT

The effects on the APT's technical bugs of reorganising the train's project structure was substantial. By early 1984 it was running reliably and from August 1984 to early 1985 one APT saw regular passenger service as a relief train. In December 1984 an APT covered the London-Glasgow run in a record three hours and 53 minutes — more than an hour faster than the fastest scheduled train.

In the end, however, success rang hollow. Market conditions had significantly changed, which meant that simply adapting what BR had in the APT was not adequate. Two other factors also played a significant role. The first was government authorisation in 1984 for the electrification of the East Coast Main Line from London to Edinburgh. Unlike the West Coast route, for which the APT had been designed, this line is relatively straight, so tilting coaches are not needed for high speed operations. A strategy therefore developed of reducing the risk involved in the APT's successors by first building a fast non-tilting train for the newly-electrified East Coast route, before tackling the more tricky, highly-curved West Coast line.

The second factor was the new rolling stock procurement policy of British Rail. Until the early 1980s, British Rail organised the design, development, building and testing of new rolling stock itself. This involved, as has been noted, a considerable management task. This has now been replaced by competitive tendering and BREL has been sold to become one of the companies tendering to British Rail for business. The firm winning a tender is now responsible for the design, development and management of the project. BR engineers cooperate with this process, but the responsibility for the project rests with the supplying company and not with BR, as was formally the case.

The shift in design and management responsibility away from its own departments to those of the project's main contractor clearly simplified BR's situation. However,

---

[3] see Twiss. 1980. Ch 7

RECORD-BREAKER: *The 0900 InterCity 225 ex King's Cross on September 26, 1991, was cleared for 140mph and set a new capital-to-capital speed record, arriving in Edinburgh at 1229. The train comprised five coaches plus driving vehicle trailer. Note the distinctive crosses on the buffers as it crosses Relly Mill viaduct, Durham.*

it meant that a whole new learning process had to be undertaken as working and managerial relationships were established with the main contractor.

The first major project to be undertaken using this new policy comprised the Class 91 locomotive and "Mk 4" coaches that made up the InterCity 225, the APT's direct successor. The InterCity 225 (the name reflects its top speed of 225kph) is a much simpler train than the APT. The lower top speed and elimination of the need for body tilt meant that only one innovation was needed. This was a mechanical design for the drive between the locomotive's gearbox and wheels in order to reduce unsprung mass and track wear. The coaches for the InterCity 225 are of conventional steel construction and do not use articulated bogies.

The management structure of the InterCity 225 used an adapted form of the matrix organisation that eventually sorted out the APT's problems. The adaptions were to allow for the increased responsibilities of the companies building the locomotive and coaches. To take the development of the Class 91 locomotive as an example (see Figure 14.1), there were dedicated project teams both in BR and in GEC, which built the train. Each was headed by a Project Director whose task was a managerial one, to ensure that the right people and resources were available. Under them was a Project Engineer in BR, and another in GEC. It was their job to undertake the coordination of engineering skills. Inputs to the project from both BR and GEC were managed by these two key people.

This management structure (coupled with extremely hard work from the individuals concerned) proved capable of meeting the exacting schedule required by the Class 91 project. The design, development and construction of this locomotive took only two years (1986-88). The Class 91 began to be used in passenger service in early 1989 with the first InterCity 225 train entering service on time in October 1989.

In June 1990, British Rail announced plans for the development of high speed trains on the West Coast Main Line, the route for which the APT was originally developed. This involved a £800 million plan to upgrade signalling and track for up to 250kph and develop a new InterCity 250 train. Although aiming for the same sort of speed as was intended for the APT, the InterCity 250 project involves considerable civil engineering work on easing curves. Some of this has already been undertaken. Although body tilt was seen as a possibility, British Rail is still very wary of this, following the reliability problems on the APT's tilt mechanism and would prefer to avoid the need for tilting trains altogether.

Figure 14.1

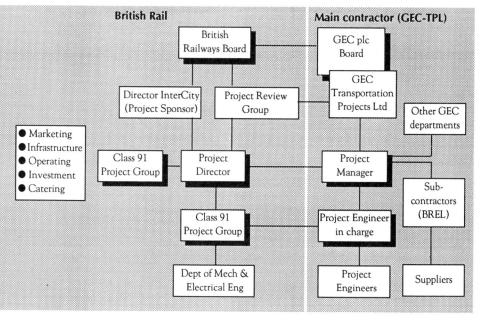

Left: *Management of the Class 91 Electra project within BR, showing the links with the main outside contractor. The Project Director coordinates inputs from the relevant areas of BR. The outside contractor liaises on technical matters with BR's Mechanical and Electrical Engineering Department through the Project Engineer.*

Right: *Management of the Class 91 project within GEC, showing the links with British Rail. The Project Manager is responsible to the Board of GEC Transportation Projects Ltd for all aspects of the project. The Project Engineer is responsible for technical development and liaises with his opposite number in BR. (Adapted by author from information supplied.)*

However, although British Rail put the InterCity 250 out to tender in 1991, the bids were not taken up and the tenders have now expired. InterCity operates under a very tight commercial remit and the 1990-92 recession added further difficulties to the InterCity 250's already marginal investment case. Furthermore, there are now the plans of the re-elected Conservative government (announced in May 1992) to allow private competitors to InterCity to operate on BR tracks. InterCity will not get additional government funding and may well have to face direct rail competition on its own lines. It appears that the InterCity 250 project is too expensive under current commercial and political circumstances. At the time of writing an upgraded InterCity 225 seems more likely than the more ambitious InterCity 250 project. However what trains new private operators are likely to use is another matter. Richard Branson has already expressed serious interest in operating IC 225 (or possibly X 2000) trains to compete with internal air services[4].

Project management lessons

The APT/InterCity 225 case study provides a number of crucial lessons for innovation management. These include:

● Radical technological innovation depends on the availability of strong R & D capabilities and is likely to involve a long period of development, testing and debugging.

● Radical technological innovation, while offering the prospect of major benefits, is inherently risky. There is probably a threshold of the number of innovative features that can be incorporated in one product, beyond which the costs and risks of development become unacceptably high. If possible, the risks of innovating can be reduced by incorporating the minimum amount of innovation at first and then incorporating more into updated versions of the product.

● Technological innovation often requires organisational innovation to succeed, and the commitment of all sections in a company is crucial. British rail was divided over the APT project and the way it was implemented did little to heal those divisions. It was not divided over the IC 225 project and had an appropriate project management organisation.

● Major innovations usually require the coordination of a team approach. The exact form of management must be appropriate to the size, nature and organisation of the company involved, However, two factors seem crucial for success: the use of a dedicated project manager, and support at senior management level through a "product champion".

● It is nearly always necessary to change the composition of the project team through the various stages of the research, design, building, testing and implementation of a new product. This was a serious problem with the APT which was addressed in subsequent projects by the use of a "matrix" team.

● Even if you have devised a potentially successful product, it may not be appropriate for you alone to develop it. The strong involvement of the railway

[4] See Ford. 1992

supply industry in research and development that is now occurring has stimulated a number of important innovations. The old BR-dominated system tended
to relegate the supply industry to little more than a production line operation.

Fast trains: Dominance or diversity?

Returning to a more strategic level, British Rail appears to have shifted away from the
approach of running a technically sophisticated train on existing track, in favour of
upgrading lines to permit high speed operations by relatively conventional stock and
(in the case of linking the Channel Tunnel to London) even planning a new line on
the French and German model.

However, despite the proliferation of high speed line projects in Europe, it would
be wrong to conclude that the convergence has been entirely towards the TGV/ICE
approach. Until about 1985, the French had considered 200kph to be the absolute
limit for trains on upgraded lines. One thing that the APT project proved was that it
was possible to run passenger trains on existing track at up to 250kph. The upgrading
of the East Coast Main line to 225kph and plans for 250kph operations on the West
Coast route have further reinforced this lesson. That this is understood is shown by
the fact that, as part of the TGV Atlantique project, existing lines linking into the new
300kph LGV have been upgraded to 220kph.

The approach of concentrating infrastructure investment to build (or improve
considerably) key trunk lines, and so upgrade a large interrelated network is very much
becoming the standard method to achieve fast rail operations. This allows for the use
of high-performance, medium-tech trains with little technical or business risk.

High-tech tilting trains have proved to be very risky projects. Only Italy and
Sweden have successfully developed tilting trains (Fiat's ETR 450 and ASEA's
X2000). Both took over 20 years to perfect. However, tilting trains do have an
important role to play. There will always be a threshold of passenger traffic below
which it is simply not viable to build even a limited amount of new high speed line.
We now know how to develop new high speed line for the busiest rail corridors. The
challenge is how to extend that benefit to the large network of rail services off the big
trunk routes. In this respect the X2000 and ETR 450 may represent the next step
forward into markets where the TGV and ICE can not go.

References

Ford, Roger. 1992. Virgin's shuttle-beating flyer, Modern Railways, March, pp 123-24

Francis, Arthur and Winstanley, Diana. 1988. Organising Professional Work: the case of Designers in the Engineering Industry in Britain, in Pettigrew, A (ed) Competitiveness and Management Progress. Blackwell, Oxford

Oakley, Mark. 1984. Managing Product Design. Weidenfeld and Nicholson, London

Potter, Stephen and Roy, Robin. 1985. Research and Development — British Rail's Fast Trains. Open University Course T362 Design and Innovation. The Open University Press, Great Britain

Potter, Stephen. 1987. On the Right Lines: the limits of technological innovation. Frances Pinter, London

Roberts, John and Woolmer, T .1984. BR: A European Railway. Transport and Environmental Studies. London

Rothwell, Roy. 1977. The Characteristics of Successful Innovators and Technically Progressive Firms. R & D Management, 7 (3) pp 191-206

Twiss, Brian C. 1980. Managing Technological Innovation, (2nd Edition). Longmans, London

Wickens, Alan H. 1985. Research and Development of High Speed Railways — achievements and prospects. Transport Reviews, Vol 3, No 1, pp 77-112

15.
Technical diversity

The integration of the European high speed train network
Douglas J Puffert, Economist, United States International Trade Commission

1. The problem of technical diversity

AS EUROPEAN high speed train systems spread beyond across national borders, they are confronted with a diversity of technical standards. Much of this diversity is inherited from conventional railways, because the high speed systems usually maintain compatibility with the older systems in power distribution, train control, loading gauge (clearnance tolerance), and other technical parameters. Other aspects of diversity are new and include the variety of designs for high speed train sets.

The problems that technical diversity poses for the development of an integrated European high speed train network are illustrated by the steps taken to develop the Transmanche Super Trains (TMSTs), which will link London through the Channel Tunnel with Paris and Brussels[1]. Although the train sets are based on the French TGVs, they must be compatible with the railway infrastructures of Belgium and southern Britain. Thus they must be able to use not only the 25kV, 50Hz alternating-current (AC) power system of France and the Channel Tunnel, but also the 3kV and 750V direct-current (DC) systems of Belgium and Britain, respectively[2]. Furthermore, in Britain, power will be collected from an electrified third rail, while in France and Belgium it will be collected from two different overhead wire systems, requiring two sets of pantographs. Multiple sets of equipment for the three power supplies will add substantially to the weight of the TMST. Notwithstanding this, the motors will still develop less power from the British and Belgian power systems — 4,300kW and 7,200kW respectively — than from the French system, at 14,000 kW. However, this reduced power potential will not greatly limit operations, for the lower quality trackbed in Britain and Belgium will not permit the high speeds possible in France and through the tunnel[3].

Furthermore, because Britain's clearance tolerances are smaller than those of the Continent, TMSTs will be less capacious than TGVs. TMSTs will also have to

[1] International Railway Journal, February 1990, p10; Railway Gazette International, May 1989, p 337.

[2] The abbreviations V and kV refer to volts and kilovolts, kW to kiloWatts, and Hz to hertz (frequency of alternating current).

[3] Over the next several years, Belgium will construct a new TMST route with a high-quality roadbed and the French system of electrification. This will permit imporved performance for future TMSTs.

accommodate differing platform heights. The presence of five different train-control and signalling systems (the French conventional system, the TGV system, the British and Belgian systems, and a special system for the Channel Tunnel) will lead to further duplication and expense. Finally, the TMST cabs will have control panels presenting information in three languages: French, English, and Flemish.

Taking these issues together, technical diversity will not prevent the linking of multiple national networks, but it will make it more costly to link them, and it will prevent the optimisation of train performance for any one part of the larger network.

These difficulties impose limits on the number of technically diverse railway systems that can be joined together. The technical solution that links London with Paris and Brussels will not work for links among other European cities. The PBKA system, for example, will overlap routes of the TMST as it joins Paris, Brussels, Köln, and Amsterdam. The PBKA system will have train sets compatible with the technical standards of four countries and four electrical power systems, but they will not be compatible with British systems. Passengers will not be able to take a direct high speed train from London to Amsterdam or Köln, let alone other cities on the Continent[4].

Thus, technical diversity will restrict the degree of integration of any future trans-European high speed train network, and the restriction of integration will limit the level of service available to passengers and shippers. On conventional railways, technical diversity can usually be accommodated by changing locomotives at stations near borders. This approach is impossible for high speed trains, because of their integrated train sets and low tolerance for delay. Furthermore, the Channel Tunnel will greatly increase the significance of Britain's variations from Continental standards.

As a result, the TMST and other high speed train projects raise the issue of technical diversity among national railway networks more acutely than at any time since the 19th century battles over track gauge[5].

2. The dimensions of diversity

Conventional and high speed train systems differ in a wide variety of technical characteristics. The characteristics that railway administrators and industry journals cite most often as important for technical harmonisation are the following (see also Table 15.1):

TRACK GAUGE — the distance between rails. Britain and most of continental Europe use the international standard of 4ft 8½ ins (1.435 metres). However, the Iberian countries use 1.668 metres on most routes, Ireland uses 1.600 meters, and Finland and the former Soviet Union use 1.524 metres[6]. The break of gauge at the border of France and Spain has become an increasingly costly

---

[4] Slower through trains will, however, travel through the Channel Tunnel to points beyond Paris and Brussels.

[5] This and other references to the history of track gauge are explored more fully in Douglas J Puffert, The Economics of Spatial Network Externalities and the Dynamics of Railway Gauge Standardization (PhD dissertation, Department of Economics, Stanford University, March 1991).

[6] In addition, there are narrow-gauge (often 1.0 metre) routes in Switzerland, Spain, Portugal, and elsewhere.

barrier as Spain's economy has been integrated into that of the European Community. In view of this, Spain has adopted the international standard gauge for its major high speed lines. Ireland's variant gauge matters much less due to its physical isolation from the European network.

LOADING GAUGE — the set of horizontal and vertical clearance tolerances. Most continental railways use a standard developed by the International Union of Railways (UIC), but Britain still has the narrower clearances developed in the early decades of its railway system. West Germany's new high speed routes (Neubaustrecken) and ICE train sets have a loading gauge broader than the UIC standard.

POWER DISTRIBUTION SYSTEMS — diesel or electric, electric voltage, AC or DC, AC frequency, and means of electric power distribution. France uses 25kV AC at 50Hz on some routes, including the TGVs, but 1.5kV DC on others. Britain recently introduced the same AC system on the London-Edinburgh route, replacing the high speed diesel service, but it uses 750V DC power south of London. Germany, Switzerland, and Austria form a contiguous region using 15kV AC power at $16^2/_3$Hz. By contrast, Portugal, Spain, Denmark, Belgium, and the Netherlands each have systems different from those of their neighbours.

TRAIN-CONTROL SYSTEMS — signalling, automatic stopping, and radio communication between the train cab and control centres. Most countries have their own systems, but efforts are currently under way to develop a standard European Train Control System (ETCS). A related issue is the language used for human communication.

TRACK INFRASTRUCTURE — characteristics such as minimum curve radius, maximum gradients, trueness of layout, smoothness of track, strength of trackbed and bridges, and extent of tunnelling. These characteristics limit the maximum speed, permissible axle-loads, and other characteristics of trains. Track infrastructure varies greatly even within countries, particularly between conventional and high speed track. It also varies among the high speed systems of different countries. High speed trains can sometimes be used on lower-quality track with some sacrifice of performance.

ROLLING STOCK CHARACTERISTICS, such as coupling and braking systems and the design of integrated train sets. While conventional rolling stock usually follows international standards, high speed train sets differ greatly among countries.

ENVIRONMENTAL STANDARDS, such as noise emissions.

OTHER CHARACTERISTICS. Among the other features that differ among railway systems are platform height and length, and organisational matters, such as management, ticketing, and billing systems.

The UIC has set standards for several features of high speed train networks, including track gauge, loading gauge, minimum distance between track centres, maximum gradient, minimum platform length, and maximum axle loads[7]. Work is currently under way to develop international standards for train-control systems[8]. There are currently no standards, or standards-setting projects, in the areas of power distribution and train set design, however.

As Table 15.1 shows, the high speed lines now in service in France, Germany, and Italy have three different sorts of electrical power and different designs of train sets. Local maximum gradients also vary substantially, although all within UIC standards. Because Germany's and Italy's routes include many tunnels, their train sets must be pressure-sealed for passenger comfort when entering and leaving tunnels — but France's train sets are not.

The German ICE train set is notable for departing from the UIC standard loading gauge: it is 3.02 metres wide, rather than 2.91 metres. German Railways has been criticised for this car width but defends its choice on the grounds that a number of connected routes, not only in Germany but also in Austria and Switzerland, will be able to accommodate the wider cars. Germany's Neubaustrecken routes will also be used for fast heavy freight service in vehicles larger than the UIC freight car standard. Thus these routes' roadbed strength, and distance between track centres will also be greater than those of other railways.

Table 15.1.

Selected technical characteristics of major European railway systems

Country	Track Gauge (mm.)	Loading Gauge [1]	Electrical Power [2]	Train Control	High-Speed Train sets
Austria	1435	UIC	15kV 16 2/3 Hz	3	Series 2000
Belgium	1435	UIC	3kV DC	TBL	TMST; PBKA
Denmark	1435	UIC	25kV 50Hz	3	IC3
France:					
Conventional	1435	UIC	1.5kV DC; 25kV 50Hz	KVB	—
High-speed	1435	UIC	25kV 50Hz	TVM	TGV; TMST; PBKA
Germany:					
Conventional	1435	UIC	15kV 16 2/3 Hz	3	—
High-speed	1435	Broad	15kV 16 2/3 Hz	LZB	ICE; PBKA
Great Britain	1435	Narrow	750V DC; 25kV 50Hz	AWS	IC 225; TMST
Italy:					
Current lines	1435	UIC	3kV DC	3	ETR 450
Future lines	1435	UIC	3kV DC; 25kV 50Hz	3	ETR 500
Netherlands	1435	UIC	1.5kV DC	ATB	PBKA
Portugal	1668	Non-UIC	25kV 50Hz	3	(none)
Spain:					
Conventional	1668	Non-UIC	1.5kV and 3kV DC	3	—
High-speed	1435	UIC	25kV 50Hz	3	AVE
Sweden	1435	Broad	15kV 16 2/3 Hz	3	X2000
Switzerland	1435	UIC	15kV 16 2/3 Hz	3	Series 2000

NOTES: [1] UIC indicates the standard of the International Union of Railways. [2] Alternating current unless otherwise indicated. [3] Local standard.

[7] European Conference of Ministers of Transport, High Speed Traffic on the Railway Network of Europe (Report of the International Seminar held in Hanover, Federal Republic of Germany, on 12th-14th April 1986). Paris: ECMT, 1986, pp. 26, 91.

[8] Peter Winter, "The Project for a Unified European Train Control and Protection System," Rail International, vol. 23, no. 6/7, June/July 1992, pp 206-9.

High speed train sets in other countries will also differ from each other, except that Switzerland and Austria will use a common design, and Spain's design is based largely on the French TGV.

3. The economics of diversity

European railway officials are certainly aware that technical diversity will inhibit the integration of a European network of high speed trains. Indeed, the need for greater "coordination, cooperation, harmonisation and standardisation" was a recurrent theme in the addresses of government ministers and railway officials at a 1986 seminar on high speed trains[9], organised by the European Conference of Ministers of Transport (ECMT). The Minister for Transport of the Federal Republic of Germany said, for example:

> "Costly investment in infrastructure will be severely devalued if we fail to remove existing obstacles and to achieve uniformity in the key technical standards."[10]

Perhaps the strongest analysis of the consequences of technical diversity was that of C Davis, EC Commissioner responsible for Environment Policy:

> Suffice it to say that the approach of the various countries active in high speed is not a common one. Herein lies the danger: by developing a whole series of certainly innovative and interesting designs, the benefits of common operation and mass production are placed in jeopardy. Although standardisation has long been an aim in the railway construction industry the progress made in that direction has been less than inspiring. Given the enormous potential for railways on the European level, a potential to open up new markets, a potential to compete effectively with the private car, the concept of an integrated European network must be given pride of place in planning for the future.

What does this mean in practice? To the European Commission, the following points seem to be imperative:

● First, that the various new lines that are being built are properly integrated and are not considered as isolated and separate sections;

● Second, to ensure that the rolling stock is built to certain common norms, so as to ensure that we avoid the absurd possibility of passengers being forced to change trains, because of differing, incompatible technical standards;

● Third, that the possibilities of European cooperation for the design and construction of new trains and other hardware are fully evaluated;

● Fourth, that common marketing and tariff-setting policies are adopted...

The reason for technical diversity, as several participants in the ECMT seminar noted, is that some aspects of railway technology developed independently in different countries. The participants explained this independence as a response to national differences in the characteristics of traffic, but there were at least four

---

[9] European Conference of Ministers of Transport, op. cit.

[10] Dr W Dollinger, Ibid, p 11.

MEETINGS CAN NOT ALWAYS BE AS THIS: *The Italian ETR 500, the German ICE, and the French TGV Atlantique pictured together in Brussels in 1992*

additional reasons.

● First, when national railways adopted their technical standards, they tended to adopt the best practice of the time. Spain's and Russia's broad track gauges, for example, were chosen because the loco-motive technology of the 1840s made such gauges more advantageous than the emerging international standard. Similarly, Germany and other countries introduced special low-frequency AC power systems, rather than use the industrial frequency of 50Hz, because such frequencies were better suited to the AC traction motors of the early twentieth century[11]. Today the industrial frequency is recognised as superior.

● Second, national railways have often preferred to support local industry rather than rely on foreign sources of technology. This is one reason for the separate development of high speed train sets in different countries.

● Third, national differences sometimes reflect historical accidents. For example, the track gauges of different countries, or even of different railways within a country, have often depended on the opinions of the particular engineers hired to construct early routes.

● A fourth reason for the variety in national technical standards is that national railway authorities have usually placed a much higher value on domestic, rather than international, network integration.

[11] Paul A David and Julie Ann Bunn, "The Economics of Gateway Technologies and Network Evolution: Lessons from Electricity Supply History," *Information Economics and Policy*, vol 3 (1988), pp 165-202.

This has affected not only the origin of international technical diversity, but also its persistence. Each national system has a stake in maintaining its own standards, for much of its operating and manufacturing infrastructure is specific to those standards. By contrast, national railway authorities tend not to take account of how their decisions affect other countries or the integration of the European network as a whole.

To put the matter in the language of economics, their decisions do not take account of externalities — the benefits and costs imposed on others. When one railway system chooses the same technical standards as a neighbouring system, the benefits of network integration are shared by both systems. Conversely, when railway systems use different standards, the costs of coping with technical diversity are shared as well.

Thus, as some recent economic research has shown, the presence of "network externalities" can easily lead to economic inefficiency[12]. Even if the total benefits to be gained by having a common European standard outweigh the total costs, it might not benefit any particular national railway system to convert, as some of the benefits go to others.

Thus the calls of officials at the ECMT conference for coordination and standardisation ring hollow. It is noteworthy that none of these officials offered to forego their own national technical standards in favour of those of other countries. Nor can they be expected to do so unless, perhaps, their own countries' internal benefits from conversion exceed the cost.

4. Prospects for the resolution of diversity

This chapter argues that technical diversity among railway systems emerged, and now continues, in part because decisions have reflected national, rather than trans-national, interests. At the present time, the costly diversity that high speed trains inherited from conventional railways is being reinforced through large new capital expenditures. Moreover, new dimensions of diversity are being created as countries develop their own high speed train sets. This development is particularly ironic given the expectation that an emerging high speed train network "represents a powerful

---

[12] This literature also shows that economic processes governed by network externalities may be "path-dependent," in that underlying incentives and technology do not necesasarily lead to a unique, predictable equilibrium outcome. This provides a rationale for understanding how historical accidents, early in the history of a nation's railways, may determine the track gauge and other technical standards. The literature on network externalities and technical standards also notes that there is an inescapable trade-off between realising the benefits of network integration through standardisation, on the one hand, and pursuing technological innovations that go beyond current standards, on the other.

For a discussion of these topics in conjunction with railways, see Douglas J Puffert, The Economics of Spatial Network Externalities and the Dynamics of Railway Gauge Standardization (PhD dissertation, Department of Economics, Standford University, March 1991). For a more general introduction to the economics of network externalities, see either W Brian Arthur, Competing Technologies, Increasing Returns and Lock-in by Small Historical Events, Economic Journal, vol 99, March 1989; or Paul A David, "Some New Standards for the Economics of Standardization in the Information Age", in Partha Dasgupta and Paul Stoneman (ed), Economic Policy and Technological Performance (Cambridge: Cambridge University Press, 1987).

catalyst of European integration"[13].

While the costliness of technical diversity is clear, one should not infer that an increasingly integrated Europe should completely standardise its high speed and conventional railway networks. That might be desirable if Europe were building a railway network for the first time. However, Europe has a huge fixed investment in railway infrastructure, and it would cost many billions of US dollars to convert it all to a single set of standards. The cost of converting Spain's broad track gauge has been estimated at $5 billion, and the cost of changing Britain's narrow loading gauge has been set at £1 billion for the major lines that will carry international traffic. The cost of converting several countries' electrical power systems would be high as well.

Some diversity of train set design would be appropriate, even if the fundamental technical parameters were standardized[14]. This is because high speed routes vary, both in the characteristics of their traffic and in their track infrastructure — particularly the gradients, curvatures, and extent of tunnelling made necessary by physical geography and environmental concerns.

Thus, the emerging European high speed train network should accommodate a certain amount of continuing diversity. A recent UIC publication makes this point in discussing the design of train sets:

> "The objective is not to develop uniform rolling stock which would be difficult to design and costly, itself a fairly theoretical objective. The idea would be to develop well-adapted modular rolling stock for similar groups of routes... Economies of scale can be realised as much at this level as through complete uniformity."[15]

This UIC statement is true as far as it goes, but it takes technical diversity in matters other than train set design for granted. Thus, it does not consider how resolving this diversity could facilitate the development of train sets that could provide direct service among cities throughout the TMST, PBKA, French, German, Swiss, Austrian, Italian, and Spanish high speed networks. The best response to Europe's technical diversity is to accommodate this diversity where necessary, while pressing toward the goal of increasing standardisation.

A strategy of accommodation is being pursued by the German Federal Railways, which is developing a "multi-system" ICE train set, the ICE-M, for service on routes from Belgium and the Netherlands to Austria and Switzerland. This is also the strategy, of course, for the TMST and PBKA train sets. In conventional railways, the Swiss Railways uses a quadri-current locomotive for international Eurocity trains. Britain is developing a special, low-profile car to carry international standard freight containers on routes with low vertical clearances.

Several national railways have chosen to relinquish national for international

---

[13] International Union of Railways, Proposals for a European High-Speed Network, January 1989, p.19.

[14] Francois Lacote, "The Myth of the Universal Train", Rail International, vol. 23, no. 6/7 (Proceedings of Eurailspeed 92 conference), June/July 1992, pp 164-5.

[15] International Union of Railway, Proposals for a European High-Speed Network, January 1989, p. 20.

standards to facilitate their integration into the emerging European network. Belgium will convert to the French electrification system for its portion of the TMST route. Italy recently announced that it will also use that system for new high speed routes. Italy's decision was motivated in part by the inadequacy of its low-voltage DC system for high speed trains.

The most notable example of technical conversion is Spain, which is adopting the international track gauge for its major high speed routes, even though it will be some years before these routes are linked to France's TGV network. Spain is also adopting the French electrification system and a variation of the TGV train set design. Spain will accommodate its internal diversity in gauge by introducing high speed rolling stock with adjustable wheels that can fit both gauges. In recent years Spanish Railways has sought government funds to change the gauge of conventional railways as well. Although funds have been denied, the railway system is preparing for eventual conversion by using sleepers suitable for both gauges wherever track is renewed.

European standardisation is also being pursued under the leadership of the Commission of the European Communities. A project for a unified European Train Control System (ETCS) is already well under way[16]. In response to a provision in the Maastricht Treaty calling for "interoperability" within trans-European networks, the Commission is currently preparing an extensive directive listing parameters to be standardised on high speed trains[17]. According to a member of the Commission, this directive will not require total standardisation but only "a sufficiently clear level of technical compatibility to enable those who wish to send their trains over the whole of the network", without being hindered by "technical obstacles of a bygone era"[18].

The extent of technical integration that will result from these efforts remains to be seen. If Europeans approve the Maastricht Treaty and pursue increasing economic, political, and cultural integration, then they may well wish to pursue a more integrated high speed train network as well. In both these efforts towards integration, the legacy of past national differences will affect the extent to which Europe is brought together.

---

[16] Peter Winter, "The Project for a Unified European train Control and Protection System", Rail International, vol.23, no. 6/7, June/July 1992, pp 206-9.

[17] Raymond Mourareau, "High-Speed Technical Standardisation Commission Proposal", Rail International, vol. 23, No. 6/7, June/July 1992, pp 186-195.

[18] Karel Van Miert, "Opening Address" (Eurail Speed 92 Conference), Rail International, vol. 23, no. 6/7, June/July 1992, pp. 7-8.

References

Arthur,W B, "Competing Technologies, Increasing Returns, and Lock-in by Small Historical Events," Economic Journal, vol. 99, March 1989, pp. 116-31.

David, PA, "Some New Standards for the Economics of Standardisation in the Information Age," in Partha Dasgupta and Paul Stoneman (ed.), Economic Policy and Technological Performance (Cambridge: Cambridge University Press, 1987).

David, PA and Bunn, J A "The Economics of Gateway Technologies and Network Evolution: Lessons from Electricity Supply History," Information Economics and Policy, vol. 3 (1988), pp. 165-202.

European Conference of Ministers of Transport, High-speed Traffic on the Railway Network of Europe (Report of the International Seminar held in Hanover, Federal Republic of Germany, on 12th-14th April 1986). Paris: ECMT, 1986.

International Union of Railways, Proposals for a European High-Speed Network, January 1989, p. 19. [place of publication not known]

Puffert, DJ, The Economics of Spatial Network Externalities and the Dynamics of Railway Gauge Standardization (Ph.D. dissertation, Department of Economics, Stanford University, March 1991).

Rail International, vol. 23, no. 6/7 (Proceedings of Eurailspeed 92 conference), June/July 1992. Note: The entire issue consists of conference proceedings. The following items cited in my paper are from this issue:

Lacote, F, "The Myth of the Universal Train," Rail International, vol. 23, no. 6/7 (Proceedings of Eurailspeed 92 conference), June/July 1992, pp. 164-5.

Mourareau, R, "High-Speed Technical Standardisation Commission Proposal," Rail International, vol. 23, no. 6/7, June/July 1992, pp. 186-195.

Van Miert, K, "Opening Address" (Eurail Speed 92 conference), Rail International, vol. 23, no. 6/7, June/July 1992, pp. 7-8.

Winter,P, "The Project for a Unified European Train Control and Protection System," Rail International, vol. 23, no. 6/7, June/July 1992, pp. 206-9.

16.
A question of image

The design of high speed trains
John Heskett, Professor, Illinois Institute of Technology, Chicago

WHEN CONSIDERING the design of modern high speed trains, it is interesting to place them in the context of the historical development of railway design, in an effort to identify some of the key influences that either have a valid continuity or require change.

Despite the use of terms such as "the Iron Horse", early locomotives had no precedents and it took a considerable period of experiment for a distinct visual form to emerge. In the earliest stages, they were basically beam engines on wheels and a distinct form recognisable as a steam locomotive emerged slowly through a process of trial and error.

In Britain, where the first substantial network evolved, many railway companies competed for business on routes between the same cities, with, for example, three separate lines between the cities of London and Birmingham. The appearance of locomotives and rolling stock, which were generally built by the railway companies in their own workshops, and of stations, their staff, and the trackside environment, were therefore all important as selling points in a highly competitive environment. Consequently, every British railway company developed an overall livery and appearance that was unique and distinctive.

It was not, however, a uniform process applicable to every country. Factors such as differences in geographical conditions, the economic and business structure of railways and their markets, and varying national traditions brought wide variations in how that basic steam technology was shaped into a visual form. In the USA, for example, a different pattern of evolution in relation to the country's distinct circumstances led to considerable variations in the form of locomotives, rolling stock and equipment, compared with, say, Britain. Further differences emerged in Europe and other continents.

By the early 20th century in Britain, a tradition of clean-lined locomotives of distinctive form, with paintwork in company colours, polished brass-work and decorative identification provided well-established company images. The decline of railways against growing competition from road, and later, air transport similarly renewed emphasis on visual form as a means of capturing public attention. The trend to streamlining in the 1920s and 1930s had some technical rationale, with wind tunnel tests used as justification, but marketing and advertising image was also a fundamental concern.

Three basic streamlined shapes emerged that still provide a fundamental typology

Gresley's A4 Pacific Silver Fox *hauls the* Flying Scotsman *northbound in the 1950s*

of locomotive form: the forward wedge; the rounded frontal plane; and the bullet- or torpedo-shape. There have also frequently been combinations of these types.

The forward wedge was typified by Sir Nigel Gresley's A4 Pacific locomotive of 1935 for the London and North Eastern Railway that set a new world speed record for steam locomotives. Gresley was heavily influenced by a railcar for SNCF by Ettore Bugatti of 1934. In Germany, Count Kruckenberg, who had experience as an aircraft and airship designer, developed what was known as the "Rail-Zeppelin" in the late 1920s, from which high speed railcars, the round-fronted *Flying Hamburger* of 1932 were developed for Deutsche Reichsbahn. By 1937, Kruckenberg had another prototype railcar that was torpedo-shaped and strikingly modern, with flush doors, double-glazed windows and air-conditioning. The war prevented its further development.

In the USA, the love affair with the automobile put heavy pressure on railroads in the period after the First World War. Prominent outside consultants were often used in an attempt to revitalise a declining competitive image. One of the most prolific designers was Otto Kuhler. Two examples of his work are locomotives for the Lehigh Railroad and the famous Hiawatha series for the Milwaukee Railroad. Among other well-known consultants, Raymond Loewy did a series of designs in flowing, streamlined form for the Pennsylvania Railroad, while Henry Dreyfuss designed steam locomotives for the New York Central's crack train, the *Twentieth Century Limited*, with spotlights illuminating the wheels and linkage to provide eye-catching imagery by night.

Changes in motive power and competition from the automobile were the driving force behind design innovations in the USA. Union Pacific's Challenger cuts a dramatic image, with its distinctive style and observation car, at Crestline, Utah. See also other pictures, Chapter 7.

Fundamental changes in motive power provided further opportunities for dramatic changes in form. The Union Pacific developed a petrol-engined unit for the City of Salina of 1934, followed two months later by an outstanding design, the diesel-powered Burlington Zephyr for the Chicago, Burlington and Quincy Railroad. Both attracted enormous crowds when put on display across the country. The future, in fact, lay with diesel power and a new unit displayed by General Motors at the New York World Fair of 1939 dominated the market for many years, providing an efficient but standardised means of power in what became a period of serious decline and contraction. In Europe too, the years after the Second World War saw a similar pattern of decline in many countries.

What emerges strongly, even from a brief historical overview, is that design in all aspects has been important whenever railways have been in a competitive situation. Designs can adapt a basic technology to many contexts, and be a powerful means of distinctiveness and differentiation. Much else may have changed, but that central fact still remains true.

174

At present, there is the prospect of a revival of railways in many countries as a major competitive form of transport over short and medium distances. The concept of the high speed train was first established in the public mind through publicity for the Tokyo Olympic Games of 1964, the first games in which television played a central role, bringing the event to a world audience. In general background programmes on Japan, a most startling image was the Shinkansen, the bullet train of Japanese National Railways, introduced in 1964 to coincide with the games. Above all, it was a potent image of the emergence of Japan as a major technological power, with its futuristic shape streaking through the countryside at high speed on purpose-built track, and a range of services and standard of comfort contrasting sharply with European and American railways at that time.

Japanese railways were heavily damaged in the war and had to be almost completely rebuilt. But as early as 1953, work began on a new generation of energy saving shapes for monocoque-built trains to run at high speeds. This early work was a basis for the emergence of the new high speed train.

Designs for the Shinkansen were primarily the work of JNR engineers and the construction companies involved, with some outside consultants. It is important to emphasise, however, that the process of design in the development and subsequent refinement of the Shinkansen differs in major respects from Europe.

JNR had established a Design Committee in 1958 to identify design needs throughout the system and provide advice on potential solutions. Although most JNR design staff have engineering backgrounds, outside consultants with expertise in industrial design, interiors and even fashion are regularly appointed. But the concept of design is not necessarily limited to the trains themselves. In an extraordinary project begun in 1977, an industrial designer studied colour psychology, public preference for colours, cleaning and economic maintenance, as the basis of a programme to make trains fit their environment better. Different colour schemes for different lines and contexts were intended to make trains part of a totally harmonious environment — a continuing emphasis in Japanese culture.

This approach is very different from the concept of corporate identity that has dominated much design thinking by European railway management in recent decades. In fact, JNR has no overall corporate identity programme in that sense.

Design is not intended to have overall impact, with once-and-for-all solutions valid for all projects, or even any single major project. Instead, there is a constant rolling programme, selecting problems one at a time, such as particular aspects of drive units, coaches, stations, services and facilities, investigating them in detail, and proposing solutions best fitted to particular circumstance. In 1957, for example, the external liveries of commuter coaches were redesigned as part of a colour-coding system for each route, that extended to signage, maps and timetables. In the early Sixties, seating was examined, with ergonomic studies of height and weight percentiles for each category of passenger traffic — express, limited express, and commuter. Different layouts were examined and determined for each category.

Other elements were similarly considered — in 1966, interior fittings such as handles, racks, and ash trays; in the late 1960s, an in-depth analysis of eye-contact, height and sight-lines to improve information boards and signage; in 1972, toilet facilities. Interiors received a major examination in 1980, and lighting in 1982. Policy decisions were subsequently implemented in new stock, with existing stock systematically retrofitted in periodical major refits.

This step-by-step process is a very distinctive Japanese approach to design. The Shinkansen stock on the Tokkaido line, for example, had been through two major refits and thirty-three minor changes by 1982, enabling constant improvement to be possible. Lines built later also have purpose-built units that vary in considerable detail from other lines.

However, some features of the Shinkansen did not apply to normal railway stock. High operating speeds, with close interval running, required new approaches. For example, automatic doors for coaches, with waiting points for each clearly marked on platforms, enabled a transfer of passengers with minimum of delay. Toilet facilities had to follow the aircraft model, with a retention tank, rather than using the track as a disposal system.

Problems emerged with operating experience and as the system extended that had not been foreseen. The radio link to the cab and computer control from a central control room made driving simpler and ensured an outstanding safety record in operation.

But there were problems of boredom among drivers, who had a very limited field of vision through the narrow windows of the cab, and had little to see and do. Experiments were made to enlarge windows, even to have television cameras giving a larger view, but, for a time, without success.

Another difficulty appeared when the Joetsu line, the second major extension of the system, was being constructed. For the first time, trains had to run through long tunnels. The high speed and different pressure levels in the tunnels caused difficulties with blow-back from the toilet tanks, that had some alarming consequences, before a solution was found.

A second phase of stock is now in widespread use, which has built on experience in operation and the incremental improvements in design. The trains have a sleeker pointed nose on the drive-units, and the problem of drivers' field of vision has been solved. Improvements in technology enabled the control panel to be reduced in size and the driver's seat to be moved six inches closer to the window. This simple solution gives the better, enlarged angle of view for drivers that was sought earlier. There are also new double-deck coaches for the Green Cars, the first-class service, with digital display units in the coaches showing a range of information such as distance to the next station, the speed of the train, and the time remaining until arrival at the next station or the final terminal. Green car seating can be reconfigured by passengers to enable, for example, a group of businesspeople to have a small conference en route.

Soon, there will be a third generation of Shinkansen trains which will improve standards still further. However, there is clear evidence that more than a quarter of a century of successful operation has brought the system on its main routes almost to a point of saturation. There is now planning for a maglev system to run parallel to the Shinkansen and provide an even faster service.

JNR is now partly privatised, with Shinkansen services detached from the rest of the system. In a sense this was made easier by the fact that, in contrast to the

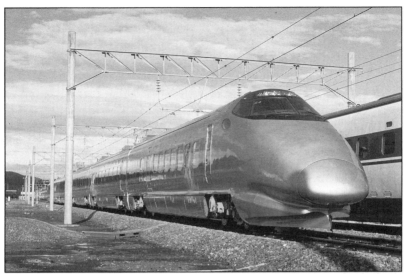

The later Shinkansen trains have a sleeker nose and improved field of vision for the driver

nationalised systems of Europe with their centralist approach to design, JNR had no overall corporate identity policy to which all aspects of its design conformed. Instead, its image emerged from the sum total of solutions to clearly defined problems. In fact, the emphasis was not on image, but on on quality of service to passengers and staff conditions, expressed, again in characteristic fashion, in great attention to detail, and with design as a critical factor. Identity emerges from this basis, rather than being superimposed as a general approach.

The British experience of designing high speed trains is very different from Japan, and has been a story both of substantial success and also of highly publicised failure.

Planning for new generation of trains began in 1967 with the Advanced Passenger Train (APT), based on radically new technology. Gas turbine engines developed in the aerospace industry with lightweight building techniques were to achieve high speed performance without the need for an electrical catenary system. A tilting mechanism in the train would enable existing track to be used at unprecedented high speeds, drastically reducing timings over major routes. However, as discussed in Chapters 8 and 14, theory did not translate so easily into practice. A prototype built in 1972 had considerable problems with its engines, that were exacerbated with the oil crisis of 1973-4.

The research team established for the APT project was substantially recruited from the aircraft industry and had therefore not graduated via the traditional route of railway engineering training. There were continual disputes with the old guard of railway engineers who criticised the attempts to make a great leap forward to a train capable of 150mph, with all the risks of untried technology. Instead they advocated a more conventional approach for a train capable of 125mph, based on railway

The ill-fated APT lacked a distinctive image, with a wedge-shaped front and badly placed windows

engineering principles, rather than those of the aircraft industry. So great was the confusion that in 1970, British Rail management also gave the go-ahead for this more conventional concept, known as the High Speed Train (HST). A prototype for this was also in service by 1972.

Meanwhile, the APT programme was also bedevilled by a long-running dispute with the rail drivers' union (ASLEF) about pay and conditions for operating the new trains. When testing eventually began, far behind schedule, the oil crisis made its propulsion redundant and necessitated a switch to electrical power. Extensive engineering redesign further delayed the project and resulted in a reduced maximum speed of 135mph. Moreover, the development and testing programme continued to be plagued by technical problems and union obstruction.

When, eventually, the APT was rushed into service in December 1981, as Britain's answer to the TGV, introduced in France three months earlier, the rival HST had been in service for four years and was providing new levels of speed and ride.

Curiously, for all its new technology, the APT did not have a very distinctive image. Its wedge-shaped front end had windows that were clumsily spaced, many aspects of its interiors were very conventional, and its livery was ill-conceived.

Questions of image, however, were a minor problem compared with technical inadequacies in operation. More than £37 million in development funding had been spent on the APT, but there were still fundamental flaws that crippled the project and, within two months, led to its humiliating collapse and abandonment.

Apart from union resistance, two major problems contributed to the failure of the APT. One was the attempt to adapt new technology from one context to another, which although not impossible, requires considerable management understanding and skill if it is to be successful. This was amplified by the traditional engineering base of the British railway industry, with its own workshops, traditions and procedures, heavily rooted in the steam age. They had great difficulty in working to tolerances which would have been second nature in the aircraft industry.

Secondly, pressure on the project from a marketing point of view led to the train's introduction before it was fully tested and all problems had been ironed out. Marketing dominates engineering in much of modern industry, with results, as in this case, that are frequently disastrous.

In contrast, British Rail's High Speed Train had the advantage of new but well-proven diesel technology and a high-profile image. For the latter, British Rail went to the London-based design consultancy, Pentagram, whose chief industrial designer, Kenneth Grange, headed the programme.

The dimensions of the HST were, of course, restricted by the overall spatial limitations of the infrastructure — factors such as loading gauges and platform clearance. The technical brief given to Grange by British Rail required a front cab window made of flat glass, which, because of air pressure at high speed, was strictly limited in size. The driver's seat was to be centrally placed in the cab. The economics of high speed running were a critical consideration, since the power required sharply increases with every extra ten miles per hour of speed. So although only commissioned for what Grange once called "a nose job" — in other words, the exterior styling — finding an appropriate style led through aerodynamic calculations and wind tunnel tests. The resulting form therefore had strong technical support and the prototype when constructed, set a new world speed record during test runs.

Grange's initial design successfully fulfilled its brief but was not put into production. At this point, the archaic system of British labour relations imposed its bizarre logic. Steam locomotives had historically required both a driver and a fireman for their function, and when diesel power was first introduced the unions insisted that two operatives be retained in the cab, even though one was superfluous. The drivers' union also insisted that this system of double-manning be retained in the HST. When the management gave way in the dispute, a redesign was necessary to accommodate both driver and his "fireman" side-by-side.

The decision meant the front window had to be reconfigured, so both men could have the same angle of vision. Grange's initial concept relied on a smooth air flow to both sides of the window for aerodynamic efficiency. Two problems now emerged: a larger window required two pieces of glass, with a central bar that obstructed forward vision; secondly, the wider window obstructed air flow, with adverse effects on performance. *See pictures, Chapter 14.*

Grange tried numerous possibilities until two breakthroughs enabled a solution. First, a new type of glass became available that could be used without a window bar.

However, the airflow problem still remained. The solution, once conceived, was very obvious. Kenneth Grange recalls nervously asking the chief mechanical engineer of British Rail why it was necessary to have buffers on the HST. They were assumed to be necessary because trains in Britain had had buffers since time immemorial. Their function enabled locomotives to be detached from trains to work different configurations of coach and goods stock. Because the HST was to be permanently coupled to its carriages as a complete unit, however, it was realised that buffers were no longer necessary.

This decision taken, it became possible in further wind-tunnel tests to divert the air flow over the top of the unit, with even greater aerodynamic efficiency resulting. The clean appearance of the new units, and their improved performance provided British Rail with a very potent image of modernity and revitalisation.

On his design, Kenneth Grange wrote:

"When a company is in retreat, torn by arguments and ridiculed by the Press, the morale of its workforce is soon eroded. This in turn affects attitudes to customers, and the downward spiral accelerates. The High Speed Train — in reality only a small part of the vast efforts made to improve British Rail — has re-awakened some of the old railway pride."

Although only a part of a programme of improvement, the HST was a critical factor in communicating the fact of change to the public by the exciting quality of its imagery, which reflected the real improvements it brought in performance.

The experience of Grange with the HST is also reflected in some aspects of the design of the trains for the cross-Channel route between London and Paris. Because of different standards in key infrastructure dimensions, the smaller British loading gauge being a major factor, and differing power systems, existing TGV designs can not be used on the route. So the basic TGV technology has to be adapted to the specific needs of the Chunnel route.

A competition for the train design was held with three design companies invited from each of the countries involved, France, Britain and Belgium. On the basis of initial concept proposals submitted by the nine participants, the British design company, Jones-Garrard, was chosen for the job. One of the principals of the company, Roger Jones, has identified three major phases in the project so far.

In the first phase, Jones-Garrard also began with extensive work on interpreting the technical brief provided by the railways. Clay models were used in wind-tunnel tests to develop basic information and explore possibilities, and their final concept form proved to be highly efficient in aerodynamic terms. Michael Rodber, a director of Jones-Garrard commented:

"These trains will be operating for thirty years and the whims of fashion are not appropriate in determining its shape."

Once parameters for the most efficient external form were established, it had to be developed in structural terms, which required many detailed models and close cooperation with engineers from the three participating countries. This element of designers' work, the detailed cooperation with other disciplines necessary to realise the concept, also often goes unnoticed, and requires considerable managerial as well as creative skills.

A full, detailed technical brief was given to the designers at this stage, which required modification of many ideas. In addition, the brief was also subject to modification as the work proceeded and problems emerged through detailed consideration. A series of regular meetings ensured constant cooperation and detailed design ideas were worked out for discussion and agreement, using small-scale models.

With agreement finally reached on the form, a second phase began, in which drawings were digitised and full-scale mock-ups prepared to elaborate the structure. Again, at this stage, working in full-scale also required further detailed modification and adaptation.

By the time the Chunnel train was proposed, the archaic arrangement of two men in the cab had been resolved in Britain and the driver's position could be centrally placed in the cab. A basic consideration was the safety of the driver, so the nose had to be able to withstand low impact forces. This required an angle different from that of the more acute aspect of the driver's window. It therefore became possible for the driver's cab to be clearly delineated on the upper part of the nose, with the form able to diverge from the familiar symmetrical wedge of the HST.

Another safety factor related to the driver's window. At speeds of 300kph, any solid hitting the window is highly dangerous. Material can be thrown up from the track or come loose from a passing train, and there is always the problem of vandalism, of objects thrown at trains from bridges or the trackside. To protect drivers, the front window was made of thick glass with as small an area as possible. At the side, another small window enables drivers to look back along the train. The interior details of the cab were also completed at this stage. With small windows and heavy padding (Roger Jones has called it womb-like), a possible problem was that the cab could be claustrophobic. However, when in the driver's seat, the field of vision is quite large.

Following approval by the railway companies, a third phase began with the designers working with the group of construction companies contracted to build the trains, headed by GEC Alsthom, of Paris. With the definition of the design on a CAD system, a new problem became apparent. The smaller British loading gauge emphasised the need to maximise floor width to make the most of the available space. French manufacturers, with a different loading gauge, built their coaches differently. This affected the basic cross-section for the train. Modifications again became necessary, which also affected the roof-line, and so the form of the train as a whole. The nose became a resolution of all the different angles, representing in a very real sense the totality of factors that had to be taken into consideration.

Through each phase, as the degree of technical refinement became more demanding, the design evolved in a process of constant input, feedback and review.

However, as with the HST, it was not simply technical considerations which dominated the design process. There was also the need to create a form for the train that would provide a visible image to capture the public imagination. It would have to cover not only the exterior and engineering construction, but also interiors and livery in a total concept. In the words of Roger Jones:

"The whole approach was, 'What happens when you decide to go on this journey to Paris?' We must control that, from the decision onwards, and make sure that's an exciting experience."

A basic consideration in the initial brief was to produce a solution that would be futuristic and exciting.

Examining models can only give a limited impression of what the final reality will be. Even full-scale mockups tend to be seen from ground level, which radically alters the perspective. Mockups of station platforms to British, French and Belgian heights, all of which differ, were therefore constructed to give a passenger's eye view and simulate their impression, when they first see the train and actually walk along its length.

With the construction of an extension for the Channel Tunnel trains at the London terminal, Waterloo Station, it also became possible to work with the architect to present a strong image to the public. The final platform stands on the inside of the train, allowing it to stand fully visible, dramatically floodlit behind a glass wall. [meaning?]

The idea that a train is not only a convenient visual image for publicity and advertising purposes, but that it represents the possibility of a "totality of experience", is important. It provides one of the outstanding opportunities for the new generation of high speed trains in renewing the public's belief in rail travel as a viable alternative to other forms of transport.

For example, the reality of air travel increasingly diverges from the image projected in advertising, of speed and convenience, comfort and caring. The reality is increasingly one of inconvenience in reaching airports, and once in the air, of discomfort, indifferent service and, sometimes on long flights, of squalor. Packed into limited space, passengers are subjected to a routine of so-called "in-flight entertainment", that has little relevance to their needs and denies any experience of the marvellous thing flight can be.

In recent decades, railway management has generally looked to the example of air transport in many aspects of change and remodelling. Stations and information systems often deliberately resemble airports; seating-layouts and the pattern of staff uniforms, services and announcements similarly imitate airlines. This can be highly successful, as with SNCF's very efficient TGV network.

An important element in the new generation of high speed trains and their associated infrastructure, however, is the possibility of changing this airline-derived pattern and once again establishing standards for railways, in their own right, as leaders rather than imitators.

For example, it is possible on a train to watch the landscape as it passes, to meet people, to dine and drink in comfort when you want to — in short, to have available a whole range of services which have nothing to do with the rigidities and artificiality of in-flight entertainment. In Germany, for example, Deutsche Bundesbahn has been experimenting with different configurations of coach layout and facilities to explore new possibilities.

Ultimately, railway design, as any other form of design, must reconcile a range of factors, such as engineering, environmental, economic and marketing considerations. In the final analysis, however, it is user satisfaction by means of a distinct product and service that will be the best guarantee of vitality in the proposed high speed network.

The possibility of travel as a distinct and pleasurable experience has always been at the heart of the great romance with railways that made it both such a powerful function and symbol in people's lives. The challenge to recreate this possibility now faces designers in developing new concepts and imagery that will not only be economic, but will also capture the imagination of the public by providing a genuine alternative in terms of quality of experience.

17.
Buildings befitting their station

Professors Jeffrey Richards and John M MacKenzie, Department of History, University of Lancaster

Part I: Historical context
Jeffrey Richards

"Over every railway station the flag of Hope waves bright."

SO WROTE railway enthusiasts Foxwell and Farrer in 1889. They attributed almost all the distinctive characteristics of the 19th century to the advent of the railways and in particular to railway speed — the spirit of competition, the cheapness of necessities, the unprecedented growth of population, the rise of realism in art, the ending of feudalism and the introduction of freedom[1].

While some of their claims may have been modified in the light of historical research, there can be no doubt that the railways in the 19th century opened up and unified nations and continents, transporting people and goods speedily and in bulk and, in the words of Sydney Smith, "abolishing time, distance and delay". Despite the recent preeminence of road and air transport, the railways remain the safest, the most efficient and agreeable, and the most environmentally friendly means of transporting people and goods in bulk. The age of the high speed train is about to demonstrate that fact once more, and beyond doubt, so that the flag of Hope can be raised again above the railway station... but what kind of station?

Theophile Gautier wrote of stations:

"These cathedrals of the new humanity are the meeting points of nations, the centre where all converge, the nucleus of the huge stars whose iron rays stretch out to the ends of the earth"[2].

Like cathedrals, they are places where all sorts and conditions of men and women mingle. They are the gateway to the countryside, the seaside, the wider world. They are the point of arrival for work, the point of departure for business, pleasure, foreign travel. Historically, stations have come in all shapes and sizes. There have been passenger stations and goods stations, public stations and private stations, racecourse stations and port stations, factory stations and military stations, coal stations and milk stations, hospital stations and school stations, pilgrim stations and royal stations, mail

---

[1] E Foxwell and T C Farrer. 1889. Express Trains English and Foreign. London. pp70-72

[2] Jean Dethier ed. 1981. All Stations. London. 6

stations and necropolis stations.

All stations are simultaneously technological and metaphysical, romantic and prosaic, communal and individual, places to work and places to dream[3]. The advent of high speed trains means that far more emphasis will be placed on the big city terminal stations, since there will be fewer stops and much less division of function.

It is no coincidence that temple, cathedral and palace are the images regularly adduced to describe the great city stations. For they dominated the landscape, both physical and mental, of 19th century people. To create them, whole swathes of housing were demolished and the railway lines demarcated new areas and sub-divisions in the inner city as the companies drove their rails as close as possible to the centre. It is this centrality which gives railways an important edge over airports, usually built outside the city and requiring additional journey time. The arrival of a station always served as a magnet for business, hotels and places of entertainment and therefore the station has latterly been used as an engine for inner city regeneration.

Whatever hardship was caused as they were being built, once they were completed stations represented a source of unending variety and delight. Like medieval cathedrals, Victorian stations combined bold and innovative modernity with heroic and comforting traditionalism. The modernity came in the form of the technological skill that went into the creation of the trainsheds, the great single and double-span roofs for which unsung engineers solved complex structural problems of weight and distribution with breathtaking brilliance. They also boldly utilised the new materials of iron and glass to construct the naves and transepts of the cathedral stations. The frontages were the work of architects and they built not in new styles but in revival styles — Gothic, Renaissance, Classical, Baroque — both to promote the civic image of the rival railway companies and to reassure those concerned about the newness of it all.

For, although it is hard for us to credit it now, many people believed that if you travelled faster than 30mph, you might actually burst and be scattered across the railway tracks. Those who, like me, suffer from catarrh, find that the speed of the TGV in tunnels creates the sensation of the ears bursting — so one can have some sympathy with this fear.

Revival styles in architecture did not mean lack of imagination or inventiveness; quite the reverse. They meant a prodigal outpouring of both. For the Victorian style was picturesque eclecticism, the creative reuse of all previous styles, putting the best of the past at the service of the present. It was a form that revelled in colour and contrast, drama and dissonance, boldness and individuality, an unleashing of the imagination, but always within the anchoring framework of rules and conventions. Since the unforgivable primal sin of the Victorians was to be boring, they poured their ingenuity into the provision of intricate wrought-iron work, stained glass, mullioned windows, canopies, balustrades, turrets, spires and crenelations. Such embellishments were functionally redundant but they engaged the eye and gladdened the soul. As John Ruskin observed:

---

[3] All these aspects are explored in Jeffrey Richards and John MacKenzie. 1986. The Railway Station: a social history. Oxford

"The most beautiful things in the world are the most useless — peacocks and lilies for instance."

It was this profusion of decoration that helped to give the railway station its distinctive mystique.

When, after World War One, in a self-conscious rejection of Victorian ornamentalism, architects turned to the Modern movement, they evolved a wholly different style based on purity, austerity and simplicity of form. It inspired some notable achievements — in Britain, Broadcasting House, the Hoover Factory, Odeon cinemas and tubular furniture — but with the aesthetic Puritanism underlying the new outlook went dogma, intolerance and the demand for uniformity.

The objective was a form which would epitomise the new age — the age of the Common Man. It did not matter to architectural gurus that the Common Man liked decoration. Roger Fry, for instance, announced that the emotional life of the populace "had been drugged by the sugared poison of pseudo-art". Fry deliberately wrote the next part of his essay in a railway refreshment room, declaring:

"One must remember that public places of this kind merely reflect the average citizen's soul, as expressed in his home."

Oozing with contempt, he proceeds to list the room's decoration: the stained-glass windows, patterned lace curtains, Greco-Roman wall mouldings, imitation 18th century satin brocade wallpaper, potted plants, neatly arranged tables:

"I say their contemplation can give no one pleasure; they are there because their absence would be resented by the average man who regards a large amount of futile display as in some way inseparable from the conditions of that well-to-do life to which he belongs or aspires to belong. If everything were merely clean and serviceable he would proclaim the place bare and uncomfortable."[4] So whether they liked it or not, people were going to be presented with a new architecture that would be classless, functional and uniform.

Architectural extremists like Berthold Lubetkin declared that "the admiration of aesthetically beautiful things is bourgeois"[5]. He set out to produce ugly things as a conscious proletarian rejection of such notions. He and his fellows sought above all else a style-less style. So began the procession of flat, boring, sterile and characterless buildings which have afflicted us, particularly since World War Two. This is undeniably a style, but it has no "style" as such (which I would define as a combination of elegance, authority and wit). As the architectural historian J Mordaunt Crook has written, we, in the 20th Century, must rediscover what the 19th century learned so painfully that "architecture begins where function ends"[6]. That means decoration, colour, variety, imagination; not bare, square boxes. It is something the Post-Modernists are discovering and implementing, to return joy to architecture. It tells us a good deal about the relative values of the 19th and 20th centuries that where the Victorians modelled their stations on cathedrals and palaces, Modern Man has modelled his on shopping centres and office blocks.

The station builders of the future would do well to consider very carefully the achievements of their Victorian forbears. There are encouraging signs that they are doing so. The architecture of a station conveys not just an aesthetic message. It often makes a political and ideological statement too. The heavily monumental stations built in Russia to replace buildings damaged or destroyed during World War Two were designed in a style that has been dubbed "Stalin's Doric revival" and bears all the hallmarks of the totalitarian regime — the massive immovable bulk of the state apparatus and the mindless uniformity of the faceless proletariat. Milan Station, designed in what one critic called "a megalomaniac delirium", remains a monument to the ambitions and grandiose aspirations of Italian Fascism. The stately Victorian Terminus in Bombay, the "St Pancras of the Orient", embodies the imperishable spirit of the British Raj in India.

Modernist architecture proclaimed internationalism, but an internationalism of the worst kind — a bland, featureless, lowest common denominator internationalism epitomised by the anonymous tower block station — Rotterdam Central, London Euston, Warsaw Central, Berne Central, München, Leningrad Finland Station, which could be anywhere and convey no sense of place at all.

Until recently, Paris Gare Montparnasse would have been on this list, but as part of its reconstruction to accommodate the TGV, the faceless tower block frontage is being embellished with concrete turrets and a perspex arch. As Sir John Betjeman, the British poet laureate and patron saint of railway preservation, said: "Railway stations

---

[4] Roger Fry. 1937. Vision and Design. London 60-64

[5] Architectural Review 71, 1932. p207

[6] J Mordaunt Crook. 1987. The Dilemma of Style. London. p11

are most important in giving places an identity."[7] Stations should be readily identifiable as belonging to the city or country where they are located. One cannot but be struck by the Spanishness of Toledo, the Dutchness of Amsterdam Central or the Norseness of Copenhagen Central, that sea-girt castle of a medieval Danish warrior king magically set down in the nation's capital. As we move closer and closer in economic and political union, it is more than ever essential that we maintain and promote cultural plurality and national diversity: nowhere more so than in our stations, for they are the gateways to the nations.

When big stations were first developed, their ground plans were modified. The earliest form was the one-sided station, where arrival and departure took place on the same side of the track. Later, in the mid-19th century, twin-sided stations appeared, with arrival and departure taking place on opposite sides. But the volume of traffic made this a problem and the result was the head-type station, with arrival and departure through a building and concourse at the end of the tracks. The Gare de l'Est in Paris was regarded as the model example of this type. The head type enabled the end building to be used as a hotel. It seems likely that this form will remain the most useful and flexible for stations.

The social functions of the station in the 19th century were highly significant. With its timetables, tickets, uniformed staff, clocks and so on, the station became one of the principal forces in society for promoting order, regularity, punctuality and discipline.

But at the same time, the station became a focus for crime and immorality. For stations have been havens for social outcasts and criminals. There is a floating population of station denizens who are there not to travel — prostitutes, pickpockets, drug addicts, luggage thieves, derelicts, dossers, drifters, the homeless and the friendless who find in the station, open 24 hours a day, not only warmth, shelter and light, but also opportunities for profit. Stations used to figure on the itineraries of the great and used to be used regularly for assassination attempts. President James A Garfield of the United States was shot at the Baltimore and Potomac depot in Washington DC in 1881. Nowadays stations are more likely to be blown up by extremists as spectacular advertisements for their cause, as in 1980 when 85 people were killed when right wing terrorists blew up Bologna Station in Italy, and in 1983 when Islamic fundamentalists exploded bombs at Marseille Station, killing two and injuring 35, and in more recent events involving the IRA in London. In these days of international terrorism, with high speed trains as prestige targets, policing and security arrangements in terminal stations are going to be essential.

Most passengers are oblivious to the fact that stations are for many thousands not a place of arrival or departure but their place of work. The coming of the railways meant the creation of major industry; in 1870 in Britain, the railways comprised the sixth largest industry in the country. In Britain in 1910, the peak of the railway age, 169,572 people worked in British stations alone. Railway staff all over Europe tended to be disciplined, skilled, hierarchic and loyal. They took pride in their work and in their concept of public service. Demoralisation and depopulation took place as the

---

[7] Sir John Betjeman, Time with Betjeman, BBC 2 Television, 13 March 1983

This Edwardian photograph of the staff at York station reflects a time when service was all, and rival railway companies sought to reflect their status through both the presentation of their staff, and the architecture of their buildings. Note the fine roof of curved arches of this, the pride of the North Eastern Railway.

Inset: *Armorial detail of the station clock*

railways declined. Both trends will be reversed by the regeneration of the railways. This means there must be adequate facilities for staff provided in the stations.

The station itself is made up of a number of different units and areas, each serving a specific function. They range from ticket office to left luggage office, from lost property department to public conveniences. In the past, waiting rooms reflected the class divisions of society. Bookstalls and telegraph offices underlined the role of the station as an information centre and the refreshment rooms, the role of the station as a source of sustenance and renewal.

The extent of the facilities varied according to the size of the station. But the Gare de Lyon in Paris in 1931 boasted the following: in the left wing, a booking hall (with 70 ticket and baggage windows), left-luggage cloakroom (departure), information and telegraph office, exchange and sleeping car company offices, 12 automatic luggage-weighing machines, five automatic distributors of platform tickets, several telephone boxes, two waiting rooms, and lavatories (including baths, hairdressing and shoe cleaning rooms); in the central block, the buffet and restaurant, left luggage office (arrival), ticket collectors' and other offices, entrance to the Underground; in the right wing, luggage arrival hall, omnibus order office, customs hall, lost property office, stationmaster's and police offices and medical room.

In American stations shopping arcades were introduced. Moscow Leningrad station introduced a crèche in 1931, Milan Station had an umbrella hire service and Washington Union Station a Turkish bath and a swimming pool — all very useful adjuncts to the station.

There is no reason why the concourse area of the station should not be part of a city centre area of entertainment, refreshment and merchandising. It should be if the station is to continue to be one of the nodal points of the city, along with such buildings as the city hall, the cathedral, the central museum and art gallery.

But most of all for the ordinary traveller the station is an arena of emotion, the focus for a hundred different reactions simultaneously: parting and reunion, joy and sorrow, relief and anxiety, rage and disappointment, excitement and anticipation, frustration and despair, optimism and fulfilment. In his essay Railway Romance James Scott sums up the maelstrom of conflicting emotions and experiences that a station represents:

> What of the passengers and their friends! Who may fathom, much less portray the thoughts and emotions surging within their minds and hearts? The grief and pain of separation, the hopes, the fears, the loving care, the prayers, the joys, the trust! Here are soldiers or sailors with troops of acquaintances to see them off. There are some boys and girls going away to school, their fathers and mothers using up their moments of waiting with many injunctions in order to shut out their anxieties which their children must not see. At another place a wife is bidding goodbye to a husband whom duty calls hence. Elsewhere an only son and brother is setting out into the great world to win a name and place...

> At another compartment a happy wedding pair is assembled and, amid merriment and showers of confetti, the 'happy pair' are getting a good send-off. These and a hundred other scenes one may witness at the departure of an important train. There may be tears of mirth or calm demeanour, but in all, the life of feeling runs high.[8]

All these facets of station emotion are visually encapsulated in WP Frith's celebrated painting The Railroad Station, which depicts a cross-section of mid-Victorian society: the wedding party, the schoolboys, the soldier, the police arresting a criminal— 80,000 people paid to see the picture on exhibition in 1862. It was reproduced in print form, recreated in stage tableaux and described in detail in a 32-page booklet, such was the public fascination.

There is no more potent evidence of the emotional significance of the station than its appeal to artists. Emile Zola said, "Our artists must find the poetry of stations as their fathers found that of forests and rivers", and the station has been securely enshrined in every aspect of art and culture[9]. Painters, poets and novelists have all responded to the drama in the station. But it is perhaps the cinema which has blended all the other art forms together to create the powerful visual and aural imagery of locomotives, billowing smoke, clattering rails and melancholy train whistles, allied to the idea of

---

[8] James Scott. 1913. Railway Romance and Other Essays London. pp71, 89-90

[9] Jean Dethier ed, op cit, p9

WP Frith's celebrated depiction of Paddington station, London, embodies a wide cross-section of Victorian life

the dramatic potential of a mixed group of passengers thrown together by circumstance. "We always seem to be meeting in railway stations," says Anton Walbrook to Moira Shearer in *The Red Shoes*, a film in which the heroine later throws herself under a train at Monte Carlo Station.

Perhaps everyone has some memory of railway station meetings and partings in films: Humphrey Bogart receiving a farewell letter from Ingrid Bergman at the Gare de Lyon in *Casablanca*; the extended parting of Jennifer Jones and Montgomery Clift in De Sica's *Stazioni Termini*, set in the newly opened Rome terminal; Anna Karenina, as played by Greta Garbo and Vivien Leigh, throwing herself despairingly under a train in a lonely Russian station; Massimo Girotti having a nervous breakdown on the concourse of Milan Station in Pasolini's *Teorema*; the sleepy Czech country station as a hotbed of sex in Jiri Menzel's *Closely Observed Trains*; and Ingrid Bergman's reunion with her lover at Stockholm Station in *Intermezo*.

Perhaps the most famous of all station films, however, is David Lean's film of Noel

Coward's *Brief Encounter*, in which that most gentle and most English pair of lovers, Trevor Howard and Celia Johnson, establish the railway buffet as the place for secret lovers to meet. Architects must bear continually in mind the fact that their station buildings will continue to be the stages on which a thousand personal emotional dramas are played out daily.

The closing of a station intangibly but significantly diminishes the spiritual life of a country and its people; for it rings down the curtain with devastating finality on a stage which has seen these dramas, both comic and tragic, played out, and has mirrored the changing moods of the nation, has etched itself into the working lives of some, the emotional lives of others. Robert Lynd summed this up when he reported his feelings on listening to a radio broadcast of the arrival of the last mail train at Dublin's Broadstone Station before its closure in 1936:

> How tenderly everybody spoke of it during the broadcast! How haunted with memories of happiness it seemed — old servants of the railway company came into the signal box from which the broadcast was given and spoke of the closing of the station as if for them it was the end of the world. Never again would the

The powerful imagery of railways as celebrated in cinema: Marilyn Monroe in an evocative scene in Chicago, from the classic movie, Some Like it Hot

Galway Mail arrive there in its midnight glory. Never again would a signalman give the signal that all was clear. A banquet hall deserted — Broadstone Station would henceforth be only that to thousands for whom it had long been associated with happiness — the happiness of the day's work, the happiness of companionship, the happiness of simply being alive on a fine day. There was a note of exile in the voices of the old railway servants who came to the microphone to say goodbye to the station...

Ruskin would surely have been surprised if he had been told that a time would come when railway stations, like lakes and mountains, would become a part of the imaginative life of men...

He would have been still more surprised if he had been told that the closing of an old railway station would one day move men to sadness no less than the demolition of a Gothic church or the violation of a landscape. Yet how natural it is? Life is brief and the removal of a long-tolerated equally with a long-loved landmark alters and injures the world in which we have been happier than we have deserved to be.[10]

---

[10] Robert Lynd. 1937. In Defence of Pink. London. pp 72, 74-5

Despite Ruskin, 19th century stations stood as monuments to optimism, aspiration and confidence in the future, as public meeting places where faith in the perfectibility of Man by his own ingenuity, and the blessing of divine providence were daily affirmed. The advent of the high speed train and the regeneration of the station means that the railway station can once again become a place of hope, faith and inextinguishable humanity. It is a challenge to which architects, planners, economists, engineers and governments must rise.

Part 2: Present and Future
John M MacKenzie

IT IS very appropriate that my colleague, Jeffrey Richards, should have sketched in the historical background to the development of new stations because, in many respects, we find ourselves back where we were 150 years ago. We have new tracks, new trains, new destinations, new passengers, and of course new stations.

Just as the railways and their stations of 150 years ago introduced a new understanding of time and a new sense of national identity, now we have new concepts of time and overland distance, of both time and community within an international framework. The high-speed network may be based on an existing passenger system, but in many respects, in its technology, its standardisation, its levels of comfort, security and safety, its capacity to mesh with other systems and cross international boundaries, it is wholly new.

There are other similarities with 150 years ago. We have similar controversies about private investment and state involvement. We have communities that welcome the new developments, others which fiercely oppose them. We have regional, civic, and national interests which are as likely to be conflicting as congruent. These tensions are exacerbated by different ideological approaches at the various levels of political control. If, in the 19th century, the railway and its stations and yards could make or break a town or city, so in the 21st century, the high-speed network may have the power to make or break a region, or even a country marginal to the system.

We also have tensions between architects and property developers. The architect hopes to build new station buildings which will fulfil the requirements of high architectural art according to a contemporary and developing canon. She or he wants to display her/his work and the technology it celebrates, while providing an experience for the passenger which will be both practical and aesthetic. The property developer wishes to use a site to maximum commercial advantage. The two are not, of course, irreconcilable, but each may well have a dramatically different effect upon the cityscape.

But 150 years ago, precisely the same problem presented itself: should the station be a station or should it be a hotel, a headquarters, an office block, or (more commonly today) a shopping centre.

If these are the similarities with the situation faced by the railway companies and their architects 150 years ago, let us now identify the new challenges posed by the stations required to serve the high-speed networks.

Let me first address the character of the terminus which is serving international routes. Such a station has to satisfy a number of requirements not faced by their great 19th century counterparts. Some of the new stations have to include closed international enclaves and require strict security arrangements. All require strict regulation of passenger flows and embarkation patterns, precise and efficient arrangements for train servicing, and a need for split-second time-keeping, particularly for trains likely to be routed to the Channel Tunnel. Let me deal with each of these in turn.

It is often said that the British are particularly obsessed with frontier controls and security because of their anxieties about immigration, political asylum and the problem of the Irish Republican Army. To a certain extent this is true, and has been confirmed by the British reaction to the proposal to remove border controls from European Community frontiers in 1992. However, there will of course continue to be frontier controls at the fringe of the Common Market and the security implications of stations and tunnels are not unique to the United Kingdom.

The Franco-British system and the Chunnel has very particular problems, but some of these do apply elsewhere in Europe. Sweden will be linked to Denmark by a bridge and a tunnel; within Denmark a tunnel will link Zealand and Funen; bridges and tunnels link Zealand to Lolland and northern Germany. Elsewhere frontiers will often lie on river or mountain systems, requiring major bridging or tunnelling.

The international enclave

It may be that post-1992 Europe will have less need of customs and passport regulation, but these are unlikely to disappear entirely. Moreover, national laws are likely to remain very different in respect of drugs, firearms, pornography, and publications generally. In the British case, for example, the alleged Thatcherite belief in free market forces is severely diluted when it comes to ideologies, political forces, so-called moral issues and publications. Thus, for the foreseeable future, both customs officers and police are likely to have a continuing interest in cross-border criminal activity, particularly in relation to drug trafficking.

Quite apart from hard drugs, there is obviously going to be a lengthy conflict, for example, between the practices of the Netherlands, where soft drugs have been legalised, and those of Britain, where adamantine prohibition is likely to prevail. This is going to be equally true in respect of various forms of censorship. Even if the British do tend to diverge from common European practice in these respects, the EC will maintain controls in dealings with non-EC countries.

In all of these respects high-speed networks will be anxious to escape from international controls at borders and will seek to place such controls, where necessary, in the stations of major or capital cities.

The departure area of such stations will hence become an international enclave just like airport departure lounges. The station, therefore, needs to be divided into two sections: firstly, the open area, where the main services will be located — inquiries, booking, catering, shopping, rest and leisure facilities. These will often be shared with a station serving national and commuter destinations. Secondly, there will be the closed area, which only intending passengers will be permitted to reach. They will pass through to it via ticketing controls and security checks.

Security

So far, trains (with a few notable exceptions) have generally not posed a security problem. The possibility of stopping them anywhere, of boarding and exiting at a multiplicity of points, of having a driving system usually cut off from the passenger compartments, have all ensured that they do not present a particularly attractive target to the hijacker or the bomber. These conditions change dramatically in the case of high speed trains. They need to be sealed, for reasons of safety and of air pressure. It might be possible to control key points, such as the driving compartment or the principal conductor's control position. In tunnels they will be highly vulnerable, presenting a striking terrorist target. Thus the station may well have to provide the full panoply of security provision for both passengers and their luggage. Fortunately, technology in this area has now been greatly improved and this can be provided with a minimum of delay or inconvenience. Moreover, there ought not to be any need, as with an aircraft, to separate passengers from their luggage. It should be stressed, however, that while these sorts of arrangements may well be judged necessary in London, Brussels or Paris in respect of the Chunnel route, the majority of high-speed stations in Europe may have no need for the international/security enclave.

Embarkation

Once in the departure area, hopefully the passengers will find large quantities of comfortable seating in an attractive environment, well provided for in respect of light catering supplies. The passengers will have to be held there until the moment of departure comes. The Anglo-French trains will carry a total of 750 passengers. Thus, assuming that two trains may be loading at roughly the same time, as many as 1,500 passengers may have to be kept in reasonable space and comfort for up to half an hour.

So far, the international part of the station sounds like an airport. But at this point the similarity ceases. High-speed trains will be very long. Those serving the Channel Tunnel, for example, will have 18 coaches and will be over 393 metres long. Whereas an aircraft is boarded by one, or at most two, entrances, embarkation and time constraints ensure that the high speed train should be boarded at the maximum possible number of entrances. It would be both inconvenient and time-consuming to expect passengers to walk up to 400 metres from an old-style ticket barrier mid-way along very long platforms.

It is therefore highly desirable that the train should be approached either from above or from below, thus providing opportunities for lifts, escalators and stairs numbered according to the car in which the passenger has reservations. This implies that the departure lounge should be roughly the length of the platforms and it may be that a moving walkway through the departure lounge, with a series of stepping-off points, would increase embarkation comfort still further.

The departure lounge will have to be carefully designed so as not to give the impression of a long cavernous space, and to avoid the possibility of people running or skateboarding its full length. The catering outlets and newsstands will have to be conveniently located and designed according to security requirements.

Of the two options, ascending or descending to the platform, clearly rising to the train is preferable. This permits the station platforms to be lit by natural light; it is possible to reproduce a modern version of the great 19th century train sheds; and the departure of the train is provided with a much greater sense of occasion. The nature of the site and the lie of the land will not always allow this, of course. The departure lounge and the platforms could be at the same level, but this is a highly inflexible system and may mean much further distances to be walked by passengers unless it were possible always to use the one platform face as a departure bay. It may be an option for the smaller station.

Descending to the train will often be necessary and this immediately raises the spectre of sopme unpleasant modern stations known to us. Taking the train can feel like indulging in a minority and persecuted interest pursued in subterranean environments. As someone has put it, such stations have the capacity to reduce the passengers to the level of sewer rats. There are, however, modern and more attractive ways of dealing with this. So long as the tunnel heights are reasonable, surfaces are bright and clean, and there are interesting features for the eye to rest upon, this can become a more pleasant possibility. The point at which the train emerges from the tunnel becomes architecturally, socially and aesthetically significant and should be given careful attention.

Train servicing

High speed train rakes will, of course, have to be used at a high level of efficiency, not only because of the considerable capital costs involved, but also because terminal stations will demand swift turn-round times. It may be that only 40 minutes will be permitted in the terminus. During this time, passengers will have to disembark and be led swiftly off the platforms and through the departure area to taxis and other forms of transport.

The train will have to be cleaned and serviced at considerable speed. This operation will be reasonably labour intensive and will require very careful supervision of a large staff moving rapidly from train to train. In this respect, it may be necessary to return to older practices. In recent years railway systems have been under pressure to reduce staff at stations. Numbers of staff have declined and both the passenger help and the staff facilities that used to exist at stations have largely disappeared. The high speed train, particularly on international routes, may bring back the very highly staffed station.

A number of consequences flow from this. The station will require clearly demarcated supervisory sectors. Arrangements will have to be made to ensure that staff flows and passenger flows do not conflict. Staff will require rest rooms and canteens. Staff operating within the station's international enclave will have to receive some form of security vetting. At the very least they will have to pass through security equipment before and after work.

Precision in time-keeping

Precision in time-keeping is particularly important on high speed networks, particularly those using tunnels. Trains have to be very precisely timed so as to slot into their booked passage periods between centres, through tunnels, over bridges and across frontiers. This is particularly the case on systems where there are no dedicated lines and high speed trains have to share track with existing services. The patterning of trains obviously conditions the flows of passengers through the terminals and has to be organised with that in mind. In the case of the Franco-British system, the trains on the British side of the Channel will have to share tracks with commuter trains. They will leave the Waterloo terminal in "flights" of two at roughly half hourly intervals. Their time of arrival at the Chunnel will have to be very precise so as to feed into the system of vehicle-carrying trains which will be operating through the tunnel on a continuing basis. This clearly has implications for signalling and driver radio-control. It also requires a high degree of efficiency during servicing and embarkation period at the terminal station.

Other stations

The through station obviously presents a rather different set of conditions. The numbers of passengers using them will be of a lesser order, except perhaps where through stations serve airports or larger centres. The train will, however, stop relatively briefly. The servicing period will be cut out, and a higher level of platform efficiency will be capable of being achieved. It will therefore be possible to have the departure lounge and platform at the same level, perhaps most conveniently in an island arrangement.

Where international trains are handled, it will still be necessary to maintain the distinction between the open and closed parts of the station. Commuter and regional services will be able to feed into such stations, but the high speed train will almost always require separate ticket and security controls and embarkation arrangements. Clearly these stations will be few in number since a multiplicity of stops destroys the point of the high speed train, but their existence should prove a spur to regional and local services feeding into them.

Architectural and social opportunities

The high speed train station presents a large number of challenges and problems, but it also presents considerable architectural and social opportunities. The airport has always been an unsatisfactory type of building. It adds nothing to the cityscape, but tends to rape the countryside. Airports have seldom been built with sufficient capacity to cover natural expansion. They therefore tend to be a series of buildings of different shapes, sizes and styles, dominated by concrete aprons and runways on one side and by roads, car parks and flyovers on the other. They attempt to provide a reasonably comfortable environment for temporary sojourners, but few visit an airport for an aesthetic or social experience.

The stations of the high speed network can bring the excitements of international travel back to the city centre. They can be approached by pedestrians and cyclists in a way that airports generally can not. They can link much more satisfactorily to other transport arrangements — underground railways, taxis, buses, suburban train services. They can act once again as city gates, the portals of business and leisure travel, be at once utilitarian and a source of romance and adventure. They should do their best to flaunt their technology which is accessible and aesthetically appealing.

The high speed train is itself a highly satisfying object. It is not something to hide away. It should be exhibited to the full within a glass shell, visible, though within a controlled environment, to the surrounding streets, taxi ranks, pedestrian walkways, and commuter platforms. It should act as an invitation to travel, a means of securing the uplifting sense of achievement that the Victorians revelled in. It should not be a source of small-minded gestures or mean-spirited attitudes. Since such stations aim to move large numbers of people — more than double that of a jumbo jet, for example — they should again become the subject of the studies of crowd movement which Victorian architects loved to place in historical contexts: like those of the Colosseum, the Baths of Caracalla, great temples or medieval cathedrals.

Stations devoted to the high speed train rank with the modern concert hall, theatre or sports stadium as environments in which large numbers of people have to be brought comfortably and safely together, held, in the case of the station despatched and received, and dispersed. It offers striking opportunities for multiple use, particularly through the shopping centres, bus stations, hotels, trade centres, leisure areas, and office blocks which can be combined with it. There are good examples of these in Bilbao, Paris, and Stockholm.

The station should not, however, become the excuse for megalopolis — cold, labyrinthine, soulless, and alienating. If multiple use is contemplated, it should be a multiple use which makes social and economic sense, which combines the station with other buildings in sensible and useful ways. The era of megalomania in railway station building in the United States came on the eve of the decline and collapse of railway systems. The megalomaniac stations tended to be those of shortest lifespan, ready for demolition soon after completion.

Despite all the constraints I have described above, the station of the future should remain a place to wander into, a place to look and enquire, to soak up the atmosphere and watch the comings and goings. If you can enjoy a sauna, drink a coffee, buy a pair of socks or underpants as you do so, then fine. But the significance of the building as a station, as city gate, portal to a European-wide system, should not be lost.

The exciting thing is that we can recreate in modern form the finest train sheds and grand concourse spaces to vie with those of the past, while using modern materials, carefully planned and integrated maintenance and cleaning systems, bright, attractive and durable materials, and strong design features like graphics, directional and functional signs, illustrations of trains and destinations (maybe in representational rather than realistic form), together with destination indicators that can thrill the viewer as well as offer bread-and-butter information.

New developments

There are, of course, a number of significant station developments taking place in Europe at the moment, together with many still at the planning stage. I have visited a few of these and examined plans and models of others.

The Gare Montparnasse in Paris is nearing completion. It comprises no fewer than three stations, together with a bus station and Metro. In the façade there is a postmodernist attempt to recreate the façade of the old station, purely as a decorative feature. There is a train shed outline and twin towers which have no functional significance whatsoever. Inside, the heavy concrete environment is to my mind unwelcoming and oppressive, despite the large number of levels, shopping areas, and station offices connected by escalators and extensive ambulatories. But the "mid-way"

The new Waterloo terminus for Channel Tunnel trains should prove an exciting addition to the London cityscape

space is narrow and unsatisfactory, and there is no provision at all for handling international departures. On a lower level there is in one place a sensation of a vast Egyptian temple, though without the mystery or the decoration. But overall the station gives exactly the impression of megalopolis that I castigated earlier. The platforms for the high speed trains are mean in width and height. There is no attempt to separate passenger flows and passengers find themselves bumping into servicing trolleys carrying meals etc for the bar-buffets. It is not going to be a great success.

The plans of Grimshaw Partners for the new terminal at London's Waterloo are much more satisfying, and it is to be hoped that they will be executed as planned, with the high speed trains visible from the street in an elevated position, rather than obliterated by an office block. Lighting the platforms is an interesting idea, though it may create cleaning problems. Foster Associates' plans for the new King's Cross Terminal are also exciting, light umbrella structures making a very restrained statement beside two grand and very different 19th century stations, St Pancras and the existing King's Cross, covering, in this case, an underground terminal. This new station may be part of a much larger development which will be spread out over a very large lozenge-shaped site, but the continuing reluctance of the British Government to commit itself to high speed developments means that it may never be built.

At Antwerp there are plans to sink the high speed tracks beneath the great 19th century "listed" station, making the high speed section a through station. It seems to be a very sensitive way to handle a building of this sort. So do the plans for Brussels Midi/Zuid. The plans for the new station at Lyon airport look particularly exciting in their external form, while the new stations on the Spanish high speed link, opened between Madrid and Seville for the 1992 Exposition, look imposing in scale but relatively restrained in form. At Le Mans some excellent solutions have been found to the high speed through station. The continental track-crossing culture of the past has been eliminated by the provision of tunnels so broad and airy as to be almost a subsidiary concourse, while a new small concourse and piazza at the back of the station have very successfully renewed what was formerly a quiet and insignificant area of the town, by providing a new hotel and offices.

German Railways have grandiose plans for the development of a high speed network which can now embrace the former GDR, whose railway system requires considerable modernisation and technical upgrading. A plan, *Bahnhof 2000*, has been produced for the development of German stations, transforming them into transport interchanges with a wide range of facilities. Stations have been divided into five categories. Not all of these will handle high speed trains, but those that do will have shopping halls, a range of different food outlets, in some cases hotels and conference centres, even facilities for cultural events. Generally, existing buildings, such as the impressively vast station at Nuremberg, are to be redesigned to accommodate these new functions.

To end on an idiosyncratic and personal note from a country not yet planning the

Opening day at Atocha station on Spain's new high speed line

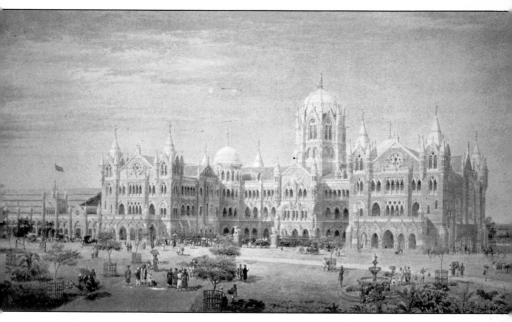

Victoria Terminus, Bombay — from an 1887 watercolour by Herman Axel Haig... will tomorrow's stations share its dramatic sense of place?

introduction of high speed trains, I well remember the first time I encountered my favourite station in the world, Victoria Terminus in Bombay. I set out from my hotel in search of it without a map. I found my footsteps leading inexorably towards it for two reasons: the street system of that area of Bombay places it at the centre of a series of radials; and in any case I could detect a distinct flow of people in its direction. When it revealed itself, the streets, street furniture, and surrounding buildings somehow fell away. It had a majestic presence, integrated yet alone, a syncretic riot of Gothic and Saracenic, bright and colourful, representing Victorian power and self-confidence yet still acting as a Bombay building, packed with workers, travellers and station dwellers. When I entered through its arches into its great central Gothic space, the destination board announced the departures of the Frontier Mail, the Rajdani Express and the Deccan Queen. I hope that the high speed train stations currently being built and those of the future will fit similarly into their cityscape, will make positive statements about the age that produced them, and will produce pleasing and exciting sensations for those who walk into them and look at their destination boards.

Acknowledgements

I am grateful to Michael Edwards, of the Architecture Department of British Rail; the architects Grimshaw and Partners; Alan Reekie and H Vanherle, for information about developments in Belgium, and Hartmut Liebs for material on German stations.

Bibliography

Barman, Christian. 1947. Next Station. London

Biddle, Gordon. 1973. Victorian Stations. Newton Abbot

Binney, Marcus ed. 1984. Great Railway Stations of Europe. London

Binney, Marcus and Pearce, David ed. 1979. Railway Architecture. London

Carter, E F. 1958. Famous Railway Stations of the World. London

Crook, J Mordaunt. 1987. The Dilemma of Style. London

Dethier, Jean ed. 1981. All Stations. London

Droege, John A. 1916. Passenger Terminals and Trains. New York

Glancey, Jonathan. 1988. 'Model Stations', Archi-

tects Journal, vol. 188, 26-31

Gregerson, John. 1989. 'Rebirth of a Station', Building Design and Construction vol. 30, 46-52

Kubinszky, Mihaly. 1969. Bahnhofe Europas. Stuttgart

Meeks, Carroll. 1956. The Railroad Station. New Haven and London

Nakayama, Shigenobu. 1988. Kawaji Onsen Station House', Japan Architect, vol 63, 47-51

Spring, Martin. 1988. 'Vaulting Ambition', Building, vol 253, 40-45

Stubbs, Douglas and Stephanie. 1988. 'The rebirth of a magnificent monument: Washington's Union Station', Architecture, vol 77, 68-75

Zardini, Mirko. 1989. 'Nuove Costruzioni ferroviarie', Lotus International, vol 59, 100-113

18.

The conquest of distance by the destruction of time

The impact of high speed trains on society
Dr John Whitelegg, University of Lancaster and Helmut Holzapfel, University of Kassel

EARLY RAILWAY builders were sharp operators who knew that railways were about much more than just offering transport services and binding together disparate bits of national territory. This was not only the case in the USA and Canada, but also in south-east England and other parts of Europe, where railway building was intimately bound up with the exploitation of land and new opportunities for creating profitable assets, where none had previously existed.

Railways have always attracted a romantic following and their record in destroying homes and landscape, and in the development of extensive and energy-greedy suburbs, is rarely rehearsed. Likewise they are rarely associated with rapacious land development and property market excesses which have in fact characterised rail development since the mid-19th century.

In more recent times rail is helped in its "user-friendly" image by the even greater environmental destruction brought about by motorised transport and air services. Indeed we frequently hear the call for more rail investment as an alternative to the far worse depradations of road construction and airport extensions. We return to the myth of substitutability a little later in the paper.

More recent history has shown rail in different colours. In the UK it has been a struggle to persuade BR to keep some lines open and to operate a service that is both reliable and comfortable. The days of aggressive entrepreneurship in European rail operations seemed a thing of the past until, that is, the idea of high speed rail came along and breathed new life into rail managements. The enthusiasm and creativity that has been in such short supply for the tedious business of running commuter trains in cities and providing attractive connections on cross-country journeys has materialised when there are big expensive toys to play with and new routes to plan. A similar point could be made for freight which, with the honourable exception of Germany, really does get forgotten when high speed trains are on the agenda.

These points have been brought sharply into focus by the Australian experience with the Very Fast Train (VFT). Observing this process is like going back in history 100 years. Stridently aggressive entrepreneurs (such as TNT) have established a private consortium of developers to build a new line between Melbourne and Sydney taking in the federal capital of Canberra and run about 300kph to cover the 900kms in three hours. The developers understand the business of high speed trains. Sir Peter Abeles, representing TNT on the VFT consortium, described the project proposal as:

Unlike the VFT idea, the InterCity XPT is an adaptation of the successful British HST which now runs at speeds of up to 180kph on a variety of routes in Australia

"the restructuring of our sociological and economic structure of the east coast"
— *Canberra Times 8.12.88*

Running through substantial suburban communities — and substantial wilderness areas — the idea of this new line would be to set out to stimulate travel demand by developing tourist facilities en route and by creating large traffic generators in previously undeveloped areas. To paraphrase Sir Peter Abeles, it would be an environmental, social and economic disaster.

The questions posed by the VFT are the same as those posed by all high speed train developments. They are simply more sharply focussed in Australia than in Europe. The main questions are, do we need this kind of development? and is there any justification for the deliberate manufacture of travel demand for purposes of ensuring a profitable return on an investment?

The conquest of distance by the destruction of time

The history of transport technology and the development of society comprise a series of distinct jerks in our ability to cover a given amount of distance in a given amount of time. Sometimes there is an element of illusion in this. We can get from Frankfurt to New York quicker today than 50 years ago, but inhabitants of a small town in North Rhine Westphalia will find their journey possibilities to another small town very much reduced if they wish to go by train or other kinds of public transport. More importantly, they will find that journeys on high speed forms of transport frequently have the time savings wiped out by stops or by the difficulties in travelling to points at which high speed transport can be joined.

Higher speeds extend the spatial domain in any given allocation of time. Thus we can compress distance by conquering time and allocate society's benefits by giving people more time to overcome distance, or giving them privileged access to modes of transport with higher speeds. In either case the results are socially skewed. The "action space" of a poor black resident of Los Angeles or a poor white resident in Montgomery, Alabama, is no greater than that of an urban resident of 100 years ago. The poor have the time to devote to travel, but no money, whereas the rich have the money to buy travel, but no time. The more we emphasise time savings, the more we skew the whole transport system to serve the needs of a privileged, wealthy, elite.

Faster modes, and more individualised modes, of transport produce serious social inequalities. All our citizens now travel much further than they used to do (30kms each per day in Germany) but they still do the same kinds of activities. Increasing the length of journey which we need to undertake in order to reach the things we need to access always leaves the "mobility-poor" with much reduced shopping, social and work possibilities.

The ability to buy distance with time savings has other serious consequences. Marchetti (1989) in Vienna has shown that there is a very rough correspondence between the amount of time we devote to travel, regardless of how fast or how much we travel. The significance of this empirical work is that, if we save time, we use it to consume more distance. We simply make more journeys and contemplate day trips to Brussels, Paris or Stockholm where previously we would have thought the idea slightly ridiculous. Thus, time savings as promised by high speed trains release time for more travel and spur on the consumption of distance to ever higher levels. The environmental consequences of this ever accelerating process are as dramatic as they are destructive.

In our home territories we must spend more time in journeys to supermarkets or leisure centres, and more time looking for somewhere to park. We add to congestion in cities on our way to airports or high speed train stops and spend as much time getting to the end-points of our HST trip as we do on the trip itself.

The high speed train is a polluter. It pollutes space, time and the mind (Whitelegg, 1993). We normally measure spatial pollution, but not the other two. The pollution of time is the transformation of useful units of human energy into something which has to be destroyed. Time is a valuable resource which should be conserved so that it can produce socially useful products. The urge to save time is fuelled by the belief that the next task is more important than the present task, and that speed and crowded diaries correspond to social importance. This is pollution of the mind, when no-one has time for a leisurely exchange of views with a friend or colleague. Indeed the very use of the word "leisurely" in this sentence would be seen by many as indicative of sloth or dereliction of duty.

The three pollutions come together to pollute locality. We are so intent on getting from A to B that the quality of the urban environment in A or B is relegated to the bottom of the list. The quality of the urban environment in Europe is generally very poor and this is well documented. Inappropriate and mismanaged transport policies produce environmental damage and fail to capitalise on the solutions which lie in high quality, local public transport at speeds of 20-40kph. The high speed traveller is making a very real contribution to the destruction of place and the diffusion of environmental problems down high speed corridors to spill over into the next urban centre. The contribution of high speed trains to the solution of these problems is as great as the contribution of landing a human on Mars is to the solution of Third World problems here on Earth.

In the next section we turn to the disadvantages of high speed rail summarised under five more conventional headings.

1 POLARISATION OF THE SPACE ECONOMY

High speed rail developments pick out a few favoured areas or cities from a much larger number of possibilities and confer on them additional advantages in terms of accessibility and the winning of inward investment. This produces problems for a national space economy and operates at several different spatial scales. Nationally it leads to disinvestment in non-favoured areas and exacerbates long-standing historical problems of structural disadvantage and job loss. This in turn produces a low level of efficiency in the use of expensive infrastructure. In the favoured areas it necessitates new investment where costs are already artificially raised by improved accessibility and attractiveness of the location. Labour and land costs will be higher and the "overheating" of the local economy will inevitably result, sucking in scarce resources in the form of investment in energy supplies, transport services, road construction, and building development — all with high environmental costs.

For the non-favoured areas the consequences are just as bad, if not worse. Expensive infrastructure already in place is in danger of underutilisation and ultimately of disuse and closure, as lower levels of utilisation raise unit costs and force reductions in levels of service. This is particularly the case for railways and for social infrastructure such as schools or post offices. After a while, outmigration of bright young people produces even lower levels of attractiveness to potential investors and a downward spiral of frightening proportions can result.

Improved accessibility at a few points in the national space economy also permits corporate changes which concentrate production or professional service activity at a small number of places. When South Wales was made more accessible through the construction of the M4 motorway it became possible for firms to close their operations in westernmost areas because they could now service their customers from Bristol. Improved journey times encourage centralisation and the concentration of employment opportunities at a few locations, in effect creating a kind of internal colonialism and a socially divisive employment market characterised in Britain by the yuppy (young, upwardly mobile) phenomenon and the lack of managerial jobs in areas which can be serviced from metropolitan centres.

2 ENERGY ISSUES

The experience of improvements in speed on the electrified West Coast Main Line and the newly electrified East Coast Main Line in Britain has shown that long-distance commuting increases dramatically, fuelling the substitution of long journeys for short journeys. Paradoxically this is exacerbated by the very success of the urban agglomeration in attracting investment and jobs. As the economy "booms" the quality of the environment declines and those with wealth move out to establish homes up to 200kms from London where a good quality environment and housing can be found at a fraction of the cost of housing in London.

This increased consumption of kilometres has energy implications, as does the inevitability of car-based trips at the new location. Those moving out take their motorised pollution with them to spread the environmental damage caused by economic success. High speed rail travel creates hyper-mobility and a psychological dependence on other high speed modes to support the rail journey. Most journeys to or from railheads are likely to be by car, and by high performance cars, as high speed rail customers strive not to "lose" the benefits of their high speed rail journey by using "slow" modes elsewhere. High speed rail has the potential to fuel higher and higher levels of car ownership and use, as well as the use of more powerful cars, and hence cancel out any gains made elsewhere in the reduction of vehicle emissions or reduction in energy consumption.

3 EQUITY CONSIDERATIONS

Transport policies always have clear social and distributional implications. Putting large sums of money into motorways or high speed rail will benefit those groups who use them most and in both cases these groups are predominantly male, aged between 25 and 45, and are more likely to be highly paid employees, or running their own business, than not. Building high speed rail links is not of much relevance to the vast majority of women, the young, the elderly, the poor or the unemployed or (in Germany) the Turkish community.

Of course this may be acceptable or even desirable to railway planners maximising revenue and winning customers from air services, but no country can build harmonious social relationships and a healthy society if it pursues socially polarised transport policies. Women with child care responsibilities and people in low paid jobs or with no job at all make shorter journeys, use more public transport and walk more. These groups are more environmentally friendly than those who consume thousands of kilometres each year by car, train or plane. They should be encouraged, not penalised, by transport investment decisions.

Germany's investment in high speed rail has taken place at the same time as over 2,000kms of "low-priority" railways have closed (Whitelegg,1988a). Investment in socially regressive transport systems signals a withdrawal from rural areas, from declining industrial areas, and from other areas of poor traffic potential.

4 ENVIRONMENTAL ISSUES

The current controversy over Britain's newest high speed line proposal to connect the Channel Tunnel with London shows just how damaging such schemes can be to established communities and to the environment. Similar struggles in France have tarnished the image of the TGV and high speed lines in Spain are threatening important archaeological sites and habitats. In south-east England an initial, brutal, plan has now been replaced by a modified version with one third of the 112kms in tunnels, and speeds reduced from 186mph to 140mph. On one sensitive stretch the line will now run alongside the M20 motorway to minimise environmental damage. Germany has more experience in the construction of new high speed lines than

Britain and so is in a better position to quantify the damage and the benefits of expensive measures intended to reduce damage. This experience shows that measures which can contain the noise problem, for example, are very expensive indeed.

On the new Mannheim-Stuttgart high-speed line, just south of Mannheim, the residents of Rheinau opposed the construction on environmental grounds. To overcome this opposition DB (German Railways) was compelled to bury its new line in a 5.4kms of artificial tunnel at a cost of DM110 million.

It should be pointed out that, in France, campaigns are often directed at securing a connection on a high-speed line which is seen as major economic boost. Similarly, in Germany, many cities (in the Ruhr area, for example) have demanded high speed train connections. This raises the interesting possibility that cities can end up with the track and the noise, but no stops.

Germany has produced important environmental arguments against high speed trains (Die Grünen, 1989). The German opposition stems from a sharper appreciation of environmental problems, based partly on more detailed research on noise and air pollution and partly on the distribution of centres of population which affords less opportunity for building new lines round urban "obstacles".

High speed trains (including maglev) are disruptive from a noise and severance point of view. The Transrapid programme will have several deleterious effects which have not been costed and which have not deterred governmental support (so far) of DM 1.3 billion. These include:

● 40 per cent more noise than conventional trains and a measured rating on the test track of 96dBa at 25 metres distance, and 60 dBa at 1,000 metres

● Energy consumption is double that of conventional trains, and at speeds over 300kph it is four times greater, due to wind resistance

● Raw material consumption is about 40 per cent higher with Transrapid, in comparison with conventional trains.

Other factors to be considered (Die Grünen, 1989) include land take, which is always much greater than the nominal width of the permanent way, damage to the finances of ordinary rail and hence the ability of ordinary rail to carry freight, and damage to employment opportunities (10,000 lost jobs per annum on DB).

In south-east England there is very strong opposition to new line construction because of noise and severance problems. A new line represents a significant barrier to movement across its route for both human and non-human populations. Arguments for new rail facilities on the grounds that these will transfer freight from road to rail are powerful ones, particularly in Kent which will take the brunt of Channel Tunnel traffic. Interestingly the arguments have not convinced local residents who probably have a better appreciation of the realities of road haulage and political influence than do the planners.

In Germany and Britain extensive motorway construction has taken place in recent years and often in the same corridors that are selected for high speed rail. While there has been anti-motorway protest this has not produced the effective opposition which is emerging to high speed rail. The reasons for this difference remain unexplained.

5. POLITICAL ISSUES

In Britain, high speed rail developments and new line construction have to be seen as a remodelling of the traditional railway operation to make it a high volume, trunk-haul service with high profitability potential and hence good potential for privatisation. This is a "re-commodification", or repackaging, of rail services, foresaking the traditional concept of public service so that they behave instead more like high volume, uniform-standard, consumer goods which can be neatly packaged as an item for sale in the eventual return of railways to private ownership.

The implications of a return of railways to private ownership are enormous and particularly so in the context of what kind of railway we will have in the future. Railways will become more like airlines in the way they behave, the customers they serve, and their irrelevance to the needs of the vast majority of the travelling public. This process is firmly under way in Britain and can not be very far from the minds of politicians, railway operators and financiers elsewhere, out for quick profits from low risk operations, with a large historical investment from state funds.

In Britain, Germany and Australia large corporate interests are moving into the promotion of rail infrastructure as a means of improving their profitability and capitalising on the state's ability to turn land grants, compulsory purchases, running rights and free infrastructure (such as associated road bridges and new road alignments) into hard cash. The promotion of the "Transrapid" maglev train between Essen and Bonn, and Hamburg and Hannover is backed by Thyssen steel and a number of other companies as a way of stimulating demand for their products and creating an export market. The arguments are persuasive and feed on the urge for technological supremacy and global leadership. High speed rail schemes play the same role in these countries as do defence industries: they consume a lot of wealth, they divert scarce resources into useless purposes and they are justified by pure ideology, with no analysis of wider social and economic costs and benefits.

Conclusion

No European proponent of high speed rail has yet explained how we really gain from increased speeds and time savings. Time savings can only be won at the expense of very few intermediate stops (Holzapfel,1982) and the time saved on journeys of up to 800kms is not necessarily reallocated to productive purposes which benefit the common good. Most journeys that are made routinely are a lot less than 800kms. In Germany, 70 per cent of all journeys are less than ten kilometres and the provision of facilities for these journeys is a deciding factor in creating a quality of life which impinges on everyone. This is a central paradox of high speed rail. High speed anything meets the needs of a very small fraction of society and consumes disproportionately large resources. High speed rail contributes to the "spacing-out" of society, which stimulates demand for travel, increases energy consumption and increases pollution.

A "spaced-out" society is less able to function in a way that nurtures social relationships and puts value on places. When speed becomes a desirable objective, places suffer. This can be measured in noise and pollution but also in community severance, damage to walking and cycling as environmentally friendly and socially nurturing activities, and damage to the way we value places. Environmental destruction is made possible because we value travelling between places more than we value the places themselves.

A balanced transport policy which reflects environmental concerns and the needs of places can not embrace high speed rail.

High speed rail will not diminish air travel as some supporters suggest. The airlines desperately need high speed trains to liberate air space and make it available for even faster rates of utilisation for longer distance traffic and tourism. High speed trains eliminate a temporary blockage on the growth of air transport and result in even more crowded skies and more air and noise pollution from aircraft and airports. There is no basis whatsoever in the suggestion that high speed trains produce environmental gains by shifting passengers from air to rail. The history of technical innovation is that we consume more of the basic product, in this case distance. The introduction of telephone traffic did not diminish letter post and as we pursue economic growth the pie gets bigger anyway. European experience shows that the main users of high speed rail come from conventional rail or are newly generated traffic. Any effect on air traffic volumes will be temporary and marginal as people consume any time-saving benefit by buying more travel.

Marchetti (1989) has shown that the amount of time people will devote to travel is remarkably constant through history. The faster we can go, the more we use up time savings to travel further and more often. High speed rail gives this upward spiral another hefty shove, with all its attendant social, economic and environmental disbenefits.

Fundamentally, high speed rail is an expensive distraction from the urgent business of transport policy. It has no relevance whatsoever to the solution of pressing urban transport problems (Whitelegg, 1989). It will make them worse, as high-earning, high speed rail-users use their high value, high speed cars to gain access to rail stations. If you travel by train at 300kph you do not use a bus or a bike to get to the station. High speed rail is irrelevant to freight movement and the most urgent problem in many countries is that caused by road freight, with its serious pollution and traffic accident penalties. High speed rail disrupts local rail services, as in the Frankfurt area where reduction in journey times on inter-city traffic leads to repeated disruption on the "poor relation" local services.

To get freight off roads and onto rail is an urgent priority. To reduce road space in cities and get people onto rapid transit, foot or bike is similarly urgent. Rail has a major role to play in both dimensions, but this is actually threatened by high speed developments. New lines and new technologies tend to ignore the question of freight. Germany, with its strong environmental tradition and bias in favour of rail freight, is very different and has pursued mixed traffic on new lines at great expense. New lines pursued as passenger only lines will kill off other lines and kill off the rail freight potential.

The time has come to recognise high speed rail for what it is and that is not a transport gain, environmental gain or social gain. High speed rail is another device for increasing consumption of scarce resources in order to increase profitability and pollution. It feeds on the environmentally friendly reputation of rail, but perverts rail

Investment in high speed railways does nothing to secure the future of lightly used rural railways, such as this one in Norfolk, UK — lines which epitomised, in the words of the then chairman of British Rail, Sir Peter Parker, the "crumbling edge of quality" symbolising government neglect of the railways, more than ten years ago

policy and creates a destructive force which is fiscally draining and environmentally ruinous.

Bibliography

Die Grünen (1989) Milliardengrab Transrapid, Bundestag, Bonn

European Commission (1989) Communication on a Community railway Policy, Brussels, 23.11.89

Holzapfel, H (1982) High speed systems of public transport- a positive trend? Proceedings of Seminar, PTRC, Warwick, 14 July

ILS (1989) Strategic Transport Axis in North West Europe, ILS Scriften No. 31, Dortmund, West Germany

Marchetti, C. (1988) Building Bridges and Tunnels: the effects on the Evolution of Traffic. International Institute for Applied Systems Analysis, Laxenburg, Austria. Document No. SR 88 01

Whitelegg, J (1988a) High Speed Railways and New Investment in Germany in Transport Technology and Spatial Change, ed Tolley,R S, Institute of British Geographers, Transport Study Group, Aberystwyth, 109-122

Whitelegg, J (1988b) Transport Policy in the EEC, Routledge, London

Whitelegg, J (1989) The future of Urban transport, Paper presented at "Public Transport in Crisis" conference in Melbourne, 29 November. Available from Public Transport Users Association, Box 324, Collins St PO, Melbourne 3000, Australia

Whitelegg, J (1993) Transport for a sustainable future: the case for Europe, Belhaven, London

Part Four: Summary

19.

The impact of high speed trains

An historic comparison

Garry Hawke, Professor of Economic History, Victoria University, Wellington

THE PAPERS in this volume, and the conference at the Stockholm School of Economics from which they derive, constitute an admirable analysis of the economic and social impact of high speed trains. They do not provide definitive answers on any specific project, but they exemplify the range of analytical techniques which need to be brought to bear as part of such answers.

The organisers thought that it would be useful to have comparisons with the historical experience of earlier railway investments. Some might wonder about the propriety of linking 19th century trains to contemporary developments. It is easy to commit anachronisms, but in my recent work as Director of an Institute of Policy Studies I have frequently found that knowledge of relevant economic history increases sensitivity to opportunities and problems inherent in current issues. And relating earlier railways to modern high speed trains is less adventurous than relating them to space exploration, as NASA did over 25 years ago[1].

As I considered modern projects concerned with high speed trains in the context of my *Railways and Economic Growth in England & Wales, 1840-1870,*[2] I thought that there would be two major differences. First, 19th century railways can be conceived as introducing into economics a new commodity — personal travel in comfort. Estimates of the social savings of those railways depend heavily on the value placed on the comfort of first-class travel. It would be interesting to learn if there was anything comparable with modern high speed trains.

Secondly, environmental issues play a much larger part in assessments of modern investment. When Stephenson built the Liverpool & Manchester Railway, the crossing of Chat Moss was regarded as an engineering triumph. There was no concern about the preservation of "wetlands", as swamps must now be called. I know from discussions of the Australian Very Fast Train project, and indeed from the importance

---

[1] B. Mazlish (ed.). The Railways and the Space Program: An Exploration in Historical Analogy (Cambridge, Mass. and London: 1965)

[2] Hawke, G. Railways and Economic Growth in England & Wales, 1840-1870 (Oxford, 1970)

of environmental issues in the whole of the recent general election campaign in that country, and from the significance of environmental issues in the emerging agenda for all international trade and investment discussions, that the current situation is very different.

I started with very little knowledge of the problems, achievements and potential of modern high speed trains, but my understanding of the issues around them was quickly improved by Professor Dahmén. It was appropriate that this was at the Stockholm School of Economics where he has been for so long a distinguished exemplar of its distinctive contribution to economic and social thinking. The development of thought interests me, and I found special interest in listening to Professor Dahmén as he deployed for the purposes of the Stockholm conference, familiar concepts such as developmental blocks, Schumpeterian entrepreneurship, and the distinction between *ex ante* and *ex post*, which the Stockholm School of Economics made part of international thinking, and which is currently receiving renewed emphasis as we explore the processes of research and development in a wide variety of contexts.

Professor Dahmén gave a very judicious account of the assessment of railways which flowed from the New Economic History of the 1960s and 1970s. He also illustrated the continuing coming together of economics and economic history which was part of that New Economic History; his concentration on "transformation processes", which draws on his long line of contributions to economic and social history, is close to the focus on "adjustment paths", which is very prominent in recent contributions to macroeconomic analysis.

Professor Dahmén invited us to concentrate on two questions.

"To what extent do high speed trains present the same dynamics as innovations in railways, shipping and trade in the experience of earlier years?"

and

"Is the current planned investment activity offensive or defensive in character?"

This clear starting point rapidly became more complex as other presentations followed. I was driven back to reflecting on the material I was bringing to bear on those questions. The economic history literature on the social savings of 19th century railways was summed up in Fogel's 1979 presidential address to the Economic History Association[3] in seven points:

● Wagons, waterways and railways should not be conceived as distinct temporal stages of transport development with increasing efficiency: rather all gained in efficiency and their functions became more specialised;

● 19th century transport improvements reduced cost most significantly for medium and long-distance transport;

● waterways and railways are good, but not perfect, substitutes for each other;

● the main transport gain of the 19th century was the replacement of high-cost

---

[3] "Notes on the Social Savings Controversy" Journal of Economic History XXXIX (March, 1979), pp.49-51; see also G.R. Hawke "Railways Revisited" VUW Working Papers in Economic History 84/6 (June, 1984)

wagon by low-cost water or rail transport;

● whether railways or waterways made the bigger saving of resources varied with country or region and time period;

● productivity advanced at a brisk pace for both waterways and railways during the 19th century;

● the capacity of countries or regions to exploit waterways or railways depended on the nature of their transportation needs, especially on the relative demand for short-to-medium and medium-to-long hauls.

As is always the case with Fogel's work, these conclusions were stated carefully and supported with persuasive argument. I would adopt all these points, but those who worked on the railways of Western Europe rather than the USA would give more prominence to passenger traffic. It is worth recalling that, while Fogel's work and the subsequent social savings literature, has often been interpreted as questioning the importance of railways, Fogel explicitly conjectured that railways had a bigger impact on economic growth than any other single innovation in the 19th century[4]. His focus was on innovations and economic growth, and his real message was that in complex economies, economic growth was not dependent on any individual innovation. "Impact on economic growth" is a subset of "importance", a significant subset, but still only a subset.

I am glad that this collection of papers on high speed trains includes some discussion of other aspects of railways — the chapter by Jeffrey Richards and John MacKenzie is a worthy continuation of studies of the symbolic significance of railways such as that of Schivelbusch[5].

Many chapters have led me to think of parallels with Fogel's summing up of the impact of 19th century railways. At the same time, I was drawing on my more recent work, which has been the public policy field. My work in an Institute of Policy Studies has led me to attach a great deal of importance to securing dialogue between people with different disciplinary backgrounds, especially between economists and educationists, and between economists and lawyers.

The contributions in this book have succeeded in producing such a dialogue among economists, economic historians, historians, geographers, sociologists and technologists. I have also been led to reflect on the nature of public policy. In recent years, policies in many countries have concentrated on securing higher living standards, not because the relatively rich have exerted selfish power, but because communities were dissatisfied with their experience as they watched Japan and the newly industrialising economies of Asia securing much greater gains in their living standards by an effective use of their resources. The thrust of policy has not been to issue commands to people to do better — the experience of Eastern Europe is not encouraging for such a strategy — but to provide opportunities for individuals and

---

[4] Fogel, RW. Railways and American Economic Growth (Baltimore, Md: 1964), p.220; Hawke G, Railways and Economic Growth in England and Wales, 1840-1870 (Oxford, 1970) p.28

[5] Schivelbusch, W. (tr. A Holb) The Railway Journey: trains and travel in the nineteenth century (Oxford: 1980)

groups to make better use of the resources under their control, while imposing or retaining a general framework of constraints so as to preserve social cohesion and national identity. Countries have sought a balance between globalisation and local particularity.

This may seem somewhat remote from the topic of this volume. I also began from a remote place in a more literal sense. New Zealand is 25 hours' flying time, plus six hours' waiting time at Singapore, from Stockholm. But my journey consisted of a direct flight from Auckland to Singapore, a flight to Bangkok for aircraft cleaning and crew changing, and then a direct flight from Bangkok to Stockholm. Earlier this year, I flew direct from Auckland to Los Angeles and then, with only a brief stop in Cincinatti, to Washington. Such flights make me think not only of the change from the position of 19th century migrants, most of whom could never contemplate a return from New Zealand to Europe, but of later generations who could seldom envisage more than one journey to Europe in a lifetime.

Even when I first travelled to Europe 25 years ago, I spent waiting time in Sydney, Manila, Hong Kong, Colombo, Teheran, and Athens. What we have seen in recent years is technological change in the airline industry which permits long direct flights. Not everybody has gained. The Cook Islands built an international airport which was intended to compete with Hawaii and Samoa as a staging post on long trans-Pacific flights. It was completed just as most flights ceased to use such stops. I was led to reflect, not only that we are seeing continuing technical progress in both aircraft and railways, as we saw with both railways and waterways in the 19th century, but that perhaps the concentration of airlines on providing long direct flights had opened up a window of opportunity for high speed trains. They now have a relative advantage on what now count as shorter journeys. In those earlier years, the appropriate concentration for railways was what were then considered to be medium-to-long journeys.

There are two major implications of these reflections: opportunities have to be recognised, and opportunities should not be assumed to be permanent — it may be that future years will see a return by the airline industry to finding ways of attracting customers to relatively short journeys.

To somebody whose preconceptions are derived from studies of the social savings of 19th century railways in England and Wales, from trends in thinking about public policy in recent years, and from benefiting directly from an ability to travel quickly without unnecessary diversions, the most striking general theme of this volume is the dominance of an economic approach to assessment of the role of high speed trains.

The approach has not been unquestioned. John Whitelegg and Helmut Holzapfel raise fundamental questions about the value of high speed trains and their case needs to be answered, not summarily dismissed. But it can be answered. Any particular innovation can be attacked as deserving less priority than improving the lot of the poor. That case would have led to some other use of resources than building railways in the 19th century. In the language of the New Economic History, the relevant counterfactual needs specification; if investments are not made in high speed trains, will resources be devoted to assisting the poor instead? Or in the language of "transformation processes" and "adjustment paths", over what time horizon are we to assess whether a sequence of investment will benefit the poor?

It is easy to dismiss any particular innovation as insignificant; that would be an extension of the misreading of the social savings literature as arguing that railways were unimportant. In particular, our sensitivity to path dependence has been much increased in recent years, both by the work of economic historians in the tradition of New Economic History which is exemplified in this volume by the impressive analysis of technical diversity by Douglas Puffert, and also by observation of the Soviet economy.

Streamlining of vehicles did seem to be a cosmetic change in the 1950s, not worth the trouble of changing production lines, but in more recent years efficient motor vehicles have depended on minimising atmospheric resistance and the former Soviet economies now seem littered with large heavy and inefficient transport devices. Consumer-oriented computers and telecommunications did look like a luxury for the rich when they were introduced, but casual observation now suggests that the Soviet economy and society will have enormous difficulty overcoming the lag introduced by not recognising what was happening in those early years. As Torbjörn Flink astutely observed, it would not be wise to assert too quickly that the current generation of high speed trains comprise merely an optional extra on an essentially completed sequence of innovations.

It is, of course, also possible to waste resources on false paths, on technical developments that prove to be economic and social failures. The challenge is to detect just which technological developments fall into that category and which, despite an initial appearance of luxuries for the rich, or even of toys for producers sheltered from market judgments, are further stages in a process which permits more effective use of resources.

Not all current analysis of high speed trains is abreast of these developments. Some conceptions of transport policy are still too much in terms of government always getting things right and being needed to prevent wrong decisions by entrepreneurs. Indeed, some such thought seems to be conceived in terms of governments being able to provide free resources; if only they would realise the significance of railways, governments could make them available. Governments can provide resources, but only by taking them from somewhere else, and policy analysis has always to consider both sides of a transaction.

Frank Dobbin has provided an account of differences between French and American approaches to the role of the state which I find generally persuasive, but which seems to me to give too much weight to the difference between public and private ownership and too little to the location of decision-making. (Indeed, in current thinking, much more weight is given to the economic disadvantages of public ownership, in that public bodies are too cautious in risk assessment and are therefore reluctant to provide investment capital which can be debilitating, especially in fast growing industries with a high level of technical change. Nor are the managers of public corporations subject to the disciplines of the capital market.) Even in more traditional thinking, it was recognised that public corporations developed lives of their own and did not automatically share the objectives of political leaders.

I would be quite sure that there are many tough negotiations between SNCF and the French Treasury over, for example, what costs are to be attributed to the TGV and what to the conventional railway system, as the railway management seeks to justify both investment in the TGV network and subsidy for loss-making conventional rail services. What I found especially interesting in the accounts given to us of the development of the French TGV by both Alain Beltran and Marie-Noëlle Polino was the implicit emphasis on getting the decision-making right. This was reinforced in a negative way by the accounts of Italian developments by Andrea Giuntini and of Spanish ones by Antonio Gómez-Mendoza, in which we see an inappropriate mixing of political and economic decision-making. (The contrast is not clear-cut. While some people welcome the French controls on TGV fares as making them available to the poor, it is by no means obvious to me that this is an efficient instrument for income redistribution or any other aspect of social justice.)

The argument that railways have to provide their own infrastructure while motorists benefit from the free provision of highways is a venerable one, attractive to railway enthusiasts. But it is part of political rhetoric rather than economic analysis. "Free" highways are provided from tax revenue, often from taxes on things like petrol, so that the incidence is located with motorists to a greater extent than if a base such as income was used. The better analysis is that the beneficiaries of highways in general are less easily identified than railway passengers and more diffused throughout society. It is therefore preferable to use a collective means to charge for the service provided, while the nature of rail traffic is such that the direct beneficiaries can be charged through individual fares. Neither solution is perfect, but the objective should be to locate responsibility for payment with those who are best placed to decide whether the benefits of the service justify the real costs involved. Apparent "justice" to rail and road is not an adequate framework.

Similarly, there is a considerable concern with the problems posed by decisions on whether the services of high speed trains should be available to particular towns. It is easy to observe that there is a conflict between those who want fast train services between two points, and those at intermediate points who want access to those services. Frequent stops mean that there is no fast train service at all.

This is not a new problem. Railways have grappled with such issues about express services from their earliest days. (The UK Parliament required "parliamentary trains" to run daily, stopping at all stations, and charging no more than one penny per passenger mile, but even at its most confident, Parliament did not think it could prescribe more than a modest average speed.) Airline managements make similar decisions now, as they schedule those non-stop journeys I talked about earlier. The issue is, who is best placed to decide such scheduling questions? I think the point about the French reliance on a public corporation which is missing from Frank Dobbin's analysis is that the French have more reason to believe that such questions will be approached analytically rather than politically than is true in many other countries.

Decision-making in railway management is complex. The discussion of Britain, by Stephen Potter, made me think of even earlier literature on railways than the New Economic History. There were echoes of the "inter-relatedness" discussion of the long-term effect of Britain's early start on railways. Sorting out the choices available, recognising that one decision impacts on another, requires skilled management. We now, in the light of discussions of "path dependence"[6] give special emphasis to decisions which can not be reversed.

This is not to deny any government role. I always think of markets as operating within constraints, and of governments operating within markets when they choose to be agents for some particular group. So a government may have reason to think that there should be some subsidy, whether explicit or implicit, in order to induce commercial managers, whether of public or private corporations, to make particular decisions about service schedules. But this requires skill in policy analysis so that interventions achieve their objectives without undesirable unintended consequences.

As I have already implied, in the case of the historical literature on social savings, it was important to specify what alternatives were being considered and to avoid double counting benefits and costs. For example, the effect of railways in lowering transport costs and of raising land values were alternative flow and asset measurements of the same effect, not separate benefits to be added together. The backward linkages from railways to iron and steel production were part of a transformation process, but it elucidated the resource cost of railways, and only an identifiable external economy was a gain to the economy additional to the benefits of cheap transport.

So, in thinking of social evaluations of modern high speed trains, it is important to have similar clarity of thinking. High speed trains might well develop some particular towns or regions, but policy analysis requires separation of aggregate effects from regional effects that are offset by compensating changes elsewhere. High speed trains might well promote employment, but if they are employment-promoting devices, the alternatives to be considered are different from those which are appropriate when considering a commercial investment project.

We do not have, even for the French TGV, the data required for the cost-benefit analysis which is the core of the historical social savings literature . My conjecture, thinking in terms of Fogel's summary which I quoted earlier, is that the gap between a social rate of return and a private rate of return is much less for modern high speed trains than it was for 19th century railways. High speed trains are highly specialised, and the gains are mostly to those who avoid journeys to airports by using quick train journeys.

The data on elasticities discussed by Chris Nash does not suggest a shortage of substitutes. I doubt if there is any substantial generalised case for public subsidies of high speed trains. I therefore adopt a middle course. I have not been persuaded that high speed trains should be discouraged as an unwelcome diversion from the more important task of building egalitarian communities or that they should be promoted as social projects. High speed trains should be judged as commercial ventures.

That requires, of course, an appropriate valuation of all the resources they use. Environmental costs are as important as any other costs. But the best procedure is likely to be evaluation by those with the best possible information, audited by others to ensure that information is appraised honestly.

This is what happened in discussion of the Australian Very Fast Train. The project involved several interrelated components. The transport development was linked with a wider proposal, known as a multi-function "polis" (after the Greek, meaning

---

[6] David, P. "So, How would it matter if 'History Mattered'?" ANU Working Papers in Economic History 158 (Canberra: July 1991)

a city state), which was essentially a proposal to link knowledge-based industries so as to utilise optimally the synergies that would arise from their combination. In the course of continuing studies, the extent of that interrelationship was markedly reduced.

The Very Fast Train proposal was mostly a separable project. One possible route had the potential to promote tourism. To assess the national gain, it was necessary to separate that part of tourist development which would have been at the expense of tourism elsewhere. The environmental costs of both tourist development and the railway route would have to be assessed analytically rather than politically. The Very Fast Train project was indeed being pushed by specific interests and opposed by others, but there was a serious policy debate going on.

What then are my conclusions about the extent to which the material in this volume has answered Professor Dahmén's questions? Are the dynamics of high speed trains similar to those of earlier railway, shipping and trade developments? There is a family resemblance, but the current decisions seem to me to be very much smaller. It is important to remember that 19th century policy decisions were about particular railway lines rather than about the overall innovation or social investment programme. It is also possible to disaggregate the notion of a railway and trace an earlier history of wheel-and-track technology and of steam engines so that the final step of putting a steam engine with flanged wheels on an iron track seems less than momentous.

Choice of perspective is an important step in any historical or contemporary assessment. However, despite these cautions, I think we are now seeing a smaller development. The parallel seems to me to be more like the development which occurred in sailing ships under competitive pressure from steamships, rather than like the invention of steamships, although I have been persuaded that railways will be a more durable part of the overall transport system of many countries than sailing ships proved to be. The general tone of discussion at the Stockholm conference was sceptical; there were some outright opponents and some enthusiasts, but the balance lay with sceptical interest, and I share that majority opinion.

Professor Dahmén's second question was whether the planned investment was offensive or defensive. To the extent that it was offensive, he suggested that its implications would be apparent only to creative entrepreneurs. I would therefore like to conclude that it is offensive, since I would then be absolved from any responsibility for assessing its likely consequences. But this volume shows clearly that it is a mixture. Railway managers have found a niche market for expansion. Some see this as the harbinger of major developments. I doubt that. Speed over reasonable distances and ability to cope with water barriers will enable airlines to respond to likely technological challenges from high speed trains. Even if the American romance with motor cars is dimming, and I remain somewhat sceptical of that since it has been announced many times, the flexibility and personal control of cars will restrict high speed trains to specialised markets. On the other hand, the material that is presented here persuades me that high speed train technology will be self-generating, and if creative entrepreneurs are allowed to manage within only appropriate restraints, the field of its specialised market is likely to widen beyond what is apparent now.

20.
Analysis and evaluation of the development of high speed trains

By the Editors

THIS BOOK has presented a number of different views and aspects of the evolution of railway systems, with a special focus on high speed trains. Here we attempt to sum up some of the most important aspects of the development and introduction of high speed trains. Clearly this is not an easy task, since railways are integrated parts of the social fabric with many and complex interdependencies. Consequently we have very much simplified the issues for the benefit of clarity. The discussion is structured according to the general analytical framework outlined in Figure 1.1 in the introduction, that is, going from the factors that determine the form of railway system , through rail operations to the impact of those operations and the related feedback loops.

Determinants

EXTERNAL FACTORS

In many countries the rapidly expanding volume of transport after the Second World War was mostly absorbed by road and air. We noted that the intensified competition stimulated the initiation of the high speed train projects. But it also pointed to the increased market potential for the railways. The mere size of the market on certain connections directed the locations of the new lines. Provided that the distance allowed for an appropriate timing, normally less than three hours, the choice of the first line often fell on providing a connection between the country's two largest cities. The enormous market potential of more than 60 million people on the Tokyo-Osaka axis was a guarantee of economic viability, despite very high construction and running costs.

Public policy is extremely influential in the development of railways. Most railway systems are nationalised and a political accord has been a necessary condition for high speed train projects to be realised. Together with an appropriate legal framework, the power of the central authority had to pave the way for the allocation of sufficient resources, for example finance and land. In some cases the process of convincing the politicians of the potential of new, faster railway services was fairly smooth, while in others it was much harder.

When choosing the mode of traction for the new trains both technological factors and the energy prices had to be considered. The oil crisis in the 1970s greatly influenced the choice of electricity as the source of energy, despite the introduction of technically promising gas turbines.

The enormous technological advancements in micro-electronics and power-electronics during this period provided the railway industry in general, and high speed train projects in particular, with invaluable new techniques and components. The new, powerful computers became an indispensable tool in design work from the 1960s onwards. Microprocessors are also used as components in the trains. The invention of the GTO Tyristor was a breakthrough in power-electronics in the late 1960s. Even though the ordinary inverters had already revolutionised current transformation technology in the early 1960s, the GTO Tyristor promised a quantum leap, although its performance was not to prove satisfactory until the mid 1980s. Nevertheless, the GTO Tyristor was a critical development in two senses. First, it made possible the use of the light and robust three-phase asynchro ous motors. Second, it facilitated multi-current operation of the traction equipment which enabled trains to run on lines with different electrical systems.

The unprecedented growth in road and air traffic during the 1970s and 1980s has in fact improved the environment for high speed trains. Increasing congestion and negative environmental effects make further expansion of these modes of transport highly undesirable . New technologies are coming in, but the shifting of technology in these vast systems is a long-term, expensive, difficult and socially disruptive process.

INTERNAL FACTORS

We have seen that the network structure of railways influences its pattern of development. In the early stages of development, the expansion of the network was propelled by economies of system scale and, of course, the fact that the railway was in many respects superior to competing modes of inland transport. Local railways were integrated into regional systems which in turn were amalgamated into national systems. Since the integration benefits were dependent on a high level of compatibility among the components, this process meant that the demand for unified national standards grew stronger and stronger. Another result was the emergence of monopolised national markets for railway transport services.

Many of the technical characteristics of the national systems thus became "locked in", a fact which would later influence the possibility of raising speeds and integrating national high speed lines.

The alternatives were either to make rolling stock compatible with the existing network — through a tilting mechanism, for instance — or to build new, straighter lines. The latter alternative was the natural choice when a higher capacity was needed anyway. These strategies, which could be pursued separately or in combination, will be dealt with in more detail below.

The different national standards are reflected also in the characteristics of the high speed lines. On the international level most high speed lines are still incompatible, a fact which poses some serious problems and has led the UIC to intensify its efforts to stimulate national producers to coordinate their standards. The PBKA network and the Channel Tunnel projects are good illustrations of the problems stemming from incompatibility between technical dimensions.[1]

The capabilities of the operator and the supplier have of course mattered, both in

---

[1] See for example, Commission of the European Communities, 1990, ch 11

qualitative and quantitative terms. The capabilities varied considerably between countries. When the Shinkansen project was initiated in Japan in the late 1950s, the operator's technical research department consisted of more than 1,000 researchers and assistants[2]. The research department in Sweden had fewer than ten people when the Swedish project started.

It is more difficult to assess the capabilities in qualitative terms. Generally though, with due respect to the technicians working for the railway operators and their suppliers, the automotive and the aerospace industry probably offered more exciting technologies to work with. However, many projects started as a result of the pervasive work of a few competent engineers. But since the problems encountered were so varied, types of capabilities other than the purely technical played important roles.

ACTIVITIES

The different contributions in this volume make clear that the process of developing and introducing high speed trains is a very complex one. The problems involved range from the purely technical to institutional, economic and environmental. To solve all these interrelated problems more or less simultaneously did in some cases demand considerable time, and sometimes, as in the USA, the only result has been paper work and a few scrapped projects. The character of the activities and the solutions chosen to different problems is highly dependent on the state of the determinants in each country. Still, we can not overestimate the enormous influence of the success of the Japanese Shinkansen trains. They mark the beginning of the era of modern high speed trains. It is not appropriate to go into details of every type of technical problem. We shall therefore confine ourselves to some important technical solutions. The conventional railway technology, that is the steel wheel/steel rail, has so far been the only one adopted. New technology, here represented by the maglev trains, still has major technical and economic uncertainties, and the fact that it is incompatible with the existing networks deprives such trains of the benefits of access to the wider network and the cumulative advantages that this would bring. From the concept of compatibility with the existing network we can define different strategies for the development of high speed rail-guided ground transport:

Figure 20.1

Strategies for high speed train investment

Source: Flink, T. September 1992, Part 2, p26.

The Shinkansen and the AVE represent trains using conventional technology but which were initially incompatible with the existing network. In the Spanish case, the

---

[2] Nishida, M. 1980, p14

plans are to change the track gauge on the old lines so that the AVE will fall into the same category as the TGV. In the meantime, Talgo trains have been developed that are capable of running on both the UIC standard, and the broader Spanish gauge. In 1992 East Japan Railways started through operations with Shinkansen high speed trains on the line from Fukushima to Yamagata by expanding the old narrow gauge to standard gauge. On this line a new series of Shinkansen trains operates to a narrower loading gauge (2.95 metres) than the standard Shinkansen trains (3.38 metres).

The choice of strategy largely determines the resultant effects. In the table which follows we have categorised these effects as high, medium or low for the three main technological options. The new magnetic levitation technology has at present no major advantages over the most advanced high speed trains. According to some estimates, maglev or Transrapid trains may use less land than traditional rail technology, have a lower noise level and will possibly have a higher speed potential. The advantages of building new high speed lines in comparison with modifying existing lines are the higher speed potential and fewer problems with mixed traffic. The outstanding safety records for all Shinkansen trains and the TGV trains operating on purpose-built high speed lines are also advantageous for new high speed lines. From 1964 to 1992 more than 3 billion journeys had been made on the Shinkansen without a single fatal accident. The equivalent volume of journeys made on roads killed nearly 2,000 people over the same time period.[3]

Table 20.1

Effects of three different technological options for investment in high speed rail

	New technology	New tracks	Old tracks
Construction cost	High	High	Low
Technical R&D difficulties	High	Medium	Medium
Use of land	High	High	Low
Time saving	High	High	Medium
Mixed traffic problems	Low	Low	High
Environmental effects	High	High	Low

The table shows that there is no unique "best strategy" — the choice involves trade-offs and is dependent on context. As already stated, the new magnetic levitation technology has at present no major advantages over the most advanced high speed trains, while its disadvantages include technological uncertainty, high construction costs and lack of compatibility with existing systems.

---

[3] Japan Railway Group, 1992. According to these estimates the same amount of travel would have produced 8 deaths in conventional rail transport and 96 deaths in air transport

Table 20.2

Railway line	Length in km	Construction cost $m 1992 (US)	Cost per km $m 1992 (US)	No. of passengers per year (millions)
JAPAN				
Tokaido	515	18,800	36.5	130
Snyuo	554	17,900	32.4	66
Tohoku	493	22,600	45.9	57
Joetsu	270	17,500	65.0	23
FRANCE				
Paris-Sud-Est	417	2,100	5.0	19
Atlantique	282	2,400	8.5	19
Nord	333	3,400	10.2	25*
GERMANY				
Mannheim-Stuttgart	99 }			
Hannover-Wurzburg	} 327}	11,800	27.7	10
SPAIN				
Madrid-Seville	471	3,500	7.3	4.2**

* 1993 forecast. ** 1995 forecast.

The already stated advantages of building new high speed lines, rather than modifying existing lines are balanced by higher construction costs and larger environmental impacts. Potential demand has been a factor compensating for this higher cost, as shown in Table 20.2. An element not included in Table 20.1 is the relative risk of accident. The outstanding safety records for the Shinkansen and TGV have already been described.

Now we turn to the problems relating to the financing of high speed train investments. It goes without saying that these projects compete for scarce resources with other possible investments. This means they have to show an acceptable rate of return. Estimating the costs and benefits of infrastructure investments is tricky, since many of their effects are hard to measure and, due to the long lifetime, appear in the distant future[4]. Another problem is that the construction phase, when most costs are incurred, is long and that the benefits will therefore be heavily deflated. A tunnel or bridge is of no use until it is completed and integrated into the existing transport system. The choice of discount rate thus exerts a powerful influence on economic viability, as do delays in construction work, the Channel Tunnel being a good case in point. Here, the financial costs were initially calculated to one third of the construction costs, but delays in construction work and rolling stock production have increased this proportion[5]. The lumpiness of infrastructural investments can sometimes be reduced by making them compatible with an existing system. A motorway can often be built in several stages, where each stretch is immediately connected to existing roads. This was also practised when the TGV Sud-Est line was built. The first half was put into service in 1981 and was not until 1983 that the new line between Paris and Lyon was completed. The costs of the new line are given in Table 20.2.

One immense problem with high speed trains is the large investment costs in high speed infrastructure and high speed rolling stock. The problem of financing has for instance blocked the development of an American high speed railway system.

The table shows that the first lines, built in Japan and France, had a relatively low construction cost per kilometre and a relatively high number of passengers. The construction cost per passenger per year increased rapidly in Japan, but slowly in France. The total construction cost per passenger per year increased from $144 for the Tokaido Shinkansen to $761 for the Joetsu Shinkansen. In France, the first line, the TGV Sud-Est, cost $111 per passenger per year, compared with $136 for the TGV Nord.

If we look at the construction cost per kilometre in relation to the number of passengers per year, the cost increases are more evident. In Japan, the Tokaido Shinkansen cost $0.28 per kilometre per passenger per year, and the Joetsu, $2.83 million. The corresponding figure for the TGV Sud-Est was $0.26, while the TGV Atlantique and the TGV Nord cost more than $0.40 per kilometre per passenger, per year. The construction costs in comparison with annual patronage in Germany and France were generally higher than in France or Japan. The Spanish high speed line is an expensive one from this point of view, despite low construction costs.

A much debated topic in recent years has been the role of the state against that of the private sector in financing infrastructure investments. For a long time the infrastructure has been thought of as a matter for public concern and indeed the specific character of infrastructure investments, outlined above, poses several problems for private investors. A major problem is the fact that the "social return" on these investments, which is the primary interest of the state, often differs from the economic or financial rate of return, which is the concern of private investors.

However, new solutions involving both private capital and private management are increasingly planned and tested and, since an important part of the investments in railways involve high speed trains, the future of these new institutional arrange-

---

[4] We do not intend to give a thorough account of all the effects, measurement problems, calculation principles etc. These are discussed in ECMT, 1992

[5] See ECMT, 1990, p23

ments will depend on the future of high speed trains.[6] Given the gigantic cost of these projects, the future of high speed rail services is probably also dependent on finding workable financial solutions.

Research and development activities have been, and still are, an important part of all high speed train projects. Most functions of the rolling stock and infrastructure had to be reconsidered in the first place. Two interrelated guidelines can be identified in the development of faster trains: the reduction of weight and the reduction of forces on the track. The former inspired, for example, the search for new construction principles and new materials, while the latter meant trying new bogie construction methods and improved suspension. To these can be added developments to the propulsion system, brakes, pantographs and, in some cases, a tilting system. However, out of 16 tilting train projects, only four led to trains in commercial service.

Effects

SUPPLY OF AND DEMAND FOR HIGH SPEED RAILWAY SERVICES

It is evident that the introduction of high speed train services has improved the competitive position of the railways relative to other modes of transport. When new lines have been built parallel to the old ones the capacity has increased as well, but where existing lines have been used for higher speeds this effect is hampered by the problems stemming from mixed traffic.

The lack of international standards in the railway networks is increasingly being felt by high speed train operators. The costs of diversity are visible in both the extra time it takes to build an international high speed network compared with a national high speed network, and in additional costs of building the rolling stock. Recently the railway operators that will be operating the PBKA network decided to buy a modified version of the TGV-Atlantique[7]. The PBKA trains will operate on four different power supply systems and this has nearly doubled the cost per train set in comparison with the standard TGV-Atlantique version. Furthermore, the trains will be shorter and only have a capacity of 377 passengers — more than 100 less than the TGV-Atlantique. In total this increases the cost per seat by more than 100 per cent.

At 1992 values, a seat on the PBKA train costs $93,000 (US) compared with $35,000 on the TGV-Atlantique. See Table 20.3. The same type of cost increases are also visible in the case of the Channel Tunnel train, on which the cost per seat is $50,000, despite the fact that the train is much longer than the standard TGV-Atlantique.

The effects on the demand for travel caused by the introduction of high speed rail services are of two main types. On the one hand there is a substitution of high speed rail service for journeys by road and air; on the other hand, the total demand for travel is expanded. The environmental effects will be dealt with in more detail below, but it can pointed out here that since a high speed train consumes less energy per

---

[6] For discussion of the problems and possibilities of private financing and management of public transport see ECMT, 1990. The Channel Tunnel is an example of 100 per cent privately financed project and the planned AV network in Italy will be semi-privately financed.

[7] IRJ, August 1992

Table 20.3

Train type	Length of train set (metres)	Number of passengers	Maximum power (kW)	Maximum speed (kph)	Price per train set ($m (US))	Number of train sets	In service
TGV Sud-Est	200	368	6,800	270	16	107	1981
TGV Atlantique	238	485	8,800	300	17	105	1989
TGV Nord	200	545	9,800	300-330	24	100	1995
Channel Tunnel	394	794	12,000	300	40	34	1994
Shinkansen 200	400	1,321	14,720	275	32	43	1985
Shinkansen 300	400	1,323	11,840	270	32	15	1992
ICE	411	759	9,600	250-270	34	60	1991
X2000	140	254	2,560	200-210	17	20	1990
ETR 450	184	344	4,700	250	22	25	1988
AVE	200	329	8,800	300	29	24	1992
PBKA	200	377	8,800	300	35	27	1996

Note: *Table based on September 1992 data*

passenger-kilometre than either road or air traffic (at comparable load factors) the substitution effect is environmentally beneficial, while the traffic generation effect will increase environmental problems.

If road and air modes use the spare capacity created by a transfer of passengers to high speed trains to expand their markets in other areas then the overall effect of high speed trains is, from an environmental point of view, entirely negative. This is almost certainly the case in European air transport where a transfer of trips on short-haul flights from air to rail will permit airlines to expand long-haul services (by using aircraft and airport "slots" thus released) to take advantage of opportunities in exotic tourism and longer distance business links. The overall effect is, therefore, more air travel, more high speed rail travel and an increase in energy consumption and pollution.

The substitution effect can be illustrated by the experience of the X2000 between Stockholm and Göteborg. Here, 60 per cent of the passengers on the new service formerly used the air service and seven per cent travelled by car. Three years after the introduction of the TGV-Sud-Est, air traffic was down by 50 per cent on the route, while it increased by between ten and 60 per cent on other lines[8]. Road traffic remained unchanged on the A6 between Paris and Lyon, while it expanded by 30 per cent on comparable motorways.

[8] France's Master Plan

The substitution effect is, of course, dependent on the relative fares charged and the time-savings. Furthermore, these examples only depict the short-run effects. The diagram below shows the effects on air traffic volume of the opening of the Fukuoka Shinkansen in 1975. It not only illustrates the substitution effect, but also the so called three-hour rule-of-thumb, implying that there is a discontinuous elasticity of demand when a journey takes less than three hours. The rationale behind this rule is probably that three hours permits a return journey on the same day. In the case below, the travel time on rail becomes shorter than on the air route at about three to four hours.

Many variables do of course intervene in the general case of substitution, and this

Figure 20.2

The substitution effect when opening the Fukuoka Shinkansen in 1975 on nine different routes.

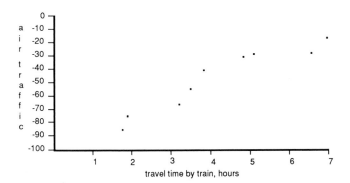

Source: *Data compiled from Okabe, S. 1980, p144.*

is just one case. But an advantage of the rich data from Japan is that cultural differences and, probably, price and quality policies, are controlled[8a].

High speed railway services have in some cases produced impressive gains in passenger volumes and market share for operators. The number of railway passengers increased by 81 per cent on the Paris-Sud-Est axis between 1980 and 1989, with the introduction of the TGV. In Spain, RENFE hopes to increase its market share on the Madrid-Seville corridor from 14 to 54 per cent.[9] In other cases, the effect on passenger volumes has been more modest. The introduction of the ICE increased the number of passengers on the Hamburg-Frankfurt-Stuttgart-München line by ten per cent, to 10 million.[10] In Sweden, the partial introduction of the X2000 between 1990 and 1992 increased the railway's market share from 36 to 40 per cent on the Stockholm-Göteborg line. But, at the same time, the number of railway passengers actually fell

---

[8a] Train fares were 64-89 per cent of the air fares on comparable routes. No strong correlation was found between fare differentials and length of route.

[9] IRJ, April 1992, p25   [10] IRJ, August 1992, p4

by ten per cent, thanks mostly to the recession in Sweden.

High speed trains also create new travel patterns on shorter distances. BR noted in the 1980s that a steadily increasing number of passengers travelled daily to and from London from towns as far as 160kms away. This pattern of passengers making daily journeys was evident as far away as York, more than 300kms north of London.

High speed trains mean that the trains generally stop at fewer stations. In addition purpose-built high speed lines run directly between large cities, bypassing a large number of medium sized towns. One recent example is Amiens which did not get a TGV station on the TGV-Nord line. As a consequence, Amiens has lost its earlier favourable position in the railway network of northern France.

DEMAND FOR AND SUPPLY OF HIGH SPEED RAILWAY MATERIAL AND INFRASTRUCTURE

An important effect that has emerged as a result of the wave of investment in high speed trains is the completion of missing links. Missing links are gaps in the railway network that have existed for a long time. An obvious example is the connection between Britain and the Continent through the Channel Tunnel. The Storebaelt tunnel in Denmark also falls into this category. Several other similar projects are planned: the rail tunnels through Switzerland, the new line connecting France and Italy, and the connection of the Madrid-Seville high-speed line with the French high-speed network. At present, the French and Spanish rail networks are incompatible owing to their different track gauge.

High speed rail services also produce demand for high speed trains. This has promoted the development in Japan, France, Britain Germany, Italy and Sweden of a national railway industry capable of producing high speed trains. The Japanese producers have so far supplied the largest number of high speed trains, but the French and British producers are not far behind.

At present, the TGV-A is the most widely found high speed train. In its original version it was sold in 105 train sets for the TGV-Atlantique system. Subsequently, it has been sold in different versions: as the AVE to Spain; as TGV-2N for the TGV-Nord system; as TGV-R for the TGV Interconnection network; and to the PBKA network.[11] In total, more than 350 train sets, more or less similar to the TGV-A, have been ordered.

The best-selling high speed train to date is definitely the Shinkansen Series O and Series 200. This type was used on all Shinkansen lines before the introduction of the Shinkansen Series 100 and the modified Series 200 No.2000 end car.

LATERAL EFFECTS

We will divide the lateral effects into two groups: those internal to the railway system and those concerning other parts of the socio-economic system. Within the railway system, for example the operator and its network of suppliers, the general accumulation of knowledge in itself has been important. More specifically, an important spin-off has been the transfer of improved bogie designs and traction equipment from the high-speed projects to ordinary rolling stock, for instance to commuter trains.

New construction of components in fixed equipment will also improve speed and comfort when upgrading the older parts of the network. Some of the examples show

---

[11] IRJ, August 1992

that new, improved principles for project management and investment calculations have emerged. It is quite difficult to tell how important these effects have been, but it is probably safe to say that these projects serve as a template for future developments. In France and Japan, where the developments have been most pronounced, the second and third generation trains have been improved in several important respects.

We have not encountered any major innovations applicable to other industries in these projects. In general, it seems that when the railway sector has been revitalised it has repeated its pattern of innovation from its early history, which was to combine existing techniques with something new. Still, the introduction of high speed trains has often moved the transformation pressure from the railways to road and air traffic. They have both stimulated and justified a demand for increased investment in new lines.

An interesting trend is the connection of the high-speed network with airports in, for instance, France, Germany and Sweden. This illustrates another outcome of the high speed train development: railways are now seen more as a complement to, rather than a substitute for air and road transport. Rail, air and road appeal to different segments of the total market and all contribute to the rising demand for transport which is at the core of the environmental impact of transport.

Environmental Effects

High speed trains have the potential to reduce energy consumption and pollution, but only under circumstances where the total demand for transport remains static and trains absorb demand "surrendered" by other modes. There is no example of a forecast of passenger travel in Europe that shows a decline in air or road passenger-kilometres. There exist several different estimates of the energy consumption of high speed trains relative to other modes of transport, ranging from 1:3, to 1:10 in comparison with air. The difference in the calculations depends partly on whether the consumption for railways is restricted to the trains themselves, or if it includes the total power distribution system.

The generation of electricity by coal, oil and gas consumes large amounts of energy which is delivered with substantial losses to the end-user (the train). The nuclear energy that powers the French high speed trains carries substantial environmental and human health penalties that are very difficult to evaluate, compared with the environmental and health-damaging effects of air transport. The balance of advantage on these grounds is, therefore, far from clear, and the environmental credentials claimed for high speed trains rests on partial and inadequate scientific evaluations.

If the energy cost of moving one passenger one kilometre by high speed train were assumed to be one third that of air transport (a conservative estimate), we could conclude that the effect on total energy consumption of high speed trains was positive, so long as the newly generated traffic effect was less than twice the substitution effect. For every trip withdrawn from air and road traffic we can thus "allow" the high speed trains to induce two new trips. As soon as air and road modes fill up the spare capacity liberated by high speed trains, however, the energy argument collapses.

Feedback and the Future

Public policy towards transport is changing throughout Europe. This development has many characteristics and high speed rail services are only one visible result. Plans for

European integration are putting increasing pressure on transport infrastructure. The general aim of privatising significant parts of the public sector is also having an effect. Internationalising the high-speed network means that the coordination of national transport policies is more important than at any time in the past. This has been the aim of the UIC since the mid 1970s.

The increased competitiveness of railways as a result of high speed services has strengthened their position. The parallel deregulation of air traffic has put further pressure on airlines. The response of the air and road industries must be to remedy two major deficiencies. Firstly, road traffic must improve its appalling safety record and its negative environmental impact. The negative environmental impact is also a problem for the airline industry.

Far more infrastructure investment is proposed for both these sectors as a solution to serious problems of congestion and pollution. This is unlikely to be effective, but the alternative of reducing the demand for transport has very little political and professional support. This is part of a more general problem of reconciling economic growth and environmental damage, which is currently being addressed in discussions on the concept of "sustainability".

We have seen that high speed trains often produce increases in demand for rail travel. What is less clear is their effect on total demand for railway passenger transport. Developments in Japan and France suggest that this effect has been slight. The total number of passenger-kilometres accounted for by Japanese railways increased by 33 per cent between 1959 and 1964 and by 41 per cent from 1964 to 1974. Similarly, total passenger traffic in France increased by 23 per cent from 1973 to 1980, and by 15 per cent from 1980 to 1988.[12] This implies that high speed trains have substituted for ordinary trains. The size of the total market for transport has increased steadily and the introduction of high speed trains also means that the railway can win a larger part of the market for medium-distance travel. This is perhaps at the cost of the loss of passengers over shorter distances.

The technical characteristics of the railway system have changed considerably as a result of the introduction of high speed services. In terms of technical performance, the best service speed has been raised from the 210kph achieved on the Shinkansen line in 1964, to 300kph in 1991.

Many of the components of the rolling stock and the infrastructure had to be drastically improved to permit this development. This was particularly the case as a result of the need to maintain safety standards and low environmental impact, as well as achieving higher speeds. In this process, the capabilities of the operators and their suppliers have been put under severe pressure, on both the technical and the organisational side. A considerable amount of knowledge about managing these innovation and development processes has been accumulated, making operators well prepared for future developments.

High speed trains have made a significant impact on those countries embarking on these major infrastructure and land-use changes. They have irreversibly altered the competitive map of European transport and they have given governments and operators a significant new planning dimension which is as relevant to the interna-

---

[12] Jane's World Railways, various years

tional sphere as it is to the national. The environmental balance sheet for high speed trains is more likely to be negative than positive but there are major counterfactual arguments. If high speed trains had not been developed it is possible that railways themselves would have deteriorated even more in status, funding and public perception. It remains to be seen whether or not high speed trains will produce a major revival of rail transport or add their contribution to the extermination of rail as a publicly supported and integrated transport option. In the final analysis this will depend on the abilities of rail operators to utilise the management and innovation skills devoted to high speed trains to the far more socially useful and environmentally beneficial rail journeys of up to 50kms.

Bibliography

Commission of the European Communities (1990) Report of the high level group on the development of a European high-speed train network

ECMT (1990) Public and private investment in transport, Paris

ECMT (1992) Evaluating investment in transport infrastructure

Fortune, April 1955

Flink, T. The development of high-speed trains — an industrial dynamics approach, EFI, Stockholm, September 1992

France's master Plan, New high-speed rail developments, not dated

GEC Alstohm, The high-speed trains, Paris

Hughes, M. Rail 300, Newton Abbot, 1988

IRJ: International Railway Journal, selected issues

Jane's World Railways, different years

Japan Railways Group, High Speed Railways in Japan — Present and Future, Eurailspeed 92, 1992

La Vie du Rail, No. 2342, April 1992

Nishida, M. "History of the Shinkansen", in Straszak, A and Tuch, R (eds), The Shinkansen high-speed rail network, IIASA, Pergamon Press, 1980.

Okabe, S. "Impact of the Sanyo Shinkansen on local communities", in Straszak, A and Tuch, R (eds), The Shinkansen high-speed rail network, IIASA, Pergamon Press, 1980.

Railway Gazette, selected issues

SJ Centralförvaltning

Utvecklingsavdelningen, Stockholm, 1969

Index

Transport books from Leading Edge

The Great Railway Conspiracy

Few books on railways have stirred so much controversy and generated so much interest as David Henshaw's remarkable account of the Beeching years. "Henshaw tells the tale well and uncovers much skulduggery," *The Daily Mail.* £14.95, hardback.

Death on the Streets — Cars and the mythology of road safety

Robert Davis turns conventional wisdom on road safety upside down in this radical critique. A deeply controversial account. £11.99, softback

Traffic Congestion: Is there a way out?

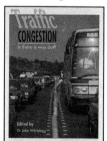

A remarkable collection of papers which shatters myths about road-building as a solution to congestion. Edited by John Whitelegg, a contributing editor of High Speed Trains. £9.99, softback

100 Years of the Manx Electric Railway

Superbly produced history of the remarkable Edwardian tram system which is little changed since it first opened in 1893. The product of painstaking research by author Keith Pearson. £13.99, large format softback

The Wensleydale Railway

Christine Hallas tells in remarkable detail the fascinating story of an English country railway and its effects on the local economy and people. £5.25, softback

Due 1993

The Line that Refused to Die

Revised and updated version of Stan Abbott and Alan Whitehouse's classic account of the six-year battle to save the Settle & Carlisle railway. £7.99, softback

Send for full catalogue, to: Leading Edge, Old Chapel, Burtersett, Hawes, North Yorkshire, DL8 3PB, UK.

☎ **(0969) 667566 (Credit card sales)**

Postage and packing charges — books under £2, add 35p; over £2, add 75p; over £6, add £1.